The Palestinians and East Jerusalem

SOAS Palestine Studies

This book series aims at promoting innovative research in the study of Palestine, Palestinians and the Israel–Palestine conflict as a crucial component of Middle Eastern and world politics. The first ever Western academic series entirely dedicated to this topic, *SOAS Palestine Studies* draws from a variety of disciplinary fields, including history, politics, media, visual arts, social anthropology and development studies. The series is published under the academic direction of the Centre for Palestine Studies (CPS) at the London Middle East Institute (LMEI) of SOAS, University of London.

Series Editor:
Dina Matar, PhD, Chair, Centre for Palestine Studies, and Reader in Political Communication, Centre for Global Media and Communications, SOAS
Adam Hanieh, PhD, Reader in Development Studies and Advisory Committee Member for Centre for Palestine Studies, SOAS

Board Advisor:
Hassan Hakimian, Director of the London Middle East Institute at SOAS

Current and Forthcoming Titles:
Palestine Ltd.: Neoliberalism and Nationalism in the Occupied Territory, Toufic Haddad
Palestinian Literature in Exile: Gender, Aesthetics and Resistance in the Short Story, Joseph R. Farag
Palestinian Citizens of Israel: Power, Resistance and the Struggle for Space, Sharri Plonski
Representing Palestine Media and Journalism in Australia since World War I, Peter Manning
Folktales of Palestine: Cultural Identity, Memory and the Politics of Storytelling, Farah Aboubakr

Dialogue in Palestine: The People-to-People Diplomacy Programme and the Israeli-Palestinian Conflict, Nadia Naser-Najjab

Palestinian Youth Activism in the Internet Age: Social Media and Networks after the Arab Spring, Albana Dwonch

The Palestinian National Movement in Lebanon: A Political History of the 'Ayn al-Hilwe Camp, Erling Lorentzen Sogge

The Foreign Policy of Hamas: Ideology, Decision Making and Political Supremacy, Leila Seurat

The Palestinians and East Jerusalem

Under Neoliberal Settler Colonialism

Bruno Huberman

I.B. TAURIS
LONDON • NEW YORK • OXFORD • NEW DELHI • SYDNEY

I.B. TAURIS
Bloomsbury Publishing Plc, 50 Bedford Square, London, WC1B 3DP, UK
Bloomsbury Publishing Inc, 1385 Broadway, New York, NY 10018, USA
Bloomsbury Publishing Ireland, 29 Earlsfort Terrace, Dublin 2, D02 AY28, Ireland

BLOOMSBURY, I.B. TAURIS and the I.B. Tauris logo are
trademarks of Bloomsbury Publishing Plc

First published in Great Britain 2023
Paperback edition published 2025

Copyright © Bruno Huberman, 2023

Bruno Huberman has asserted his rights under the Copyright, Designs
and Patents Act, 1988, to be identified as Author of this work.

For legal purposes the Acknowledgements on p. ix constitute
an extension of this copyright page.

Cover design: Adriana Brioso
Cover image © MB_Photo/Alamy Stock Photo

All rights reserved. No part of this publication may be: i) reproduced or transmitted
in any form, electronic or mechanical, including photocopying, recording or by means
of any information storage or retrieval system without prior permission in writing from the
publishers; or ii) used or reproduced in any way for the training, development or operation
of artificial intelligence (AI) technologies, including generative AI technologies. The rights
holders expressly reserve this publication from the text and data mining exception as per
Article 4(3) of the Digital Single Market Directive (EU) 2019/790.

Bloomsbury Publishing Inc does not have any control over, or responsibility for,
any third-party websites referred to or in this book. All internet addresses given
in this book were correct at the time of going to press. The author and publisher
regret any inconvenience caused if addresses have changed or sites have
ceased to exist, but can accept no responsibility for any such changes.

A catalogue record for this book is available from the British Library.

Library of Congress Cataloging-in-Publication Data
Names: Huberman, Bruno, author.
Title: The Palestinians and East Jerusalem :
under neoliberal settler colonialism / Bruno Huberman.
Description: London ; New York ; Oxford ; New Delhi ; Sydney : I.B Tauris, 2023. |
Series: SOAS Palestine studies | Includes bibliographical references and index.
Identifiers: LCCN 2023020405 | ISBN 9780755649013 (hardback) |
ISBN 9780755649051 (paperback) | ISBN 9780755649020 (pdf) |
ISBN 9780755649037 (epub) | ISBN 9780755649044
Subjects: LCSH: Palestinian Arabs–Jerusalem–Economic conditions. |
Palestinian Arabs–Jerusalem–Social conditions. |
Palestinian Arabs–Government policy–Jerusalem. |
Palestinian Arabs–Jerusalem–Politics and government. |
Jerusalem–Politics and government. | Economic development–Jerusalem. |
Settler colonialism–Jerusalem. Classification: LCC DS109.95 .H83 2023 |
DDC 305.892/740569442–dc23/eng/20230731
LC record available at https://lccn.loc.gov/2023020405

ISBN: HB: 978-0-7556-4901-3
PB: 978-0-7556-4905-1
ePDF: 978-0-7556-4902-0
eBook: 978-0-7556-4903-7

Series: SOAS Palestine Studies

Typeset by Newgen KnowledgeWorks Pvt. Ltd., Chennai, India

For product safety related questions contact productsafety@bloomsbury.com.

To find out more about our authors and books visit www.bloomsbury.com
and sign up for our newsletters.

Contents

Acknowledgements	ix
Maps	x
Introduction	1
The neoliberal settler colonization of East Jerusalem after Oslo	5
History: Settler colonialism and resistance in Jerusalem in the twentieth century	9
Israeli settler colonization of East Jerusalem from 1967	14
Palestinian resistance in East Jerusalem since 1967	18
1 Neoliberalism and settler colonialism	25
The political economy of settler colonialism	25
Settler colonial government and racial capitalism	31
The two faces of neoliberal settler colonialism	36
Resisting neoliberal settler colonialism	45
2 Neoliberal apartheid in Jerusalem	51
The neoliberal apartheid paradigm	55
Settler colonial neoliberal urbanism in post-Oslo	58
Contradictions of neoliberal apartheid and workers' revolts	66
Race and class divide at the root of neoliberal apartheid	76
3 Neoliberal Israelization of East Jerusalem	81
The neoliberal Israelization paradigm	85
Neoliberal counterinsurgency in Israel and the OPT	87
Decision 3790: The framework for neoliberal Israelization in East Jerusalem	94
De-development of Palestinian economy, capacity-building and industrial zones	104
Completing neoliberal Israelization: Culture, education and police	114

4 Neoliberal anti-colonialism in the Palestinian resistance 125
   Neoliberal anti-colonialism and the resistance economy paradigm 128
   Neoliberal urbanism, the right to housing and Palestinian urban planners 135
   Entrepreneurship, indebtedness and proletarianization of Palestinian women 140
   Palestinian youth, tech entrepreneurship and Israeli neoliberal mask 148
   Elites, tourism and the commodification of Palestinian identity 156

Conclusion: Refusal and emancipation in East Jerusalem 165

References 173
Index 191

Acknowledgements

I'd like to thank my PhD advisor and mentor, Dr Reginaldo Nasser, for all the help and encouragement he's given me over the course of my academic career. To my co-supervisor, Dr Adam Hanieh, who during my time at SOAS in London was extremely generous for the enriching experience in the British academic world and in the field of Palestine/Israel studies.

To the professors who made up the doctoral defence committee – Dr Cecilia Baeza, Dr Mariela Cuadro, Dr Samuel Alves Soares and Dr Sebastião Velazco e Cruz – I thank you for the feedback that was fundamental in converting my thesis into a book. To Dr Desiree Poets for the help with the final draft.

To all those professors and researchers, whose works are fundamental references for the results of this research, who agreed to give their time to engage with my reflections during my doctoral internship. In the UK: Dr Rafeef Ziadah, Dr Gilbert Achcar, Dr Laleh Khalili, Dr Sai Englert, Dr Elian Weizman, Dr Ilan Pappe, Dr Mark Neocleous, Dr Mori Ram, Dr Haim Yacobi and Dr Sharri Plonski. In Palestine/Israel: Dr Sobhi Samour, Dr Toufic Haddad, Dr Raja Khalidi, Dr Marik Shtern, Dr Hila Zaban, Dr Oren Shlomo, Dr Noga Keidar, Dr Emily Silverman, Dr Gillad Rosen, Dr Nufar Avni and Dr Shir Hever. I would also especially like to thank my friends in Palestine – Dr Magid Shihade, Daoud Al-Ghoul, Zakaria Odeh, Rashed Khudiri, Jamal Juma, Shahaf Weisbein, Sahar Vardi and Dr Jeff Halper.

To the staff of I.B. Tauris.

To all my family members. To Anna and Madalena.

Maps

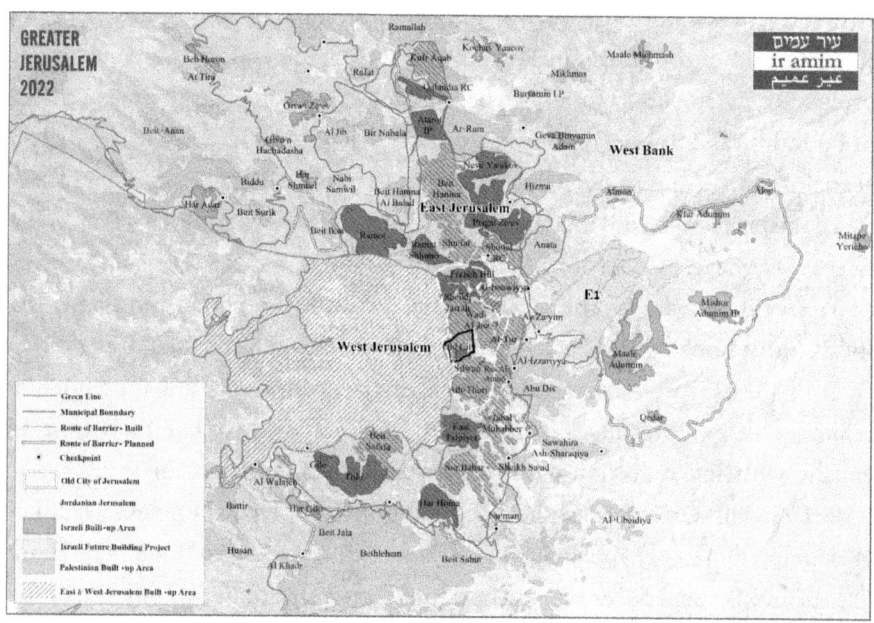

Map 1 Greater Jerusalem.

Source: Ir Amin (2022).

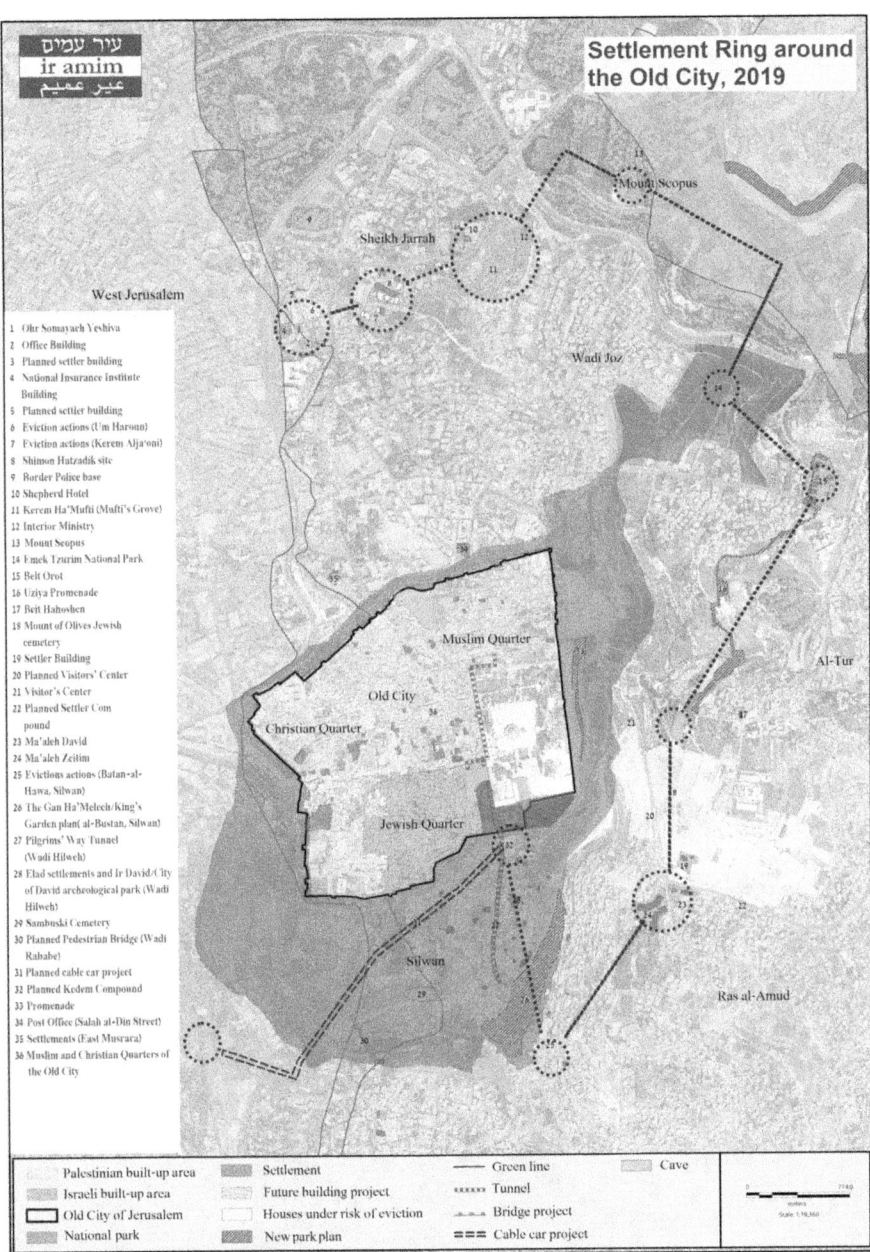

Map 2 Settlement Ring around the Old City.
Source: Ir Amin (2019).

Introduction

Yom Yerushalaim, 'Jerusalem Day', marks the annexation of East Jerusalem after the 1967 Israeli military occupation of the Palestinian territories of the West Bank (including East Jerusalem) and Gaza Strip. Every year on Yom Yerushalaim, ultranationalist settlers march at Palestinian sites in East Jerusalem and invade the al-Aqsa Mosque, the main Muslim holy site in the city and a symbol of Palestinian nationalism. And every year, crowds of Israelis can be seen waving the Israeli flag and heard shouting 'death to the Arabs'.

The 2018 Yom Yerushalaim was probably one of the most significant of recent years, but not because of any violent clashes. On that day, the Israeli government launched development plans for the city that encompasses both Israeli and Palestinian residents. Its stated aim was to 'strengthen Jerusalem' (International Crisis Group, 2019). The plan for 'Narrowing Socio-economic Gaps and Promoting Economic Development in East Jerusalem', prepared by the Ministry for Jerusalem Affairs in conjunction with the municipal administration, is the most comprehensive Israeli project ever developed for Palestinian Jerusalemites and was intended to promote a 'revolution' in Palestinian neighbourhoods in the city (Hasson, 2018). It is likely not a coincidence that Decision 3790, how the development project for Palestinian in East Jerusalem is formally named, was launched after the Donald Trump administration recognized Jerusalem as the capital of Israel in 2017, in violation of the consensus whereby Israel's annexation of East Jerusalem is not recognized by the international community. Trump's successor, president Joe Biden of the Democratic Party, has so far not reversed the decision to recognize Jerusalem as Israel's capital.

Jerusalem, the greatest symbol of both Jewish and Palestinian nationalism, also has the highest rates of poverty and inequality in the country. In 2020, about a third of Jerusalemites were living below the poverty line (Assaf-Shapira et al., 2022). The city is also a site of friction between different sections of the Jewish population – orthodox, religious, secular – and, above all, between Israelis and Palestinians. Materially, Jerusalem is far from being Israel's unique and indivisible 'sacred capital' and far from reflecting the technological modernity that has led Israel to be recognized in recent decades as a 'start-up nation'.

Decades of racist urban planning policies have ensured a Judaization of East Jerusalem. And still, since the redrawing of the city's municipal boundaries in 1967, Jerusalem's population has become proportionately less Jewish. Between 1967 and 2020, the percentage of the city's Jewish residents fell from 74 to 61 per cent, while that of Palestinian residents rose from 26 to 39 per cent. This ratio would be even more unfavourable for Israelis were it not for the high birth rate of the ultraorthodox population, which counterbalances the constant emigration of secular Jews to the Tel Aviv region or abroad (Assaf-Shapira et al., 2022). A majority of emigrants are young people, who leave in search of better employment opportunities and a modern lifestyle (Keidar, 2018; Shlay and Rosen, 2015).

Jerusalem is the most Palestinian under Israel's formal sovereignty. An estimated 366,000 Palestinians live in the city; of these, 57 per cent were living below the poverty line in 2020. The number of poor Palestinians has been growing at higher proportionate rates than those of Jews since the 1967 occupation (Assaf-Shapira et al., 2022). In recent decades, this growth has been further accentuated by the construction of the wall that divides the Palestinian territories of the West Bank. This wall forced many Jerusalemites who had lived in West Bank towns and villages, and where they enjoyed a much lower cost of living, to move back to East Jerusalem to avoid having their residency permits revoked by the Israeli authorities (Dumper, 2014). According to the Israeli Ministry of the Interior, between 1967 and 2013, 14,200 Palestinians from Jerusalem lost their right to reside in the city (Nasara, 2019). The prospect that Palestinians will become the majority of residents within a few years causes a demographical anxiety in Israeli policymakers and representatives that serves to 'justify' Israeli racist measures to make the Palestinians' lives so impracticable that they are forced to move elsewhere (Mansour, 2018; Shalhoub-Kevorkian, 2015).

Half a century of efforts to drive Palestinians out of the city have not proved effective. East Jerusalem is an issue that sticks in Israelis' collective throat. As a result, within the scope of Israeli policies related to Palestinians, the settler colonization of East Jerusalem appears to have been expanded to mean more than mere measures to facilitate the settlement of Jews in the Palestinian parts of East Jerusalem. Since the 2000s, in the 'post-Oslo' period, that is, after the peace process that led to the 1993–5 Oslo Accords and which culminated in the Second Intifada (2000–6), neoliberal urban development policies have aimed to integrate the Palestinian population into Israeli economy. Increasing numbers of Palestinians began to be seen in workplaces, public spaces, centres of consumption, schools and universities of West Jerusalem.

Since the 1990s, Israel has been implementing several urban policies that are guided by an entrepreneurial and neoliberal rationale and aim to make Jerusalem a 'global city'. The Israeli State, the private sector and the Third Sector have worked together to carry out socio-spatial reforms that market the city's sociability and global image as culturally attractive, technologically efficient and safer for new investors, tourists and residents – preferably Jews. Decision 3790 was a consolidation of this trend towards neoliberal modernization across Jerusalem's entire urban fabric. What was new about the plan was that its policies also focused on the socio-economic development of Palestinians. This shift was a response to internal and external criticisms of the social conditions of Palestinian residents. For instance, many Israelis have long criticized the exclusion of the Palestinians from the settler economy as an irrational policy, because it 'wastes' and stymies their productive potential.

The inclusion of the Palestinian population through integration into the Israeli labour market and through consumption aimed at Decision 3670, however, raises questions about the meaning of such policies. Are these inclusion policies a means to an end of historical alienation, dispossessions and several other forms of excluding Palestinian Jerusalemites? Do they mark a new era for Palestinian–Israeli relations towards reconciliation and peace? Some aspects of these new inclusive policies justify this understanding. Firstly, the focus on Jerusalemites' economic needs contrasts with the thousands of reconciliatory initiatives led by civil society organizations in the post-Oslo years that aimed to 'bring voices together' and 'build ties' between the two peoples through cultural, leisure and sports activities. Decision 3670 also departs from previous measures in East Jerusalem that were solely guided by security concerns. In sum, the vision that Israeli politicians painted at the 2018 Jerusalem Day pictured a global, developed and integrated city where Palestinians would finally have an essential material role, not just a symbolic one.

Despite major criticisms of these more 'inclusive' measures from various sectors of Palestinian society, there is support and collaboration from Palestinian individuals, groups and organzations in East Jerusalem. Many Palestinians and Israelis do not see the economic measures of neoliberal development and the political decisions of settler colonial dispossession as the result of the same mode of government, but as distinct sectors that compete in the concrete policies. Several Palestinians, most of them from the middle and upper classes, have adopted entrepreneurship as a resistance tool to fight settler colonial racism and fulfil their rights in Israeli society. That is, they have sought a transformation of Palestinian–Israeli relations through the market, such as cooperation in high-tech sector.

However, the recent integration policies conflict with persistent continuity – strengthened during the 2016–20 Trump administration and sustained during the Biden administration – of forced eviction, revocation of the right of residence, demolition of houses, confiscation of properties, construction of settlements, abusive surveillance and violent repression of social upheavals of the Palestinian residents. The coercive and arbitrary characteristics of the Israeli settler colonial process in East Jerusalem were by no means interrupted to make way for new and inclusive development measures that could be adopted without hindrance. Therefore, Israel aims to both include and exclude the Palestinians in East Jerusalem at the same time and in the same space.

Jerusalem's Palestinians have always lived in a regime of *exclusive inclusion* common to settler colonial contexts. Although the legal status of Palestinians in Jerusalem is not Israel's main concern, the native population's social reproduction has been subject to greater control and investment by the Israeli settler regime. Decision 3790 has intensified Palestinian education and training in East Jerusalem to make Palestinian labour more productive for Israeli capital. For example, Israelis need Palestinians to work at high-tech companies which lack skilled and cheap labour to compete in the global market – historically, the settlers excluded Palestinian workers from higher positions and confined them to low-skilled sectors such as construction and agriculture. To achieve this, Israelis have increasingly opened new entrepreneur and technological capacity-building programmes exclusively for Palestinians. Therefore, the lives of Jerusalemite Palestinians have become less disposable to the Israeli society than before. Consequently, Israel has increasingly switched between settler colonial technologies of elimination and exploitation. The result is a more ambivalent mode of domination of the Palestinians that enables the building of a more productive and stable social order according to Israeli economic, political and security concerns.

This book investigates recent Israeli inclusion and development measures aimed at the Palestinian population of East Jerusalem. It aims to understand how they impact the Israeli settler colonial rule and Palestinian resistance. It shows how the political objectives underlying what are portrayed as benign, neoliberal and rational policies allow the reproduction of Israeli settler colonialism as a natural consequence of the market. The result is that neoliberal reason washes Israeli apartheid and creates new subjectivities and practices among the Palestinians that avoid anti-colonial action and liberation.

The neoliberal settler colonization of East Jerusalem after Oslo

The Israeli settler colonial power in East Jerusalem works through complementary repressive and productive mechanisms. In East Jerusalem, both aspects of Israeli settler colonialism intersect with neoliberalism to produce a more elusive form of power. Neoliberal settler colonialism gives the impression that the outcomes of the settler colonial process are the result of the private actions of Israelis and Palestinians in the market. In this manner, Israel would be absolved of responsibility for its racist, violent, and exclusive behavior toward Palestinians.

On the one hand, coercive force is used to expel Palestinians and replace them with Jewish settlements. This socio-spatial Judaization is an expression of the settler colonial technology of elimination. Judaization has also comprised the essence of municipal urban planning since 1967 and the main manifestation of Israeli settler colonial power in East Jerusalem. It has already resulted in the construction of twelve settlements within the municipal boundaries. Such settler colonial processes have been intertwined with neoliberalism. An example of this was the construction of the City of David in the Palestinian neighbourhood of Silwan, where the settler NGO Elad had built an archaeological tourist park surrounded by small settlements inhabited by ultranationalist Jews. These settlements have torn up the socio-spatial fabric of Silwan.

The Old City and its surrounding area are the main sites of Palestinian elimination and Judaization in the city since 1967. The forced eviction of Palestinians in the neighbourhoods of Sheikh Jarrah and Silwan have instigated several acts of resistance, solidarity and violence. In May 2021, the resistance of the El-Kurd family to a settler organization's attempt to take over their home in Sheikh Jarrah has motivated Palestinian demonstrations from Jerusalem to Gaza, resulting in yet another violent Israeli attack on the strip. In recent years, displacement actions, nightly raids, arrests, beatings and harassment have become commonplace in Silwan, where dozens of families are the target of expropriation actions by settler NGOs and the state. Tunnels dug by settlers for supposed archaeological reasons have caused the collapse of numerous Palestinian houses. In the Batan al-Hawa neighbourhood, in the heart of Silwan, dozens of Palestinian families have received eviction orders. While Israeli plans to expand settlements are promptly approved, Palestinian projects to regulate their residences are immediately rejected. In Silwan, we find the direct continuation of the Nakba in the present.

But there is another side to Israeli settler colonial power. Israeli settler colonialism in East Jerusalem also attempts to govern local Palestinians through seemingly more moderate forms of power. Since the beginning of the Israeli occupation of East Jerusalem, an emerging Israeli settler colonial governmentality has developed and applied policies of inclusion that serve to contain social upheavals and exploit labour while advancing Judaization. This Israelization of East Jerusalem also intertwines with neoliberalism. We can call this form of power 'neoliberal Israelization'. Neoliberal Israelization does not necessarily seek to expand the Jewish presence in East Jerusalem's territory and expel Palestinians from the city. It aims, rather, to extend Israeli domination and exploitation over Palestinian ways of life and spaces. Nevertheless, neoliberal Judaization and neoliberal Israelization may intertwine.

This book's time frame is the period after Oslo and the Second Intifada, particularly the administration of the Israeli mayor Nir Barkat (2008–18), responsible for the main neoliberal reforms in the management of urban space in Jerusalem as well as for the first initiatives to include Palestinians from East Jerusalem in the city's plans. The book also covers the first years of the Decision 3790 implementation period beginning in 2019, when Moshe Lion was already the mayor of the city. The interviews included in the book were conducted in Jerusalem in 2019 during fieldwork. The book approaches this present context through a reading of Jerusalem's economic-political history based on settler colonial theory. According to Wolfe (1999), settler colonization is a structural and uninterrupted phenomenon. It is based on a logic of elimination, that is, the destruction of indigenous nation to allow for the construction of a settler colonial society through continuous settlement. Their primary means of expropriation would be the expulsion, death and confinement of indigenous populations. This type of settler colonialism is distinct from colonial occupation, which prioritizes the exploitation of native labour. The settlers do not leave in settler colonialism. Furthermore, the indigenous people are portrayed and subjugated as redundant, discardable and eliminable.

Elimination would also take place in less obvious ways, such as assimilation through education, recognition and multiculturalism policies. In other words, it involves material and subjective forms of indigenous government in order to achieve its main goal: the expropriation of land in order to build a nation based on white racial supremacy, that is, to build a state that ensures the privileges of the settler population according to the dynamics of global capitalism.

This book, however, is associated with the authors who have criticized Wolfe's settler colonial theory for failing to account for the exploitation of indigenous labour in its analysis (Englert, 2020). This is based on historical examples, such as in Latin America, where settlement and land expropriation are combined with native exploitation (Poets, 2020). Despite the importance of the land for Israelis, Palestine is a case in which native workers have been consistently exploited by settler bourgeoise. Understanding the political economy and governance modes of settler colonialism would become more complex than originally portrayed by Wolfe. It would require a more specific historical interpretation of each case to understand the dynamics of exploitation and elimination.

The making of Jerusalem a global city according to neoliberal urbanism created a demand of cheap white- and blue-collar labour. Palestinian lives became less disposable than the rest of the native population of the West

Bank because of Israeli economic and political needs under neoliberal global economy. Therefore, the reproduction of Jerusalemite Palestinians according to Israeli capital needs required a new mode of government that also met historical settler colonial anxieties, such as the establishment of demographic majority in the city. The neoliberal reason has been an important tool of exploitation and government of the Palestinians in East Jerusalem.

Through neoliberal development, settlers attempt to produce a new, more inclusive and multicultural sociability in Jerusalem capable of co-opting the agenda and efforts of the exploited and oppressed through practices that Nancy Fraser (2017) calls 'progressive neoliberalism'. That is, policies that are framed as subaltern empowerment and viewed as the most effective means of promoting political transformation in your community. A good example is the entrepreneurial capacity-building programmes promoted in East Jerusalem by Israeli and Palestinian NGOs such as Mati and Jest. These NGOs, which are funded directly or indirectly by the State of Israel, seek to frame Palestinian subjectivity through an entrepreneurial mindset and adapt their skills to the demands of the Israeli market. Instead of empowerment and inclusion, the result has been a deepening of debt and the breaking of community bonds of solidarity among Palestinian workers. Debt can be used to allow the expropriation of the Palestinian entrepreneur's real estate that was used as collateral for their credit.

Therefore, Israeli policies of economic inclusion and development serve only as a deception; they merely dynamize the subjugation of Palestinians. While some Palestinians may become wealthy in the process, the majority remain subaltern and impoverished. And while the exploitation of the Palestinian workforce may become more important to Israeli capital and the Israeli State, their 'integration' will only be a complementary policy to the generalized elimination and settlement of Palestinian lands. Capacity-building programmes naturalize settler colonial dispossession and the racist structures on which it relies. Neoliberalism allows settler colonialism to continue with greater acceptance of the colonized population and the international public opinion. Jerusalem's neoliberal settler colonialism reproduces racial hierarchies, settlers' privileges and the pacification of natives in elusive and depoliticized manner as if they were natural consequences of the market.

Thus, we seek to interpret how Israeli domination is formed by elimination and exploitation technologies in the context of neoliberal hegemony in Israel, which expands new forms of exploitation and domination of Palestinian labour. The objective is to reveal how the global dynamics of capitalism, imperialism and racism impact the local particularities in Jerusalem. Such an analysis intends to demonstrate that, despite its important specificities, neoliberal settler colonialism is part of the universal dynamics of capitalism and the history of colonialisms in different geographies of the world, not only in Palestine/Israel.

In Chapter 1, the limitations of using settler colonial theory and the counterinsurgency framework to comprehend the situation analysed in Jerusalem are discussed. Additionally, it seeks to comprehend the relationship between settler colonialism and neoliberalism, and it concludes with a discussion of resistance to neoliberal settler colonialism. Chapter 2 employs the concept of neoliberal apartheid to analyse the political economy of Jerusalem after Oslo and recent popular uprisings, particularly the Jerusalem Intifada. Chapter 3 examines the Israeli justification for neoliberal inclusion policies in East Jerusalem, particularly Decision 3790, and the mode of operation for implementing neoliberal Israelization in the city. Contradictions observed in Palestinian forms of anti-colonial resistance that adopt neoliberal rationality are discussed in Chapter 4. The conclusion emphasizes the limitations of Israeli neoliberal inclusionary measures in East Jerusalem and the significance of refusal as orientation for Palestinian praxis in the city.

History: Settler colonialism and resistance in Jerusalem in the twentieth century

Although Jerusalem is the justifying and legitimizing principle of Zionist claims to the land of Palestine – the term 'Zionism' is a direct reference to the city – Jerusalem did not occupy a central role in the claims of Jewish settlers in the first decades of the twentieth century. The Zionist movement was mostly secular and socialist, concerned with the formation of a Jewish working class that would build the Jewish nation in Palestine with its own hands, through working the land. The Jewish community that lived in Palestine before Zionist settler colonization, almost all of them in Jerusalem, were integrated into the local society, were mostly conservative and saw the Zionist settlers as distorting Judaism (Khalidi, 2010). For this reason, the Zionists concentrated their settler colonial project on arable land near the Mediterranean and Jaffa, the country's main port, where goods and new waves of Jewish immigrants arrived from Europe (Shafir, 1996). It is not by chance that Tel Aviv, the city symbolizing Zionism in Palestine, was built there.

During the Ottoman period in Palestine, from the sixteenth century to 1918, Jerusalem was not only central to the identity of the region's many religious and ethnic groups but was also administratively important to the Ottoman Empire and the region's local elites, being the capital of the southern district of Palestine (Khalidi, 2010). Elected representatives from that district made up the Ottoman parliament on behalf of emerging Palestinian national interests. This made Jerusalem a key educational, intellectual and cultural centre of the Levant[1] at the beginning of the twentieth century. Jerusalem was a cosmopolitan and global city, where different religions, nationalities and ethnicities came together and enjoyed political freedom, a free press, social clubs and international schools, and where they formed thriving artistic and intellectual communities. This scenario was the result of the city's centrality to many religions, which attracted businessmen, tourists, diplomats and missionaries from imperial powers who wanted to have a presence there.

Until the beginning of the twentieth century, Jerusalem was circumscribed within the walls of the Old City with a great ethnically religious diversity (Tamari, 2011). The division of the Old City into ethno-national quarters, such as Moroccan, Armenian and Jewish, took place in the 1930s under British colonial rule. At this time, the Jewish community comprised a religious minority that coexisted with Muslims and Christians from the city and villages in the region, such as Silwan, Deir Yassin and Lifta, nurturing bonds of solidarity and mutual economic dependence despite possible frictions in relations between ethnic groups that did not take a nationalist dimension. Businesses, neighbourhoods and real estate were shared by Palestinian Christians, Muslims and Jews, and social mobility was not linked to belonging to a particular group.

---

[1] A region in the far west of Asia bounded by the Mediterranean Sea and the Arabian Peninsula that includes the present-day nation states of Iraq, Jordan, Syria, Lebanon and Palestine/Israel.

The construction of the Jaffa–Jerusalem railway increased the commercial and tourist activity as well as the population of the Old City. As a result, the Old City's bourgeoisie and petty bourgeoisie, mostly Christian, moved to new neighbourhoods that were being built in the surroundings, such as Baq'a. The construction of New Jerusalem provided impetus to the building industry, which brought about the integration of the city's economy and labour markets with the region's villages and led to the growing proletarianization of Palestinian peasant populations (Khalidi, 2010; Radai, 2015).

Of the sixty thousand Jews living in Palestine in 1914, between twenty-five thousand and thirty thousand lived in Jerusalem, where they made up almost half of the population. Participating in the political, economic and social life of the city, Jews came to be seen as settlers by the rest of the native population as Zionist settler colonialism spread over Palestine. The good relation between Jews, Christian and Muslim indigenous population in Jerusalem never meant a political alliance or the formation of a national identity opposed to the advance of Zionism (Khalidi, 2010; Wallach, 2016). The peaceful situation in Jerusalem began to change from the 1920s onwards, under British rule (1918–48). At first, the city's elites and middle classes sought to overcome growing nationalist differences between Zionist and Palestinian identities in the name of urban and economic development and to attract international capital. Under the British rule, Jerusalem became a stronghold of middle-class intellectuals, merchants, professionals and bureaucrats, attracting a growing number of Palestinian peasants and workers from various locations to live in the villages in the region. These became true suburbs integrated into the cosmopolitan life of the metropolis (Barakat, 2016). The villages provided raw materials and highly skilled and cheap labour for the construction of new Palestinian neighbourhoods and the Jewish settlements around Jerusalem (Ross, 2019).

To maintain peace and social order, the British administered the Mandate of Palestine according to the old colonial counterinsurgency strategy of divide and rule (Khalidi, 2006). As the British permitted Zionist settler colonization[2] and redrew the city's borders to include Jews and exclude Palestinians – creating

---

[2] The British supported the Zionist colonization of Palestine because it perceived Zionists as more reliable allies than the Arabs for their imperialist goals in the Middle East. See also Khalidi (2006).

the historically false perception that Jews became the majority in the city during the Mandate – they were forced to make concessions to native urban elites when Palestinian nationalism was strengthened after the First World War[3] (Barakat, 2016). In 1921, the British appointed Haj Amin al-Husseini, a Palestinian nationalist intellectual and a member of an influential Jerusalemite family, to the role of Mufti of Jerusalem, a traditionally religious office that was given political and administrative functions during the British rule. The August 1929 conflict over the control of the access to the Western Wall, known in Arabic as al-Buraq, was a watershed. It left 113 Jews and 116 Arabs dead and ended up – spreading throughout Palestine – in a national anti-colonial uprising that had an impact on the social life of the city and the country. One of its consequences was that the British colonial government became harsher and more repressive in the following decade. According to Barakat (2016), the Buraq Revolt signified the political rise of Palestinian Jerusalemite workers and peasants. These Palestinians took on a leading role in Palestinian anti-colonial resistance, hitherto restricted to the elitist strongholds of notable Jerusalem families. The working class constituted not only the basis for the prosperity and growth of the city; it also suffered directly from the racist and dehumanizing oppression of the Zionist and British colonizers. Although the spontaneous revolt took place around a religious site, it was effectively born out of the race and class contradictions resulting from Zionist and British colonization. Workers from villages were stigmatized as dangerous and disruptive and were persecuted by Zionist settlers and British security forces with the consent of the Mufti Haj Amin al-Husseini (Barakat, 2016).

These conflicts and the racist stigmatization of peasants and workers in Greater Jerusalem ended up influencing the future of Palestinian village populations, who were harshly repressed by the British troops during the Arab Revolt of 1936 and became the target of Israeli-led ethnic cleansing efforts between 1947 and 1949 (Barakat, 2016; Khalidi, 2006). The village of Lifta, for example, was devastated by Zionist troops during the capture of Jerusalem in the last weeks of the Nakba.[4] Its ruins are visible to this

---

[3] Arab nationalisms grew in influence in the Middle East after the involvement of leaders and the population in the battle against the Ottoman Empire at the First World War. See also Khalidi (2006).

[4] *Nakba*, disaster in Arabic, is what Palestinians call the events of 1948–9, when Zionist militias and the Israeli Army conducted an ethnic cleansing process in Palestine. More than 700,000 Palestinians

day. The ethnic cleansing of Palestine and Jerusalem did not only have a class dimension, however. It also had a racial dimension and targeted Palestinian bourgeois neighbourhoods in the western portion of the city, such as Baq'a. The Israelis Judaized the district and changed its name to Baka (Pappe, 2006; Radai, 2015). But of all the episodes of ethnic cleansing, the most striking was the massacre of Dayr Yassin, a village of 750 families near Jerusalem. In 1948, Israeli State leaders authorized Zionist militias to murder between 100 and 110 Palestinian non-combatants, among them the Zionist leader David Ben Gurion. The event terrorized the population of Jerusalem, causing fear and flight, and was decisive in the Israeli conquest of West Jerusalem.

Jerusalem was one of the only places in Palestine that witnessed a violent confrontation between Palestinians and Jews during the Nakba. Despite the efforts of the Israeli military to take control of all of the Jewish settlements in the Jerusalem region, this was not possible due to Palestinian resistance in alliance with troops from Arab countries, particularly Transjordan (Radai, 2015; Shlaim, 2015). Resistance to Zionist aggression was greater among lower-class Palestinians living in the Old City and villages than in the affluent neighbourhoods of New Jerusalem (Radai, 2015). At the end of the war, in 1949, the armistice lines between Israelis and Jordanians in the Old City became a national border that divided the city in two: West Jerusalem, under Israeli sovereignty, and East Jerusalem, under the jurisdiction of Transjordan. All Palestinians remaining in West Jerusalem and Jews in East Jerusalem were expelled. Consequently, cosmopolitan and plural Jerusalem suffered two simultaneous processes of racial homogenization that ruptured the social fabric and the bonds of coexistence between Arabs and Jews. At least sixty thousand Palestinians were removed from West Jerusalem during the Nakba and became refugees on the other side of the city (Abowd, 2014). In the end, settler colonial and anti-colonial nationalism spoke louder than Jerusalem's cosmopolitanism.

The Palestinian population of East Jerusalem, under Jordanian rule, suffered a long period of neglect by the Jordanian government in terms of basic services and infrastructure until 1967. Transjordan annexed Jerusalem

---

were expelled and more than four hundred villages were destroyed for the purpose of building a Jewish demographic majority in the newly created State of Israel. See also Pappe (2006).

and the rest of the West Bank in 1951, but sought to strengthen Amman as the Jordanian capital and undermine Palestinian national identity. This sparked popular protests that eventually led to the assassination of King Abdullah by a Jerusalemite linked to local elites (Cohen, 2011). This neglect, however, did not prevent East Jerusalem from maintaining itself as an important cultural reference point and tourist destination for the Arab and Muslim world, as well as a political centre for the Palestinian cause, which has never stopped claiming the city as its capital. The Palestine Liberation Organization (PLO) was founded in Jerusalem in 1964. Its first pro-liberation actions against Israelis and Jordanians took place in the city. In 1966, when the Jordanian government finally launched a development project for Jerusalem, the Israeli occupation thwarted their plans.

Israeli settler colonization of East Jerusalem from 1967

By 1967, the part of the city known as West Jerusalem had already undergone an intense process of settler colonization that had Judaized the population, the landscape and the names of streets and neighbourhoods to make it the capital of the newly created State of Israel, thereby erasing Palestinian history. Palestinian private property was confiscated as 'abandoned', became Israeli State property and fell under the administration of parastatal institutions such as the Jewish Agency and the Jewish National Fund.[5] Concern abounded about the return of Palestinian refugees to their properties. These potential returnees were known as 'infiltrators' (Shalhoub-Kevorkian, 2015). Soon, Zionist elites began to promote the strengthening of the Jerusalem border between East and West through the settlement of newly arrived Jewish settlers from Arab countries and post-war Europe (Zaban, 2016). Some of these districts, such as Baka, were stigmatized as dangerous due to their large presence of poor Mizrahim.[6] When Israel took East Jerusalem in 1967, the plan of the Israeli elites was to continue

---

[5] These private colonial institutions work for the exclusive benefit of the Jewish population as they have more freedom of action than the state itself. This has made apartheid in Jerusalem less legally evident.

[6] *Mizrahi* (Eastern, in Hebrew) is how Jewish populations from Asia and Africa, also known as Sephardi, are racialized in Israel. See Shohat (1988).

the same racist settler colonial policy that had already been carried out in the areas under their domination. The key difference between 1967 and 1948 was that the Palestinian population was not systematically expelled from the city.

The Old City of East Jerusalem became the stage on which the Israeli modus operandi in the Occupied Palestinian Territories (OPTs) was revealed. A few days after the 1967 occupation, without any judicial authority over the occupied eastern part of Jerusalem, the mayor of West Jerusalem, Teddy Kollek, ordered the destruction of the Mughrabi Quarter, located at the foot of the Western Wall. In the middle of the night, Colonel Yaakov Salman ordered 135 families in the neighbourhood to get out of their beds and evacuate their homes within minutes. When they refused, Salman ordered the excavators to start the Quarter's summary demolition, thus killing many of the residents who had not fled (Gorenberg, 2007: 42–3). In place of the houses, an esplanade was opened so that Israelis and foreign tourists could freely access the remaining ruins of the ancient Jewish Temple – the Western Wall. Subsequently, more than three thousand Palestinian refugees were expelled to make way for the new Jewish Quarter. Two months after the end of the war, the entire Old City was declared a historical heritage site, and today no construction is allowed without a state-approved archaeological permit (Weizman, 2017: 38).

In 1967, the Israeli government annexed almost 70 square kilometres of land from East Jerusalem and incorporated some sixty-nine thousand Palestinians within the newly expanded borders of the municipality of Jerusalem (Weizman, 2017: 25). The new boundaries included empty areas to be used for urban expansion and excluded from the city's official perimeter as many of the areas densely populated by Palestinians as possible, thus combining, in the same metropolitan area, the western Israeli city, the Old City, the rest of the city previously administered by Jordan and twenty-eight Palestinian villages. Palestinians living in the annexed area were given the option of becoming Israeli citizens, but to do so, they had to relinquish their Jordanian citizenship. Only a small portion of residents accepted. The absence of citizenship left them vulnerable to various bureaucratic mechanisms that sought to transfer them out of the city and thus reduce the Arab-Palestinian population of the municipality, such as by revoking their right of residence (Salem, 2018).

Teddy Kollek, mayor of Jerusalem from 1965 to 1993, orchestrated this 'unification' with a vision of what was to be a 'mosaic of different cultures and civilisations living together in a single city'. His mission would be to foster a multicultural 'Goulash' in Jerusalem (Wallach, 2016). While Kollek's government espoused a discourse of tolerance, cultural diversity and voluntary self-segregation, in practice it aimed to legitimize eminently racist policies of social, economic and urban development that favoured Jews to the detriment of native Palestinian residents. Under Kollek, Palestinian neighbourhoods were neglected and deprived of adequate urban planning and essential public services. As Kollek himself came to admit, the 'interventions' to improve the Palestinian neighbourhoods were essentially cosmetic (Cohen, 2011). The main Israeli actions in East Jerusalem comprised the confiscation of land, the expropriation of houses and the persecution of activists and guerrilla fighters who sought to resist the first acts of occupation and colonization of East Jerusalem.

Behind the Israeli discourses of Jerusalem's redemption, unification and multilateral governance after 1967, there is a combination of racial violence, legal instruments and economic incentives manifested mainly in security policies and urban planning in East Jerusalem (Alkhalili, 2017). In the aftermath of 1967, settlers and the Israeli government have confiscated Palestinian houses and properties for the most diverse juridical 'reasons': national interest, archaeology, environmental protection, modernization, development, betrayal and terrorism, among others (Alkhalili, 2017; Chiodelli, 2016). The Judaization of East Jerusalem has continued through the construction of new gated communities, highways, government buildings and ordinary infrastructure, such as roads and tunnels. From the beginning, urban planning proved an effective tool of Israeli settler colonization and for the control of the Palestinian population, precisely because it provided a technical, neutral and objective veneer to the exercise of spatial reproduction within a racist logic (Yacobi, 2016). In this way, Jerusalem's urban apartheid was an exercise of 'good administration' according to the city's official master plan. The Israeli obsession with planning represents, according to Khalidi (quoted in Arafeh, Samman and Khalidi, 2016), in allusion to Lenin, the 'highest stage of settler colonialism'.

Israeli settler colonization of East Jerusalem advances on two spatial fronts: one internal and one external. The 'inner ring' encircles the Old City and the Hebrew University of Jerusalem. Some settlements for the Jewish middle class next to the border of East Jerusalem, such as French Hill, have always been treated as regular 'neighbourhoods' of West Jerusalem in order to depoliticize their settler colonial character and differentiate them from settlements built for frankly nationalist and religious reasons in other OPT locations. From 1977 onwards, the Israeli government has adopted neoliberal policies and a more aggressive settler colonization strategy on the margins of East Jerusalem, in locations that would become suburbs for secular middle-class Jews (Weizman, 2017). The offer of state incentives to those interested in living on the colonial borders, at the very moment when the social welfare system in the formal state was being dismantled by neoliberal reforms, allowed the Zionist project to attract economically motivated Israeli workers to live in larger, better-quality housing beyond the colonial border (Newman, 2017).

The settlements also began to be configured to serve the interests of the ultra-Orthodox low-income population, engulfing in the Zionist hegemony a group that originally held positions contrary to the settler colonization project for religious reasons. A below-market cost of living has attracted Israeli Jews, often from impoverished communities in Europe and the Middle East who had not been able to thrive in other parts of Israel. The government built a network with high-speed roads, tunnels and viaducts superimposed on the Palestinian road system that allowed settlers to transit through militarily occupied Palestinian territory to workplaces in Israel without noticing the transition from one jurisdiction to another and without coming across a single Palestinian resident (Weizman, 2017). In this way, settler colonization has become as banal as moving to a suburban gated community typical of Western post-industrial societies (Gutwein, 2017; Newman, 2017).

In the 1970s, Israeli leaders hired architects and urban planners who had built California's famous suburbs to design settlements in Jerusalem. One of these settlements was Maale Adumim, currently the largest Jewish community in the OPTs and one of several suburban complexes that make up 'Greater Jerusalem' (Weizman, 2017). International capital, urban planning and the real estate market have thus acted as agents of both the expansion and normalization of Israeli settlement in East Jerusalem. In practice, normalization means the incorporation of East Jerusalem settlements – where more than 500,000 Jews live – into Israel's socio-economic and administrative complex, erasing the division between East and West Jerusalem, known as the Green Line (Shlay and Rosen, 2015).

In addition to being built on illegally confiscated Palestinian land, most of the settler colonial infrastructure was built with cheap unskilled Palestinian labour, which, even in times of heightened political tension, never ceased to be employed by Israeli civil construction (Englert, 2017; Ross, 2019). Settlement construction work represented the biggest source of employment for Palestinian Jerusalemites during the 1970s and 1980s. In 1980, the Jewish sector in Jerusalem employed 8,600 Palestinians from East Jerusalem – approximately 40 per cent of the local workforce – in addition to ten thousand from the West Bank (Shtern, 2017). The exploitation of Palestinian labour in low-skilled and low-wage sectors allowed the social ascension of Mizrahi workers to higher positions in Israeli society. They began to occupy white-collar positions previously restricted to Askenazi, while skilled Palestinian professionals were barred from the best job openings in the Israeli market (Englert, 2017). These economic and political contradictions of settler colonial power in the OPTs led to the outbreak of the Intifada in 1987, a time of peak and decline in East Jerusalem's social, political and cultural life.

Palestinian resistance in East Jerusalem since 1967

After the 1967 occupation, the PLO continued its activities in the city, including through armed guerrilla groups now led by Yasser Arafat and his party, Fatah. However, as in other OPT locations, in the first decades after the occupation, the settler colonial policy of pacification applied by the Israeli forces managed to contain Palestinian anti-colonial resistance and normalize the occupation (Cohen, 2011). Pacification consisted, on the one hand, of the repression of guerrilla groups and other forms of organized political mobilization and, on the other, of increased employment of Palestinian workers by Israeli capital. Although the main PLO leaders were exiled, local organizations weakened and the regional Palestinian movement decentralized, Jerusalem managed to retain considerable centrality within Palestinian society due to the reasonable political freedom that the Jerusalemites enjoyed compared to the remainder of the OPTs. This happened because East Jerusalem was under the local civilian municipality rule, granting local Palestinians some rights that the Jewish residents also enjoyed, while the West Bank and Gaza were under military occupation. As a result, during the 1970s and 1980s, East Jerusalem became the de facto Palestinian capital, housing national institutions, the headquarters of major newspapers, labour unions, political leaders' meetings and major cultural events.

The First Intifada, which began in 1987, signified the ascension of the Jerusalemites among the leaders of the Palestinian movement within the OPTs. This movement happened mainly around the figure of Faisal Husseini, who not only had close political connections to Arafat, Fatah and the PLO but also belonged to one of the most traditional families in the city and was the son of an important martyr in the resistance to the Nakba (Cohen, 2011). Through grassroots popular mobilization, Husseini activated a resistance movement in Jerusalem beyond Fatah. This movement represented Jerusalem society more fully by including Marxist and Islamic organizations as well as representatives of the commercial, industrial and workers' sectors. These different groups were able to come together in the space known as Orient House, which was owned by Husseini and became the most important Palestinian cultural, political and social centre in East Jerusalem. During the Intifada, the Palestinian resistance in the city gained a certain social cohesion and was able to organize a major shutdown of economic activity as well as violent attacks against the Israeli presence in Palestinian neighbourhoods. Buses, ambulances and people were pelted with stones hurled by Palestinians. In so doing, Palestinians openly contested any rhetoric of a 'United Jerusalem'. Furthermore, the resistance permitted the rise of Husseini and other Jerusalemite militants within the Palestinian movement, whose leadership was disputed among Fatah leaders in the OPT, PLO leaders in exile and the Hamas on the rise.

The rise of Husseini within the Palestinian movement has paralleled the growth in dialogue with Israeli figures from West Jerusalem. Initially restricted to anti-Zionist circles sympathetic to the Palestinian cause, Husseini extended his network to other sectors, including Mayor Teddy Kollek (Cohen, 2011). This movement was approved by the PLO leadership, which in 1988 recognized the State of Israel and reduced its claims of sovereignty to the OPTs. Husseini advocated for an 'open Jerusalem', if a political agreement between the PLO and

Israelis could be arrived at. For him, the city should be administratively shared between Israelis and Palestinians, and no new walls should be erected to divide the urban space. That is, all Jerusalem would be 'open' for all its residents.

Husseini was named one of three Palestinian representatives who participated in preparatory meetings for the 1991 Madrid Conference, held at Orient House with US diplomats, for the creation of the State of Palestine (Cohen, 2011). The opening of a secret negotiation channel with Israel in Oslo by exiled PLO leaders, however, not only alienated the internal leaders who participated in the Intifada but also excluded the Jerusalem question itself. Eager to secure territorial autonomy and faced with the difficulties surrounding the partition of Jerusalem, Palestinian negotiators led by Arafat accepted in the Oslo Accords (1993–5) the constitution of the Palestinian Authority's (PA) jurisdiction in the OPTs without including East Jerusalem. This decision was the beginning of a growing process of isolation, depoliticization and impoverishment of the city in relation to the rest of the West Bank.

With the establishment of the PA initially in Jericho in 1994 and later in Ramallah in 1995, Jerusalem lost its status of de facto capital of the Palestinians and became a symbolic capital. As PA bureaucracies and resources from the international community were established in Ramallah and other OPT locations, Jerusalem gradually lost political relevance and underwent economic de-development (Shalhoub-Kevorkian, 2012). This process was reinforced by a series of terrorist attacks by Palestinian suicide bombers in West Jerusalem. These attacks aimed to sabotage the political negotiations that these resistant groups saw as a Palestinian surrender to Israeli settler colonial interests. The opposition coalition spread from Islamic movements to the socialist groups the Popular Front for the Liberation of Palestine (FPLP) and the Democratic Front for the Liberation of Palestine (DFLP) (Cohen, 2011). As many of the perpetrators of the attacks were Jerusalemites or had family members in Jerusalem, security forces began to punish Palestinians with house demolitions and surprise night-time police raids. From potential peace partners, all Palestinians came to be seen as potential terrorists and were threatened with the collective revocation of their residency permits.

Surveillance of political activities began to be monitored by Israel in conjunction with the newly deployed security force of the PA (Cohen, 2011). Although East Jerusalem was outside the PA's jurisdiction, the PA's bureaucratic apparatus and security forces began to operate in Palestinian neighbourhoods under the condescending gaze of the Israelis. Palestinian bureaucrats saw coordinated work with the Israelis as a solution to ensure national independence and monitoring of opposition Islamic groups. As a result, Palestinian residents linked to the PA began to vie with the Israeli bureaucracy for control of order in the Palestinian neighbourhoods of East Jerusalem. Although many Palestinians adhered to the government's project of greater de facto penetration of the PA over East Jerusalem and regarded such a possibility enthusiastically, the situation of dual authority began to generate animosity between the city's residents and the PA.

The contradiction for local Palestinians between the commitment to a Palestinian government in East Jerusalem and the material implications of living under formal Israeli sovereignty created an impasse for many non-formally organized Jerusalemites: how to reject the Israeli government and at the same time turn to the settler regime when necessary? Instead of joining the establishment running the PA or siding with the opposition, many Palestinians in Jerusalem preferred to maintain a channel of communication with the Israelis on security and other civil matters (Cohen, 2011). The Israelis made life as difficult as possible for the Jerusalemites in order to produce disharmony with the rest of the OPT. Added to these power struggles was the inability of the Palestinian authorities to stop the vigorous construction of settlements in Jerusalem (which intensified even more in the 1990s) that was encouraged to guarantee control of the territory, regardless of the political agreement with the Palestinians (Weizman, 2017).

The consequence of this set of transformations during the 1990s was the increase in the exclusion and depoliticization of Palestinian Jerusalemites. They became increasingly concerned with their immediate survival, with securing food and a roof over their heads, and were increasingly alienated from the political decisions reserved for the elites of Ramallah and Bethlehem, which had replaced Jerusalem as economic and cultural centres (Shalhoub-Kevorkian, 2015). On a daily basis, they faced the fear of forced removal by the Israeli authorities, for a simple mistake vis-à-vis a technical parameter of the master plan, fear of punishment for involvement in political activities, fear of property confiscation by a settler organization or by the government for a new urban infrastructure project. Subtle means were also employed to expel Palestinians, such as gentrification produced by planning restrictions, the curtailment of family unions between Palestinians from Jerusalem and the West Bank, the revocation of residency aimed at taking Jerusalem away from being a 'centre of life' and the lack of opportunities for employment – all part of the so-called silent transfer (Arafeh, 2020; Shalhoub-Kevorkian, 2015).

On a day-to-day basis, vexatious searches, ostensible policing, arbitrary arrests and murders began to affect mainly young people because of their involvement in demonstrations and the detachment from the rest of the West Bank. The ban on public funerals and blackmail to return bodies of martyrs murdered by settler forces also added to the human rights violations that Jerusalemites faced. All this pressure created an identity crisis and greater passivity among Jerusalemites towards political events (Cohen, 2011).

Frustration with the Oslo Accords was one of the main causes of the Second Intifada (2000–6) in Palestine/Israel. Despite the armed violence that characterized the new Palestinian uprising, the Jerusalemites' adherence to the armed struggle was quite low compared to the rest of the OPT (Cohen, 2011). Violent clashes took place in neighbourhoods such as Jabel Mukabber, Isawiyye and Ras al-Amoud, some of the places that have suffered the most from aggressive Israeli settler colonization. However, the fear of being denied the right of residence, the strategic decisions of Palestinian armed groups and penetration of the intelligence and security services by a significant number of collaborators among the Palestinians limited the armed confrontation in East Jerusalem. By mid-2001, after violent Israeli repression, the situation in the Old City and central East Jerusalem had returned to normal. Of the nearly four thousand Palestinians killed by the Israelis in the Second Intifada, only sixty-four were Jerusalemites (Cohen, 2011: 63).

But it was not just Palestinian bodies that were targeted in the Second Intifada. The clash served for the Israelis to liquidate major Palestinian political and social centres in August 2001, such as Orient House and the Chamber of Commerce and Industry, by eliminating all types of formal representation and official connection to the PA – a process that continues. Faisal Husseini, who had led an effort among Jerusalemites to build a political agenda in line with local priorities and for the valorization of the Palestinian national identity among young people, died in the same year (Cohen, 2011). His passing brought an end to the political coalition that had revolved around his leadership. Left groups lost ground to Islamist movements and internationally funded NGOs. Political activity in the city became more episodic and localized around the dispute over the al-Aqsa Mosque.

In 2001, the start of the construction of the West Bank Wall, which crosses Palestinian neighbourhoods in East Jerusalem, served, on the one hand, to promote a union of movements in Jerusalem and West Bank opposing its construction; but, on the other hand, it deepened the main features of the settler colonization project since the 1990s: the separation of Jerusalem from the West Bank, the socio-spatial fragmentation of the Palestinians and their economic de-development. As a result, the struggle for Jerusalem moved further and further outside the city, and the city increasingly became a symbol of national resistance, inhabited by a trapped population.

Palestinian resistance continues to oscillate between resistance and adaptation, subversion and submission (Alkhalili, 2017). The Oslo period, however, did not mean the end of the Palestinian anti-colonial struggle in Jerusalem, but a moment of reproduction of its contradictions with the advance of neoliberalism in the heart of the city.

1

Neoliberalism and settler colonialism

How the historical connections between settler colonialism, capitalism, and racism can be (and are) reproduced in the neoliberal present

The political economy of settler colonialism

The concept of *settler colonialism* is not new and has been used by Palestinian, anti-Zionist and Marxist authors since the 1920s – it is as old as the debate on whether or not Zionism is a colonial project. In spite of the distance in time, the contemporary relevance of these themes is clear from the quantity and quality of publications on the Palestine/Israel issue, which returned to the concept of settler colonialism in dialectical analyses based on historical materialism in the 1980s and 1990s (Abdo and Yuval-Davis, 1995; Pappe, 2015; Shafir, 1996). Among the first contemporary studies were those of two Marxist theorists (and PLO members): Sayegh (2012), a key source for Western authors, who in 1965 defined Zionist segregation in Palestine as 'racial self-segregation, racial exclusivity and racial supremacy', and Jabbour (1970), who authored a comparative study of three recent settler colonial experiments: Palestine, South Africa and Algeria.

French Marxist Maxime Rodinson's *Israel: The Colonial-Settler State* (1973) was also of great importance, as were those of other Palestinian intellectuals who were precursors of colonial studies, such as Edward Said (1979) and Elia Zureik (2001), who also flirted in their own ways with historical materialism.[1]

---

[1] The contribution of the anti-Zionist Israeli Marxist movement Matzpen, critical of the colonial character of the State of Israel, is responsible for important analyses of the relations between class, race and the Zionist-Israeli colonization of Palestine (Englert, 2017).

It is worth remembering that the contemporary revival of the concept of settler colonialism was due to the Israeli Gershon Shafir (1996) in his effort to understand the origin of the Palestine/Israel question from the perspective of historical materialism, and to highlight that the seminal work of Wolfe were heavily influenced by Shafir's theories (Piterberg, 2015).

Considering the Israeli project through the lens of settler colonialism has profoundly altered the way we understand the relationship between the two peoples: seeing them no longer as adversaries in a conflict between two nationalisms of the same nature (Pappe, 2015) has revealed historically hidden layers and provided a new understanding of the power relations between Israelis and Palestinian and given moral legitimacy to the Palestinian struggle in the eyes of the world (Busbridge, 2018).

A significant part of the contemporary bibliography on settler colonialism is based on the model developed by Wolfe (1999, 2006) and Veracini (2010, 2015), two Australian authors who have been greatly influential on research on settler colonial processes by applying temporal and geographical cross-sections to various cases, in particular the British settler colonization of the United States, Canada, Australia and New Zealand. Settler colonialism is one of the forms of imperialist expansion of modern capitalism; the bias adopted in the most advanced studies reveals singularities ignored by most traditional studies. The settler colonial theory brings back the settler/native cleavage as a dialectical relationship through which it is possible to understand the multiple unfoldings of the past and present history of Palestine/Israel (Barakat, 2018).

The dynamics of racial difference historically produced by Zionist-Israeli settler colonialism are thus placed at the heart of the conflicts and contradictions existing in the social relations of that territory. Wolfe (1999: 2) substantiates his interpretation of the phenomenon by stating that 'settler colonies were (are) premised on the elimination of native societies'. The use of the present and past forms of the verb reflects a defining characteristic of settler colonization. 'The colonizers come to stay – invasion is a structure not an event.' In several subsequent writings, Wolfe and Veracini reiterate the main characteristics of settler colonialism as a continuous, eliminatory and structural phenomenon. In other words, in contrast to exploitation colonies, settler colonies are essentially geared towards the accumulation of indigenous lands rather than value added by native labour. While exploitation colonies are dependent on the reproduction of the native body and labour, settler colonies aim to reduce its dependence on indigenous society to the *minimum necessary*. The land is, therefore, the central element, as it involves the dispute for life spaces in which the new settler nation can be established. Dialectically, the right to land and existence is denied to the indigenous peoples by the settlers. The dispute between settlers and natives over control of land is characterized by this existential and self-determinational particularity.

Violence in settler colonial contexts is aimed at the material elimination of the natives, through expulsion, genocide, symbolic elimination, the denial of the indigenous identity and its cultural, economic and social ways of life. Wolfe (2006: 388) concludes: 'Settler colonialism destroys to replace.' Settlers aim to build a new settler nation on the ruins of the native society to become the new 'natives', appropriating not only their lands but also their practices, customs, culture, ways of working, history and myths. Wolfe further notes that settler colonialism involves the social death of 'nativeness'. As the identifications of settlers and indigenous people are mutually constituted and reproduced (Mamdani, 2001), only with the disappearance of the latter is it possible to naturalize the former as an autochthon that belongs to that land. Indigenization is fundamental for the normalization and naturalization of settler colonialism (Morgensen, 2011).

There is a difficulty in post-colonial literature in recognizing the particularity of settler colonization. Most post-colonial literature rests its observations primarily on issues of labour exploitation and the racial subjugation of the colonized. Memmi (1974), for example, sees the extermination of indigenous people in the United States as a contradiction of the supposed basic logic of colonialism, which is the forced exploitation of native labour.

> It has not been so long since Europe abandoned the idea of a possible total extermination of a colonised group. It has been said, half-seriously, with respect to Algeria: 'There are only nine Algerians for each Frenchman. All that would be necessary would be to give each Frenchman a gun and nine bullets.' The American example is also evoked, and it is undeniable that the famous national epic of the Far West greatly resembles systematic massacre.

> In any case, there is no longer much of an Indian problem in the United States. (Extermination saves colonisation so little that it actually contradicts the colonial process.) Colonisation is, above all, economic and political exploitation. If the colonised is eliminated, the colony becomes a country like any other, and who then will be exploited? Along with the colonised, colonisation would disappear, and so would the coloniser. (Memmi, 1974: 193)

Thus, if natives in contexts of exploitation are racialized and reproduced in a way that constitutes submission and overexploitation, indigenous peoples in settler colonies are racialized and reproduced as spare, unwanted, disposable and eliminable populations. It is not by chance that Blacks are racialized according to their bodies and indigenous peoples in relation to the land (Wolfe, 2016). The need to reaffirm settler colonialism as a distinct field of study leads Veracini (2015: 51) to state that 'colonialism [by exploitation] and settler colonialism should be interpreted as antithetical modes of domination, even if they always interact and overlap in complex and fluid ways in the real world'.

The reassertion of settler colonial specificity, however, limits the understanding of complex forms of colonial settlement in the historical material process. Clarno (2017) notes that despite Wolfe recognizing the links between colonialism and capitalism, the essence of settler colonialism gave rise to investigations that privilege the exclusive analysis of colonialism without connection to capitalism. Cases of settler colonialism in Latin America and Africa, such as Brazil, Chile, Mexico, Algeria, South Africa and Rhodesia, are examples in which the exploitation of native labour was combined with its elimination. In all of them, the colonial demands for native land and labour coexisted, thus constituting ambiguous cases that challenge the central claims of the model of settler colonialism. Mamdani (2015), for example, observed that Africa and America, respectively, reveal two distinct cases of failure and success of settler colonialism. It was precisely the dependence on indigenous labour and the constitution of a native resistance movement that suppressed the economic capacities of reproduction of the settler population that limited the expansion of white supremacist regimes on the continent and made decolonization possible in countries such as Algeria, Uganda, Rhodesia and South Africa. In other words, labour and class relations in the political economy of settler colonization are fundamental, even at the level of reflecting on the possibilities of decolonization.

Palestine, as demonstrated by Englert (2017, 2020), Ross (2019) and Farsakh (2005), is no different. The literature based on settler colonial theory places at the centre of the struggle between Israelis and Palestinians the settlements, invasions, expansion of borders and territorial dispossession throughout historic Palestine during the more than hundred years of Zionist-Israeli settler colonization of the country (Dana and Jarbawi, 2017; Salamanca et al., 2012). Although the continuity of the Nakba and settlement demonstrates the structural importance of settler colonial theory to understand the reality and history of that territory, the exploitation of Palestinian labour has been of equally perennial importance to the settler regime, despite fluctuations in demand for various reasons. Therefore, it is an analytical requirement imposed by reality to dialectally analyse race–class and exploitation–elimination relations. That is, the land–labour dichotomy is limited. Instead of elimination or exploitation, as Wolfe's model proposes, the fate of the dispossessed could be proletarianization, as occurred in Canada and Brazil (Harris, 2004; Poets, 2020). The case of Palestine, in general, and of the Palestinians of East Jerusalem, specifically, requires an analytical framework that allows for a joint understanding of the processes of elimination and exploitation by Israeli settler colonialism.

Fieldhouse (1966) developed a classic typology of settler colonization models observed from a less essentialist approach. In his classification of 'settlement colonies', he established three categories: pure, mixed and plantation. The first case, based on the American and Australian models, is the one addressed by Wolfe and Veracini, in which the creation of white societies based on white labour and the expulsion of natives was central. Mixed colonizations are those in which the considerable presence of white settlers and settler labour coexisted with the presence and centrality of native labour, as in Mexico and Algeria. Plantation settlements are the cases of Brazil, the Caribbean and the south of the United States, where the importation of slave labour to plantations was the basis of colonial economies. However, Fieldhouse (1966) regarded the ability of colonial processes to develop according to the historical conditions between one model and another as fundamental. Varying strategies could be adopted for the expansion of the frontier in relation to indigenous populations and the metropolis.

Shafir (1996) demonstrates how the presence of Palestinians, particularly in the labour market, significantly influenced the actions of the Zionist movement on the ground. Zionist settler colonization went from a plantation model to one of pure settlement through the separation of the Zionist settler economy and the native Arab-Palestinian economy. Zionist leaders deliberately adopted a model of colonization inspired by the Prussian 'internal colonization' of Poland and the 'racial barrier' between white and Black workers in South Africa (Shafir, 1996). As Said (1979) notes, Zionism was only possible thanks to previous European colonial experiences, which were reproduced in Palestine. Therefore, we can observe the centrality of native resistance and the current capitalist modes of production as factors that have historically determined the form of colonization that took place in relation to the land and the indigenous population.

Englert (2020) argues that settler colonialism is better understood as a form of accumulation by dispossession, that is, a manifestation of the structural nature of primitive accumulation in capitalism. In other words, instead of a process with its own logic – 'elimination' – settler colonialism operates, like all colonialisms, within the logic of capital. This framework allows us to understand why settlers may seek the exploitation or elimination of natives as an accumulation strategy according to the material conditions they encounter. As Coulthard says, based on a dialogue between Wolfe's settler colonial theory and Marx's concept of primitive accumulation, the particularity of settler colonial accumulation is 'perpetual territorial acquisition'. Elimination turns out to be a result of the process, rather than the logic driving it.

Therefore, the settler colonial theory is fundamental because it places land as the main objective of the settlers, but this does not mean that in the material historical process the settler economy does not need to have greater control over the native life to better explore their work as a secondary goal. There is a dialectical relationship between the processes of elimination and exploitation, in which the native population is not understood only as redundant. The settler mode of domination may begin to impose new forms of government to enable a subaltern integration of the natives into the settler economy. It is important to emphasize that the balance between elimination and exploitation is not Cartesian, but is the result of the contradictions between the needs of different sectors of the settler society, such as the bourgeoisie, the settler movement, the middle class and their ability to face indigeneous resistance.

Settler colonial government and racial capitalism

Settler colonialism is a phenomenon that operates through racial policies of devaluation and dehumanization of native populations that offer ethical and legal resources for dispossession that endure and lead to the formation of permanent racial structures of domination (Wolfe, 2016). The process of settler colonization does not end with the closing of the frontier or the declaration of self-government by the settlers, but perpetuates itself as a permanently unfinished process (Wolfe, 2011). However, to prevail as a policy of domination, settler colonization tends to constitute a liberal governmentality based on consent and recognition on the part of the colonized subjects. This is the way to ensure the continuity of the more humane and liberal domination, dispossession and exploitation of the racial domination (Coulthard, 2014).

Coulthard's work on the policies of recognition and inclusion of indigenous populations in Canada shows that the forms of primitive accumulation and territorial dispossession are eternalized in gentler and more elusive ways, which is fundamental to understanding the complexity of the relationship between colonialism, capitalism and racism. It occurs through forced integration, the imposition of citizenship, miscegenation, multiculturalism, military confrontations over natural resources and disputes over private land ownership (Coulthard, 2014; Wolfe, 2011). In other words, the liberal state uses the centuries-old struggle of Amerindian peoples for dignity as a real trap when exploiting the identitarian vulnerabilities of the indigenous population. This has allowed the state to access the natural resources in an easy and peaceful way, an achievement that would otherwise have been more difficult to realize.

Singh (2016) notes that understanding the continuous and structural centrality of racism and colonialism to the process of primitive accumulation involves recognizing that racism and capitalism are mutually and permanently constituted, and not only in moments of expansion, the opening of new markets or crisis. These may well be the moments when these contradictions are most explosive, evident and apparent. This does not mean that in other more stable and peaceful periods they were overcome by the maturing of capitalism, rather that they were hidden and naturalized (Singh, 2016). This means that capitalism, which operates through class distinctions to reproduce itself, also uses racial differences to make possible distinct forms of accumulation that use force to extract even more wealth, such as forced labour and dispossession, to meet the consumption and production demands necessary for its global reproduction.

Chatterjee (1993: 13) observes that the defining particle of a colonial regime is 'the government of colonial difference', that is, the principle of government in which the colonized is ideologically and materially represented as inferior, radically the Other. 'Race' is therefore the specific defining element of colonial rule. Racism, for Fanon (1994), is both a 'product' and a process by which the dominant group resorts to dismantling the resistance capacities of the dominated, destroying their 'values, reference systems and social panorama' to make colonization possible together with brute force. After the social ordinances of the colonized were dismantled, a new system of references and values is imposed on the natives to ensure their subjugation and differentiation, together with violence (Fanon, 1994). In addition to promoting the material expansion of the capitalist mode of production, racialization and racism are internalized by the colonized in order to construct their subjectivity. Therefore, racism directly impacts the possibilities of a relationship between colonizers and the colonized, as well as the forms of resistance and emancipation of the colonized (Faustino, 2018).

By giving meaning and value to human spaces and identities, white supremacy organized all individuals and collectives into a deeply unequal global social order according to their relative worth (C. J. Robinson, 2000). On a macroscopic scale, capitalism established an uneven and combined development process that built a global system composed of interdependent central and peripheral nations. Barros argues that this relationship is also reproduced on a microscopic scale, where racism serves to contain the spare population produced by capital. The places for whites and Blacks are, respectively, inside of and outside of, included in and excluded from the labour market and the social space (Barros, 2019). Such a structure, far from being stable, is dynamic for both the dominant and the dominated. Certain individuals can rise socially through state inclusion policies that boost power structures without changing the racial hierarchy. Kelly (2017) argues that the central point of the idea of racial capitalism is that the fictions of race and racism are so weak that they end up revealing themselves. Therefore, for white and capitalist supremacy to remain, they need to keep changing for the structures and hierarchies to remain the same.

Harvey (2003) notes that the mode of accumulation by dispossession has the aspect of fraud or farce that are found in financial pyramid schemes, junk bonds and mass indebtedness. The violence of capital needs to be constantly masked by ideological constructions that hide reality. Racism makes these violent operations legible and justifiable through the domination of entire populations and nations in the name of civilization, progress and 'modernizations' promoted by capitalism (Wilson, 2012). In this way, development and capitalism could be portrayed as ways of resolving racialized inequalities and subjugations, while old colonial practices would remain under new signs and in new guises to allow the necessary accumulation for the privileged forms of life of the dominant classes (Bhattacharyya, 2018; Kelley, 2017).

Fanon (1994) observes that the disguise of brutal racism occurs from the moment in which the conditions of capitalist production demand more collaborators to increase productivity. This economic need results in modes of recognizing the existence of the colonized in a way that no longer reduces him to the status of an object, but instead to that of a colonial subject. This does not mean a decrease in racism or its end, but the imposition by the oppressor of new ways of seeing and understanding themselves in a covert and alienated way. Fanon observes that in the face of such depreciation, the consent to new ideological ways of living imposed by the colonizers or attempts to imitate the colonizer are means of escaping racial devaluation and the search for humanity denied by the colonizers.

Strakosch (2015) notes how the settler state's recognition that ostensibly coercive measures of early colonization were 'illiberal' makes liberal measures of inclusion, recognition and reconciliation a means for making the state less colonial, despite continuing dispossession by novel means. The previous exclusion of indigenous people is then justified by a discourse that alleges previous ignorance of their abilities. The recognition of the abilities and humanity of indigenous people justifies the extension to them of citizenship as well as other measures of inclusion by the settler society that are portrayed as acts of decolonization rather than the de facto return of indigenous land and jurisdiction. Thus, Strakosch understands social policies as ways of including indigenous peoples in the spheres of settler government and sovereignty.

Social colonial policies sought to counterbalance the high economic, political and social costs caused by the violence of genocide, looting and colonial slavery in different opportunities (Khalili, 2012). They also sought to contain resistance and bring stability to colonial productivity through more 'humanized' and tolerant forms of government that might be capable of incorporating rather than alienating colonized peoples. This mode of government was developed by parallel and connected efforts by several colonial agents around the world as a rationalization of the use of force against colonized peoples (Khalili, 2012). Repression of anti-colonial uprisings should be just enough to contain and persecute the insurgents, as the main objective would not be to destroy but to build a new pacified social order that facilitated capital accumulation. Colonial wars would no longer end with the cessation of weapons, but would continue permanently using social policies, such as the construction of schools and health clinics, the training of teachers and doctors, the opening of markets and the development of such infrastructure as highways, railways and ports (Khalili, 2012; Neocleous, 2011; Owens, 2016).

Khalili (2012) notes that liberal counterinsurgency strategies understood as 'unconventional' forms of engagement in asymmetrical conflicts against native populations began to be developed at the end of the nineteenth century to soften the genocidal practices of colonialism and allow the unimpeded transnational functioning of laissez-faire capitalism. One of the first exemplary cases of this phenomenon was the US settler colonization and the Indian Wars of the nineteenth century. At the time, the settlers who worked on the frontier simultaneously played the role of combatants and police. They were responsible for securing the frontier against any 'threat' after the expulsion of the indigenous populations through violence, disease and hunger. The extermination and dispossession of the natives, according to the Indian Removal Act issued by President Andrew Jackson in 1830, were justified on the basis of protection, paternalism and the 'humanity and national honour' of the American settlers (Khalili, 2012: 17).

The surviving natives were confined in 'reservations', often in inhospitable and infertile terrains under the monitoring and surveillance of the settlers, while the fertile lands were made available for white settlement.

Administration and pacification procedures developed in the expansion and consolidation of colonial authority over indigenous land in the United States – such as specific policies according to the 'level of development' of each tribe – became techniques in West Point manuals. They went on to be used in US foreign policy in the colonization and occupation of the Philippines, Latin America and the Caribbean (Grove, 2016; Khalili, 2012). In the war against indigenous nations, the US government also developed the country's first social welfare system through the creation of the Bureau of Indian Affairs (BIA), administered by the Department of War and to this day the body responsible for governing indigenous life. Since 1830, education and other welfare services have been used to attract indigenous people to the reserves and to 're-educate' them based on the logic of 'kill the Indian, save the man' (Grove, 2016).

One of the most influential characters in liberal pacification techniques was the French general Joseph Gallieni, who combined mapping territory to be conquered, mobile military units and protection of natives in rebellious regions with the construction of an autonomous government for the colonized (Khalili, 2012). The *politique des races* aimed to create a form of indirect government in which settlers provided conditions for loyal native groups to rule, patrol and enforce development policies on civilian populations. This technique of population management facilitated the construction of trust and consent to the colonial project, since native intermediaries were used in direct dealings with civilians. As a European bureaucrat aware of the interests of the metropolitan ruling classes in extracting long-term wealth and lowering the costs of colonial plunder, Gallieni always had the central objective of (re)building a favourable order through the implementation of an agenda of development and improvement of the natives. The *politique des races*, viewed by the French as a project for modernizing colonized societies with the collaboration of the natives, also involved the appropriation of land, the imposition of wage labour and the resettlement of populations in new villages governed by local chiefs. French colonial agents created the illusion among both colonizers and colonized that it was a sign of progress and civilization. However, there was never any intention of providing real development for the colonized, in the sense of equating them with the settlers, other than offering 'enough to keep them alive' (Fortier and Wong, 2019).

The pacifications aimed at conquering the 'hearts and minds' of the 'silent majority' of the civilian population by virtue of the 'armed social work' have become so widespread that their typically colonial origins were not noticed in contemporary wars, such as the US occupation of Iraq and the Israeli occupation of Palestine (Khalili, 2012; Neocleous, 2011; Owens, 2016). For Khalili (2012), Israel is a state that acts permanently according to the logic of counterinsurgency against the Palestinian population. The entire organization of the Israel Defence Forces (IDF) and its native governance strategy were profoundly influenced by British colonial servants in Mandate Palestine in the early twentieth century. The English official Orde Wingate, for instance, who served in Sudan before going to Palestine, was a friend of Israel's founding father David Ben-Gurion (Khalili, 2012). Wingate saw Arabs as 'ignorant and primitive' and was responsible for leading joint patrols by British forces and Zionist militias during the suppression of the 1936 Arab Revolt. Wingate also inspired central figures in Israel's early years, such as Moshe Dayan, who was responsible for the 'enlightened occupation' of the first decades of rule over the OPT. Dayan reproduced the traditional colonial logic of the carrot and the stick in order to pacify the Palestinians through policies of economic infrastructure development and free access to the Israeli labour market to create a dependence, along with surveillance and repression, which would build a stable social order (Hanieh, 2013). Neoliberalism has influenced distinct aspects of Israeli settler colonization since the 1980s. Such was the case with Israel's governance of the Palestinians.

The two faces of neoliberal settler colonialism

Neoliberalism is a term with multiple meanings, whose use can therefore be trivialized. Originally a doctrine developed by thinkers like Hayek and Mises as a means of reinvigorating liberalism and the values of Western civilization against all forms of collectivism in the post-war period, neoliberalism became a transnational political movement divided into different schools that intended to promote political change in European states and then all over the world. From the 1970s onwards, with the presence of Chicago School economists in the Pinochet dictatorship in Chile, neoliberalism took the form of a government policy for structural reforms that mainly dealt with fiscal responsibility, primary surplus and market liberalization, supposedly in pursuit of a 'minimal state' through cuts to the civil service and workers' social benefits – particularly those seen as racially distributive – in order to redistribute wealth to the bourgeoisie (Harvey, 2007). Neoliberalism represented a structural transformation of the organization of capital to provide the human and institutional conditions that could account for the internationalization of capital and the speed of its reproduction on a global scale characterized by the increasing prevalence of finance capital within the accumulation process (Hanieh, 2013; Saad Filho, 2015).

To understand the intertwining of neoliberalism with settler colonialism, it is necessary to consider the particularities of each system and how these two expressions of capitalism behave. One possible way of understanding them is through the concept of accumulation by dispossession, which has been recovered to address the violent dimension of the different reproductions of neoliberalism in recent decades. An example of this is the violent expulsion of poor populations to enrich sectors already favoured by neoliberal reforms (De Angelis, 2001; Harvey, 2003; Neocleous, 2011). This form of violent accumulation that affects the peripheries of cities and the planet is a consequence, as Harvey (2003) explains, of structural reforms that configure a new type of imperialism, in which international institutions, financial markets and organizations aligned with neoliberal doctrine promote imperialist interests.

The coercion of the empire of capital unleashed an 'endless war', such as the 'war on terror', in which violence became an everyday occurrence (Wood, 2005). This phenomenon can be clearly seen in the various diffuse 'wars' against terror, drugs and immigration, as well as in the proliferation of asymmetric conflicts and in the growth of surveillance of civilian populations formed by masses of precariously employed and surplus workers (Neocleous, 2011). Neocleous (2011) draws on liberal colonial counterinsurgency strategists to unveil what he understands as the fraud of security policies everywhere in the neoliberal capitalist world – whether in the centre or on the periphery – as a means of normalizing the violence inherent in the ongoing primitive accumulation of capital. He argues that security is a way of pacifying populations in order to build stable and predictable social orders for the valorization and reproduction of capital. The objective of pacification is not only to silence but also to permanently ensure the original and basic conditions necessary for the accumulation of capital, that is, that private ownership of the means of production remains in a few hands, and alternatives to selling their labour in the market remain absent for the rest of the dispossessed population (Neocleous, 2011, 2017).

Dardot, Gueguen and Laval (2021) see features of civil war in the way neoliberalism works in various parts of the world. Exceptional measures and sovereign resolutions are articulated against internal enemies, against those who are not identified as loyal members of the political community: immigrants, accused of wanting to destroy the country's potential and harm its competitiveness; unions; social movements; and spare populations, labelled incapable and unproductive. There is a logic of counterinsurgency at the severe punishment of strike movements, popular uprisings and social movements in central capitalist nations, such as the UK and France, which refer to their colonial experiences in Northern Ireland and Algeria, respectively. Torture, terror, arbitrary arrests and mass identity controls, once relegated to the peripheries of the system, have become common and widespread practices against civilian populations.

Several authors have observed how racism occupies a central place for neoliberalism by allowing the reproduction of conditions in which populations can be violently denied, excluded, expelled, repressed, confined, discarded and killed in a unpunished, accepted, legal and legitimate way (Barros, 2019; Gilmore, 2007; Goldberg, 2011; J.-A. Mbembe, 2003). The greater the number of unemployed and precarious workers, the greater the number of dissatisfied workers who need to be controlled so as not to disturb the social order and interfere in the accumulation process. The profiling of populations considered naturally 'dangerous', based on supposedly technical criteria of 'risk' that end up reinforcing previous racial criteria or racializing new population groups, is part and parcel of racial neoliberalism. Racial discourses on the subjects of Arab/Muslim/Palestinian terrorism and Black/poor/favela crime that frame the 'dangers' of large urban centres are disseminated locally and globally, forming a racialized surplus population to be subjugated, plundered and contained (Clarno, 2017; Gilmore, 2007; Goldberg, 2011).

The coercive process itself is commodified by security corporations (Neocleous, 2011). It is not by chance that Israel occupies a prominent place in the global market of surveillance and force, selling technologies, techniques and military tactics of control and repression to states and private corporations as universally compatible with their anxieties for the pacification of their subaltern, superfluous and disposable populations (Halper, 2015; Machold, 2015). Neoliberalism allows Israeli settler colonial practices to be exported globally as insecurity, precariousness and expropriation proliferate; on the other hand, it promotes the identification and solidarity of expropriated populations with the struggles of the Palestinians and other indigenous peoples (Collins, 2011).

Lloyd and Wolfe (2016) argue that neoliberalism and settler colonialism share the same *ethos*. The commodification of public goods promoted by neoliberalizations acts as substitutes for the old enclosures of common and indigenous lands at the dawn of capitalism (Lloyd and Wolfe, 2016). The growing irrelevance of racialized urban populations leads one to think that these populations are being 'indigenized', while settler colonialism's logic of elimination may have become global (Veracini, 2016). Mbembe (2003) argues that neoliberalism has promoted necropolitical projects to eliminate the racialized poor as the demand for their work declines and their existence is considered redundant, expendable and as constituting a threat of violence and disorder to the ruling classes. For him, Gaza is *the* necropolitical space. He identifies a universalization tendency of the Black condition in the systematic denial and epidermal reduction of the imperatives of neoliberalism around the world. Racialized elimination, exploitation and confinement are privatized as 'natural choices' made in the market (Melamed, 2011). Clarno (2017) uses the concept of 'neoliberal apartheid' to explain how the situation of racialized populations in South Africa and Palestine is maintained by the precariousness of the worker, increasing exploitation in informal activities, precarious housing on the margins of urban spaces and the promotion of the securitization of the bodies and residence spaces of these populations.

For Clarno (2017), neoliberal projects around the world intersect with a series of other projects not always aimed directly at capital accumulation. This requires attention to the complex formations that result from the articulation of simultaneous projects which tend to reorganize forms of domination by promoting partial autonomy for historically oppressed groups or the reduction of inequality, but without erasing racism (Melamed, 2011; Tilley and Shilliam,

2018). In addition to racist and colonial projects, neoliberalism could also contradict and falsely intertwine with anti-racist and anti-colonial projects. Coevally with the crisis in the Keynesian mode of production, which gave rise to the neoliberal reforms of the 1980s, these projects were intertwined with demands for independence, civil rights, recognition and multiculturalism by subaltern populations around the world. Neoliberalism's ideology of liberty, national progress and individual independence was linked with the libertarian claims of colonized and racialized populations. The technocrats and neoliberal leaders of global powers and international financial institutions knew how to *sell* neoliberal restructurings as *bitter* remedies towards the end of colonial and racial domination, such as in the Oslo process (Clarno, 2017). Clarno also identifies the relationship between legal equality, partial autonomy for the colonized and continued colonization by the ruling classes as characteristic of the 'neoliberal apartheid' of South Africa and Palestine that followed the 'decolonizations' of the 1990s. That is, it involves a combination of coercive and soft practices that aim to maintain racial hierarchy by new means, now mediated mainly by the neoliberal market.

Strakosch (2015) considers that the joint examination of neoliberalism and settler colonialism must involve not only exclusionary practices but also inclusive ones, such as commodification, individual economic participation and capacity-building. In an analysis of training programmes for indigenous peoples in Australia, she describes how these policies make it possible to classify indigenous people as responsible for their own disadvantages and failures in the market. Indigenous populations are obliged to daily prove their ability to belong to the settler political community and to enjoy the right to citizenship. They are locked into a kind of *exclusive inclusion* in order to be better governed and for disputes over the legitimacy of the settler state to be resolved.

Foucault (2010) noted how neoliberalism should be understood as a new form of government of subjects based on the administration of their freedoms, and not merely on coercion. This new rationality governs individuals through their own self-responsibility, making them independent of state social protection policies. Laval and Dardot (2017) argue that *management* is a central element to understand neoliberalism, which is, in their view, primarily a new form of government of subjects, families and states according to an entrepreneurial rationale of efficiency, improvement, responsibility and planning in the free market competition. This entrepreneurial governmentality 'is [to] govern through liberty – that is, to actively exploit the freedom allowed individuals so that they end up conforming to certain norms of their own accord' (Dardot and Laval, 2017: 10). Neoliberalism is therefore a political rationale for a new social regulation of capitalism based on the entrepreneurial form and according to the principle of competition – a transition from 'welfare to workfare'.

Neoliberal ideologues and their interventions in society, just like former colonial agents, were concerned with the *construction* and *management* of a social order that would sustain the legal, socioeconomic and subjective conditions for the accumulation and reproduction of capital in a predictable and sustainable way (Dardot and Laval, 2017; Neocleous, 2017; Whyte, 2019). The defence of the private sphere of civil society is aimed not only at increasing the productivity of capital but also at containing the violence of politics. The market order would only occur within an 'open society' formed by individuals with an 'open mind' to the dynamics of the market and exchange with other economic actors, even if they have contradictory political interests, transforming opponents into partners (Whyte, 2019). This governmentality by *liberal freedom* creates the illusion of separation between economics and politics as distinct spheres; the 'end of politics' allows for the rise of non-state actors over the sphere of government, imposing the privatization of risk management, empowerment techniques and the action of market forces and business models. *Self-government* allows individuals to participate actively in solving problems that were previously the state responsibility (Lemke, 2015). Self-entrepreneurial neoliberal subjects can ensure all their 'rights' in the market: health, housing, education, as well as dignity, freedom and even the 'fullness of the soul', as Hayek (quoted in Dardot and Laval, 2017) puts it.

Fraser (2017) notes that in the United States, the formation of a *progressive neoliberalism* occurred through the alliance between new social movements – feminism, anti-racism, multiculturalism and LGBTQIA+ – and the service sector – Wall Street, Silicon Valley, Hollywood. The agendas and leadership of these movements began to be led by the market, which represented supposedly emancipatory values of empowerment, diversity, entrepreneurship, self-sufficiency and freedom of action for 'talented' and 'capable' individuals who should not 'waste' their 'human capital' in activities that do not bring material results to their communities (Fraser, 2017). For example, the socio-economic rise of some individuals through policies linked to 'Black entrepreneurship' raised the status of a more realistic alternative means of combating racism, but transformed them into managers of the neoliberal capitalist order with legitimacy to their social base (Haider, 2018; Taylor, 2021).

Another example of this logic put into practice was the adoption of neoliberalism by the formerly socialist and social democratic lefts around the world, such as in the case of the European Third Way of the 1990s and 2000s, which was based on the understanding that 'there is no alternative'. The market has become an ally to which countries, parties and institutions should at least minimally adapt. In Palestine/Israel, this turn occurs precisely in the 'Oslo process' of the 1990s, when the Israelis left and the Palestinians consented to the neoliberal agenda of the US and international financial institutions as a basic condition for the normalization of political relations and the construction of the Palestinian State (Haddad, 2016; Hanieh, 2013). Neoliberalism's discourses and entrepreneurial development practices have thus proved to be frauds capable of provoking accommodation between opposing forces, emptying them of their radical content, and making them into managers of the new capitalist social order. This was the case for the PLO leaders who accepted the Oslo Accords (Hanieh, 2013): the soft policies of progressive neoliberalism acted as domestication of those who originally opposed neoliberalism.

Progressive neoliberalism was adopted by international institutions, in particular the World Bank (WB), in the constitution of a 'soft imperialism' (M. Davis, 2006). The promotion of 'good practices' of governance entered the international agenda from the 1990s onwards, particularly for the Third World: policies of democratization, combating corruption and so on were pushed together with structural economic reforms and the strengthening of market-friendly NGOs as the main promoters of programmes to fight poverty through entrepreneurship and microcredit, among other initiatives (Anghie, 2005; Saad-Filho, 2005). The WB provides millions of dollars to projects around the world that put the idea of citizen empowerment into practice, from India to Brazil, including Palestine and other Middle Eastern countries in situations of 'asymmetric conflict' or 'social vulnerability' (Hanieh, 2016). In the multilateral occupation of Iraq in the 2000s, for example, entrepreneurship was used as an 'unconventional' arm of counterinsurgency to 'attract' the civilian population and build favourable social conditions for foreign capital and Iraqi development. With the help of international NGOs and the WB, the occupying government promoted capitalization and financing programmes aimed at unemployed youth and women, apparently in respect of human rights and freedom (Owens, 2016).

The Peruvian Hernando de Soto, for example, is a neoliberal economist enthusiastic about popular entrepreneurship as a solution to poverty and who had a great influence on WB policies for the development of Third World nations from the 1980s. The poorest populations of underdeveloped nations came to be seen – instead of as a problem – as a solution for capitalism (Botelho, 2013). Soto argues that the 'mystery of capital' lies precisely in the informalized surplus populations deprived by structural reforms. And that the survival strategies of subaltern populations contain an immense entrepreneurial potential condemned to informality and illegality by the totalitarian action of the state. Therefore, it is up to the state to act together with civil society to unhinder the free initiative of the poor and stimulate the skills, conditions and opportunities for these 'heroic' protocapitalist individuals to be empowered by entrepreneurial activity and to actively participate in the competitive market (Botelho, 2013; Davis, 2006).

Thus, these subjects could promote development by themselves, 'free' from permanent dependence on welfare assistance. In addition to microcredit and capacity-building programmes, Soto saw land tenure regularization (of slum areas, for example) as a magic solution that would simultaneously promote the capitalization and self-responsibility necessary to make them true entrepreneurs and, therefore, the owners of their destinies (Davis, 2006). Granting land title to urban squatters would immediately create enormous wealth for the working poor at little or no cost to the government. Part of this new wealth could serve as capital for microentrepreneurs to create jobs in slums.

Neoliberal social policies do not imply a permanent and universal right, but minimum welfare focused on specific target audiences, such as 'pockets of poverty', to help them develop the specific skills required and that are measurable by the neoliberal market – in other words, to include them in the game of competitive self-entrepreneurship (Davis, 2006; Whyte, 2019). Empowerment, microcredit and popular entrepreneurship[2] programmes have led to NGOs taking the place of left-wing social movements, unions and community associations in the organization and representation of the demands of working and peripheral populations and have proven to be particularly adept at co-opting former leaders and fostering new ones (Davis, 2006). This is why the discourse of 'empowerment' is a consensus between the 'new left' and the 'new right', which defends the insertion of the poorest into the market as an inescapable reality and a humanitarian act (Hanieh, 2016).

In Rio de Janeiro, entrepreneurship was used as a social policy conducted by NGOs as part of the process of pacifying favelas through police and military occupation – this model was exported to Haiti during the Brazilian occupation (2004–17). Subjects were encouraged to promote the transformation of their communities through entrepreneurial practices, understood as more rational and efficient than other forms of popular mobilization in the fight against exclusion, genocide and racism. Entrepreneurial activity managed to carry with it both a rebellious do-it-yourself dimension and an economic and social morality of responsibility and efficiency that, due to its ambiguity, promotes an approximation between the discourses of economic liberalism and left-wing utopias (L. D. Tommasi and Velazco, 2016). In this way, neoliberalism spreads across the outskirts of large cities inhabited by racially subaltern populations and contributes to the counterinsurgency goals of the ruling classes.

These apparently progressive measures allowed slum subalterns to enter the formal economy, but they almost always mean increasing the cost of living and taxes for tenants and landlords, the population most susceptible to official government instruments and financial inspection, collection and confiscation institutions. This created inequalities among the residents of slums, dividing them between residents of regularized and non-regularized housing and individualizing the struggle for housing by breaking fundamental bonds of solidarity (Davis, 2006). Thus, instead of reducing social inequality and generating prosperity, inclusion can promote expulsion either through direct

---

[2] In the context of flexibilization of labour relations and the growth of unemployment, the definition of entrepreneurship acquires new contours. Ludmila Abilio (2019: 4) argues that entrepreneurship today refers to a means of obscuring the 'processes of informalisation of work and transfer of risks to the worker, who remains subordinated as a worker, but can now be presented as an entrepreneur'.

dispossession, with the confiscation of property due to financial indebtedness arising out of a property being mortgaged for an entrepreneurial initiative, or by indirect removal through real estate appreciation and gentrification resulting from infrastructural improvements. Therefore, the socio-spatial development and regulation of a subaltern population to neoliberalism can mean a form of predatory inclusion (Davis, 2006; Taylor, 2021).

Neoliberal urbanization and settler colonization are two processes that merge quite easily; such are the cases of Rio de Janeiro and Jerusalem, allowing the racial structure to normalize itself as a market choice and, dialectically, for the market to benefit from racial structural inequality to accumulate capital (Huberman and Nasser, 2019). Most studies point to the continuity, within neoliberal capitalism, of settler colonizing policies of exclusion, removal, impoverishment and the ostentatious policing of indigenous spaces, as seen in studies of Winnipeg (Canada), Minneapolis (the United States), Johannesburg (South Africa), Rio de Janeiro (Brazil), Townsville (Australia) and Jerusalem (Blatman-Thomas and Porter, 2018; Dorries, Hugill and Tomiak, 2019; Poets, 2020; Shalhoub-Kevorkian, 2015). The urban condition structured by settler colonialism tends to produce specific socio-spatial configurations: permanent racialized property regimes; ongoing dispossession of indigenous populations; denial of indigenous sovereignty or of the presence of indigenous people in cities, their ways of life, economic and cultural activities; and preservation of the settlers' naturalized privileges in urban daily life. The construction of a city materially means an advance, a stage in the 'progress' and 'development' of the process of settler colonization through the urbanization of space (Porter and Yiftachel, 2017). Under the banner of development, the inclusion of East Jerusalem's Palestinians through neoliberal mechanisms examined in this book represents a new stage in the Israeli settler colonial process. This is not an event in which neoliberal capitalism would promote setbacks to the Israeli urban apartheid, but rather its reproduction.

Resisting neoliberal settler colonialism

It can be said that settler colonialism and neoliberalism are essentially counterrevolutionary projects, which act preventively and permanently within the main lines of dispossession. The brutality of popular entrepreneurship reveals the fraudulent nature of the 'human face' of neoliberalism and merely recalibrates the same dehumanizing practices of the processes of accumulation by dispossession in ideologically more palatable forms. For this reason, neoliberal practices have been deliberately used as an 'unconventional' arm of counterinsurgency from Baghdad to Rio de Janeiro, via Jerusalem. Their effectiveness on the most underprivileged and dispossessed layers of the subaltern classes, however, rests not only on the masking of neoliberal propaganda about populations with little formal education or a 'bad conscience', but also on the material relationships that constitute the condition for entrepreneurship to present itself as an inescapable social fact. Confronted with the contradictions that subaltern subjects face in a world dominated by racial capitalism, resisting the traps set by settler colonialism through neoliberal instruments presents numerous difficulties.

Fanon (1963) defends the importance of the violent rejection of colonialism – its symbols, institutions, ideologies, rationales and discourses – by the natives as a way of provoking a collective catharsis that breaks not only the space the colonizer reserves for the colonized. The hierarchical ordering of differences between classes, races, genders, sexualities and other identities necessary for the progression of capitalism and colonialism needs to be destroyed – not reformed. Otherwise, the colonized can fall into a trap and become a reproduction of the colonizer.

Fanon (1963) points out the dangers of the essentialist assertion of racial and national identity by liberation movements. He indicates that national juridic independence over a post-colonial territory could lead to the adaptation of nationalist elites to the global system that originally oppressed them. (Post-)colonial peoples would continue to be subject to the brutalizing will of commodity and racism, even if by gentle, humanized and consented-to means.

Fanon also defines the limitations of individual solutions as a way of promoting the emancipation of colonized men and women. Adaptation to hegemonic values brings the illusion of independence and freedom suited to (neo)colonial interests, which are organized to maintain colonization in the post-colonial context from the moment that anti-colonial violence starts (Fanon, 1963, 1994). Fanon describes revolutionary violence as a form of *catharsis* for individuals and peoples dehumanized and objectified by colonialism. He understands that revolutionary praxis serves as a form of humanization, transforming the colonized into truly emancipated subjects. And he adds that the affirmation of the existence of the colonized must be a temporary stage in the liberation process, which must be followed by a policy of universal emancipation. Violence and rejection of the colonial system of oppression are at the core of this cathartic process of subjectivation of the colonized.

Neoliberal traps, such as entrepreneurship, reinforce essentialist and individualist forms of action and resistance among subaltern populations, impeding their actual emancipation. For this reason, several authors question the emancipatory potential of (neo)liberal multiculturalism projects in racially structured contexts, both among Afro-descent populations and indigenous and other migrant ethnicities (Barros, 2019; Coulthard, 2014; Haider, 2018; Melamed, 2011; Simpson, 2017; Tatour, 2016).

In the government of Palestinian citizens of Israel, Tatour (2016) notes that the ambivalence of liberal human rights norms is intertwined with the hybridism of the Israeli settler government, which always leaves open the possibility of inclusion and represses the most radical Palestinian resistance movements aimed at transformation and rejection of the Israeli State. The concept of human rights created illusions among Palestinians that led them to an accommodation with Zionist hegemony (Tatour, 2016). But they also paved the way for radical forms of transformative and anti-colonial resistance, such as queer Palestinian movements that reject Israeli pinkwashing.

The chances of equality and freedom in liberal bourgeois society, as Marx noted in 'On the Jewish Question' (2010), will always be limited to the illusion of such equality and freedom in their legal forms, since the institutions that construct religious and ethnic diversity as racist differentiations that are interesting to capital will continue to act and reproduce this social reality. Neoliberal and colonial intellectuals, such as Hayek and Jabotinsky, have been clear that the only options available to those who wanted to live outside the hegemonic order are conversion or destruction. At best, oppressed people may hope for autonomy within the dominant structure. The Oslo Accords represented this type of political project by coming under the framework of Palestinian autonomy. The promotion of neoliberal development by international financial institutions and NGOs was key to enabling Palestinian autonomy under Israeli settler colonial sovereignty (Haddad, 2016).

Some sectors of the Palestinians have been seduced by neoliberal developmentalism, convinced that it is the only alternative for the liberation of Palestine. The reality is that the PA is stuck on a path of state-building that is supported by foreign aid that does not drive it towards emancipation as it should have, but instead keeps it in continuous subjection for the benefit of the political and economic elites of the OPTs (Dana, 2019; Haddad, 2016; Seidel, 2019). The NGOs occupied the place previously held mainly by left-wing political parties and fostered a liberal middle class dependent on foreign aid (Dana, 2016). This model compromises an economy of resistance, impeding, for instance, family farming practices that would allow for food sovereignty, solidarity and mutual aid. But this model requires the rejection of neoliberal forms, such as that of commodity-exporting agribusinesses, which only increase economic dependence.

The global campaign for Boycott, Divestment and Sanctions (BDS) is an example of a movement against the normalization of settler colonial power, refusing any activity with Israeli institutions or projects that normalize settler colonial power and present the situation as a mere conflict between two equal parties (Hanieh, 2016). The BDS movement connects the Palestinian struggle to the struggles of other peoples and social groups oppressed and exploited by colonialism and capitalism. The refusal to pay taxes or consume Israeli products in combination with the efforts to seek alternative and independent forms of development was central to the success of the First Intifada in 1987. Refusal has also been a form of struggle among Palestinian Jerusalemites, who, despite having the right to participate in municipal elections for the Israeli mayoralty, have historically refused to do so in order not to legitimize the settler colonial claims of sovereignty over the city (W. Salem, 2018).

Indigenous and anti-colonial authors stress the importance of rejection as both a necessary condition and a pedagogical stage that exposes the brutality of colonialism, removing its veils and the masks of colonial illusions and traps (Coulthard, 2014; Fanon, 1963; Simpson, 2017). The colonial entity needs to be totally rejected to allow its dismantling and to pave the way for emancipation and decolonization (Fanon, 1963). Only through the rejection and destruction of the colonist/native dialectical positions can true decolonization occur (Mamdani, 2001). In the words of Memmi (1974: 171): 'Revolt is the only way out of the colonial situation, and the colonized realizes it sooner or later. His condition is absolute and cries for an absolute solution; a break and not a compromise.'

In the context of contemporary Palestine, this involves neoliberal policies, including some that are relatively benign and inclusive and some that do not necessarily have an Israeli face. As Hanieh (2016) says, the struggle against neoliberalism must be inextricably linked to the larger struggle against Israeli power, which, in practice, means defending the extension of social and economic rights and repudiating the myth of market neutrality.

2

Neoliberal apartheid in Jerusalem

How the contemporary formation of a
neoliberal apartheid leads to the reproduction of the
socio-spatial segregations of settler colonial racism in the
urban fabric

The summer of 2014 in Palestine made international headlines because of the deadliest air strikes ever launched by Israel against the Gaza Strip. These led to more than 2,251 Palestinians being killed and more than eleven thousand being injured, in addition to the destruction of local infrastructure (Hasan, 2018). That same summer, the city of Jerusalem also suffered. After Jewish settlers kidnapped and murdered the young Palestinian Mohammed Abu-Khdeir, a resident of the Shuafat neighbourhood of East Jerusalem, a series of mass protests and violent conflicts broke out across the city (Ihmoud, 2015). Knife attacks and random hit-and-run attacks by young Palestinians against Israelis led to some commentators suggesting links to the Islamic State (Bartal, 2017), while others noted the growing disorganization of the popular uprising (W. Salem, 2018). In response, armed Jewish settlers murdered Palestinians in the streets after the mayor of Jerusalem asked people to react (Hever, 2018).

The security forces collectively punished Palestinians with night-time raids on their neighbourhoods, vexatious searches and the imprisonment of many youths, as well as gas attacks, closures of businesses and the encircling of entire neighbourhoods with concrete blocks (Mansour, 2018). Palestinian workers, such as bus drivers, resigned out of fear of Israeli violence, while ultranationalist Jewish groups began to persecute Palestinians moving around West Jerusalem and called for boycotts of Israeli companies that employed

Palestinian workers (Shtern, 2015, 2017). Although the individual attacks resulted in some instances of commentators baptizing the movement the 'Knife Intifada', the most notable mobilization among Palestinians took place in response to an attempt by the Israeli authorities to place metal detectors at the entrances to the Temple Mount. Thousands of Palestinians mobilized in unprecedented collective prayer sessions for the right of free access to this part of the city (Hassan and Alsaafin, 2017).

All these conflicts took place at the height of the West Jerusalem urban redevelopment process led by Mayor Nir Barkat, to make Jerusalem a global city attractive to international capital, to tourism and to Jews wishing to live in Israel's 'unified and indivisible capital'. Since the late 2000s, the city has undergone a socio-spatial transformation to sell itself to internal and external audiences as a blend of the ancient and the modern: of Jewish tradition and Zionist high-tech innovation (Alfasi and Ganan, 2015; Arafeh, 2016b; Yacobi, 2012a).

The analysis of the political economy of Jerusalem is a better way to understand the social conflicts in the city, as opposed to the view that the violent dynamics are the result of religious fundamentalism (Bartal, 2017) or the 'shocks' caused by the socio-spatial configurations of the city or of urban mobility (Rokem, Weiss and Miodownik, 2018). The dispute over Jerusalem is not only of an ethnonational nature, as stated in much of the literature (Dumper, 2014; Pullan, 2011; Rokem and Vaughan, 2018; Shlay and Rosen, 2015), but it is also a class conflict entangled with the racial division.

In East Jerusalem, settler colonial disputes between Palestinians and Israelis are intertwined with the conflicts around the neoliberal project across the socio-spatial fabric of the city (Clarno, 2017; Mansour, 2018; Margalit, 2018; Yacobi, 2016). The combination of the dispossessing characteristics of the modes of accumulation and reproduction of neoliberalism and settler colonialism, which operate through the racial differentiations existing in spaces and social relations, produce ever more conflicts and crises in the city. Settler colonial violence also occurs through neoliberal practices. The advance of settler colonialism in Israel occurs naturally and appears to be the result of relations between actors in the market.

The Jerusalem Intifada that has been going on intermittently since 2014 was characterized by the Palestinian urban precariat of East Jerusalem reacting to the way in which the Israeli neoliberal settler colonialism government plunders the city. The spontaneous, fragmented and disorganized mobilization of the Palestinians is the result of the neoliberal apartheid that has made the Palestinian population of Jerusalem into a highly informal, precarious and impoverished working class.

Because of the expansion of commodification, the class struggle and social movements under the neoliberal regime increasingly resemble anti-colonial and anti-racist struggles, which never had labour-related demands as their sole focus. In a study of revolts against neoliberalism during the 2010s in Brazil, South Africa and Portugal, Braga (2017) discusses how the demands of urban precariats go beyond the exclusive universe of labour, to address other elements that make up social reproduction, such as housing.[1] Mobilizations against the oppression of unemployed populations – who were deprived of dignity or access to public spaces and services, systematically expelled from their homes, with their relatives victimized by arbitrary arrests and murdered by violence committed by the state and large corporations – are the reasons historically central to the anti-colonial struggle (Fanon, 1963). As Fanon (1963: 126) writes, formal waged workers are not the basis of the social order in a colonial context that will bring about the emancipatory decolonial revolution in urban spaces, but the so-called lumpenproletariat of the urban masses:

> In fact the rebellion, which began in the country districts, will filter into the towns through that fraction of the peasant population which is blocked on the outer fringe of the urban centers, that fraction which has not yet succeeded in finding a bone to gnaw in the colonial system. The men whom the growing population of the country districts and colonial expropriation have brought to desert their family holdings circle tirelessly around the different towns, hoping that one day or another they will be allowed inside. It is within this mass of humanity, this people of the shanty towns, at the core of the lumpenproletariat, that the rebellion will find its urban spearhead. For the lumpenproletariat, that horde of starving men, uprooted from their tribe

---

[1] There are disagreements in the literature around the definition of the 'precariat'. For Guy Standing, the precariat is a 'new social class'. Braga departs from Standing by stating that the precariat is not external to the wage relation that characterizes the capitalist mode of production. Therefore, the precariat belongs to the proletariat, being only the 'precarized proletariat'. See Standing (2011) and Braga (2017).

and from their clan, constitutes one of the most spontaneous and the most radically revolutionary forces of a colonized people. (Fanon, 1963: 128)

Therefore, the dynamics of the class struggle under a settler colonial regime should not be reduced to that which in orthodox terms is understood as a formal waged working class, excluding the racialized dimension of the equation. It must be understood in a broader way, including all of the oppressed and exploited. Using South Africa as an example, the union between the exploited and the oppressed in Palestine is a possibility for overcoming apartheid through unity (Hussein, 2015). This is especially pertinent when considering the liberation of Jerusalem. Jerusalem should not be physically divided between Israelis and Palestinians, as Faisal Husseini has argued, but should remain geographically open in the event of reconciliation. Neoliberalism brought the Jewish and Palestinian precariat/lumpenproletariat to the streets: the Israeli precariat demonstrations against rising cost of living in 2011, and the Palestinians' Jerusalem Intifada of 2014–17. Although both popular movements had a common target in the effects of the same neoliberal urbanism process – after all, gentrification and real estate speculation have caused the dispossession both of Palestinians in East Jerusalem (Alkhalili, 2017) and of Jews in West Jerusalem (Zaban, 2016) – there was no possibility of a class alliance across racial divisions. The Israeli government remains structurally stable despite instabilities on the surface, as it is based on the hardness of the racial division produced by decades of settler colonialism that both facilitate neoliberalization and prevent popular protests against the ever-increasing plunder of public goods from turning into a revolutionary movement capable of overcoming the hegemonic mode of production and Zionist racial supremacy.

Settler colonialism and neoliberalism combine in both the western and eastern parts of Jerusalem, as opposed to traditional approaches that see neoliberalism only on the Israeli side, and settler colonialism only on the Palestinian side. This is not to say that neoliberal settler colonialism works identically in settler and native social spaces, but that the reproduction of inequalities and differentiations between racial groups occurs in specific and different ways. Also, neoliberal government is not infallible. Its vulnerability lies precisely in the increasing dependence of Israeli capital on the exploitation of Palestinian labour and territories, quite different from the historic separation and alienation of native labour by the Israeli settler regime during the hegemony of Labour Zionism until the 1970s (Englert, 2017; Ross, 2019; Shtern, 2018b).

The neoliberal apartheid paradigm

For theorists such as Clarno and Yacobi, the concept of neoliberal apartheid in Jerusalem is a conjugation of settler colonial racism with neoliberalism similar to the situation today in Johannesburg after the end of the formal legal-institutional apartheid regime. In this type of government, inequalities between racial groups are reproduced on a daily basis and normalized by market relations. Urban planning, the commodification of space by the real estate market, gentrification and securitization processes have become key means for advancing settler colonization (Clarno, 2017; Yacobi, 2016). This interpretation is in line with the assessment that other scholars make of the intersection between neoliberalism, settler colonialism and racism in urban spaces in different countries, such as Canada and Australia, where racialized violence takes on harder or softer facets according to the racial group, the social class and the space in which it occurs (Blatman-Thomas and Porter, 2018; Dorries, Hugill and Tomiak, 2019; Poets, 2020).

Clarno (2017) defines as common features of neoliberal apartheid observed in Palestine/Israel and in South Africa as the combination of extreme inequality with the constant crisis of fragile regimes. In Palestine/Israel, one of the particular features is the formation of enclaves, such as Ramallah, surrounded by highly securitized gated communities, which have served as the most accurate portrayal of the settler colonization of indigenous lands in recent decades. Yacobi (2016) defines neoliberal apartheid as a radicalization of the ethnocratic regime in force in Jerusalem and the other 'mixed cities' in Israel, which are urban spaces divided between and contested by Israelis and Palestinians, such as Haifa, where the prevalence of Israelis over Palestinians gives an illusory appearance of democracy thanks to the legitimacy conferred by the legal system and the official decisions of the state.

Despite the many similarities in the institutional-legal fields between the racially segregated regimes of South Africa and Israel, apartheid has become an important paradigm for both the *praxis* of the Palestinian national movement, through BDS, and the resurgence of the paradigm of a binational state (Hussein, 2015), as well as critical theories on the Palestinian question (Makdisi, 2018; Soske and Jacobs, 2015). Labour relations, however, have always been a point of fundamental divergence, both analytically and politically (Clarno, 2017; Greenstein, 2015; Makdisi, 2018). In addition to being central to understanding the social order and the legal apparatus, the issue of labour is fundamental to shaping the possibilities of the resistance to, and the overcoming of, the apartheid regime. The organized mobilization of the Black labour movement was essential for building up internal economic and social pressures that, together with the external influence of the BDS campaign, put an end to official apartheid in South Africa in the 1990s (Greenstein, 2015).

Although South African and Israeli apartheids are historical products of settler colonial processes by white European settlers, there are theorists who argue that this situation could not be repeated in Palestine/Israel because the Israelis are free from economic pressures that oppose their segregationist racist imperatives as they do not depend on the exploitation of Palestinian labour (Greenstein, 2015). While the South African regime was constituted to exploit the native labour on which it was dependent to sustain white privileges, the Israeli form of government was structured for the accumulation of native land by the dispossession of Palestinians, without necessarily taking advantage of them as a workforce, which makes them marginalized, disposable and eliminable (Greenstein, 2015; Makdisi, 2018). This characteristic can be more clearly perceived when observing the much more relentless and genocidal violence of Israeli apartheid when compared to the South African model. As Mbembe (2015: 8) observes, Israeli apartheid 'is not South African-style apartheid. It is much more lethal.' This is not to say that the Afrikaners were more benevolent or less racist than the Israelis, but that the political economy of the historical settler colonial process of conquest and resistance in these countries made South African racial capitalism organize itself differently from Israeli racial capitalism.

The analysis of the issue of labour in the Israeli system in the literature on settler colonialism in Palestine is usually restricted to the process of creating employment opportunities with 'European wages' in the early twentieth century so that the Jewish settler population can live well on indigenous lands, while Palestinian labour is exploited in exceptional circumstances when appropriate (Shafir, 1996; Wolfe, 2016). However, Israeli capital increasingly came to depend on Palestinian labour throughout the twentieth century until the First Intifada, when dependence on native labour put significant economic pressure on Israelis. The separation policy imposed on Palestinians in the Oslo years combined with the importation of foreign labour allowed Israelis to reduce Israel's economic vulnerability to native labour (Englert, 2017).

Some researchers have noticed a change in this trend towards the exploitation of native labour since the end of the Second Intifada on both sides of the Green Line (Englert, 2017; Ross, 2019), including Jerusalem (Clarno, 2017; Shtern, 2018b; Yacobi, 2016). Normally, neoliberalism seeks to reduce the power of labour in the face of capital, but, paradoxically, this process of greater exploitation of Palestinian labour accelerated with the deepening of neoliberalism in Palestine/Israel, which occurs mainly in the most precarious, informal, dangerous and poorly paid situations (Englert, 2017). It can be said that there is a 'South Africanization' of the relationship between the Zionist project and the indigenous Palestinians, in the opposite direction of the total separation that the settler regime originally aspired to. The country's political economy is moving towards mutual dependence between Palestinian labour and Israeli capital in sectors such as construction and agriculture (Englert, 2017; Ross, 2019; Shtern, 2018b). Finally, the bibliography has also pointed to the emergence of independent Palestinian labour struggles and trade union movements in both the West Bank and Israel (Alva, 2016; Englert, 2017).

Although the critical literature on Jerusalem correctly identifies the mechanisms that combine settler colonialism and neoliberalism and their fractures, conflicts, instabilities, removals, repressions, exclusions and deaths in the socio-spatial fabric of Jerusalem, these facts have long since been normalized and trivialized. The re-emergence of the labour issue in Palestine/Israel and in Jerusalem reveals another fracture produced by settler colonial racism that is little analysed in the main theoretical corpus: that of the Jerusalemite working class, racially divided between privileged Israeli-Jewish workers and overexploited Palestinian workers. Understanding the dispute for Jerusalem also as a class struggle within a neoliberal apartheid allows us to understand the struggle for decolonization in new ways and formats. Indeed, the struggle for the decolonization of Palestine/Israel from the point of view of Jerusalem does imply a confrontation not only against the Israeli settler state apparatus but also against the neoliberal project of the ruling classes that exploit and oppress the Palestinians and the Israeli working classes at the same time, although in different ways based on the compositions of race and class. It would, in theory, allow for the forging of a class alliance across racial cleavages to constitute a movement that challenges the hegemonic order. The rise of a multiracial working-class movement could be a real possibility for decolonization. However, this is not the story of Jerusalem after Oslo.

Settler colonial neoliberal urbanism in post-Oslo

Jerusalem after the Second Intifada was an even more impoverished and unattractive city for Israeli, Palestinian and international investors than it was at the start of the Oslo negotiations. Instead of the privatized economic peace promised by the Labour Zionists, the result of Oslo was for Jerusalem to become an even more precarious city, not only in its Palestinian neighbourhoods but also in its Israeli ones. The poverty rate among Jewish families was 27 per cent, the highest in the country. It is highest (64 per cent) among the orthodox community, who make up the majority of Jerusalem's Jews. Of the approximately 584,000 Jews living in Jerusalem in 2020, 35 per cent were ultra-Orthodox and 18.9 per cent were secular (Assaf-Shapira et al., 2022). The emigration of Jewish residents to other parts of the country and abroad has caused economic and demographic concerns for Israeli leaders. Indeed, the city has recorded a negative net migration rate of Jewish citizens since 1986. In 2020 and 2019, approximately 7,900 and 8,100 Jews emigrated from Jerusalem, respectively. The highest emigration rate since 1980 was recorded in 2012, when 8,500 Jews left the city (Assaf-Shapira et al., 2022). The construction of Jerusalem as a global and prosperous city, connected to the transnational circuits of capital, is closely linked to the project of Judaization of the city to contain the possibility of the Palestinian population constituting a majority in the near future.

The initial response of Jewish Jerusalemites to these problems was the election of the first ultra-Orthodox Jew to govern the city, Rabbi Uri Lupolianski (2003–8). His religious orientation did not prevent him from adopting neoliberal measures in accordance with the hegemonic order to attract Jews and capital to the city at the same time, in continuity with the neoliberal urbanism agenda initiated by Ehud Olmert (1993–2003) under the golden promises of Oslo. The mayor offered monthly grants to workers in the high-tech sector who were living in the city, and aid to young Jews who were going to study at local universities (Lis, 2005). But his deliberately racist and conservative position created friction with the Palestinian population and the Jewish LGBTQA+ community and hindered his measures to encourage economic development and Judaization (Erlanger, 2005).

High-tech entrepreneur Nir Barkat, who succeeded Lupolianski as mayor in 2008, was elected on a pledge to economically develop Jerusalem for both Israeli Jews and Palestinians. As an organic representative of neoliberal Zionism, Barkat came into municipal politics from philanthropic involvement in online entrepreneurial skills training during the Oslo years. After his defeat in the 2003 election, he became the leader of the opposition and helped create the NGO StartUp Jerusalem, an incubator focused on creating jobs for young people in the city's tech sector (JTA, 2004). Barkat was also one of the supporters of the creation of the NGO New Spirit by young Jewish Jerusalemites who wanted to make Jerusalem more attractive to Zionist youth around the world.

Unlike his predecessor, Barkat used discursive resources and material instruments from the repertoire of neoliberal urbanism to revitalize the strategy of settler colonial government originally constructed by Teddy Kollek. With Barkat, the combination of multicultural discourse, Judaization through socio-economic development and the farcical inclusion of Palestinians for their pacification took on a neoliberal guise. The illusory neutrality of the market played a central role in the strategy of executing urban infrastructure projects to attract foreign capital to be portrayed as a policy that would benefit all Jerusalemites, regardless of their nationality, gender, religion, neighbourhood or sexual orientation (Margalit, 2018). Instead of appealing to a liberal rhetoric of tolerance and coexistence between the different parts of the mosaic that make up the effervescent 'goulash', as Kollek did (Wallach, 2016), Barkat sought to undertake a union of Jerusalem around the neoliberal projects of

Israeli elites and transnational corporations that would supposedly bring a materially better future for all the city's inhabitants after the disillusionment of the Oslo period.

In addition to making the city more attractive to business and tourism, Barkat also aimed to make municipal management more transparent, fiscally responsible and guided by business management principles, imposing goals on municipal bureaucrats, with accountability vis-à-vis the use of the budget. The objective was to create the understanding that the municipality would act in an exclusively rational manner for the economic and social development of Jerusalem (Magalit, 2018). Through these ideological and practical instruments offered according to neoliberal rationales, Barkat sought to distinguish himself from Lupolianski's racism and homophobia and from the corruption associated with Ehud Olmert, who had been arrested for a scandal involving real estate market benefits during his administration. In this way, Barkat, a right-wing politician, won the support of the entire Zionist political spectrum and of anti-Zionist Jewish and Palestinian sectors, particularly businessmen and local leaders alienated from the Palestinian Authority's (PA) zone of influence.

The Israeli neoliberal settler colonialism in Jerusalem has been translated into several master plans designed to maximize the number of Jews and reduce the number of Palestinians as a goal of adapting the city to neoliberal globalization. Jerusalem's urban planning involves local, district and national governments, as well as the aspirations of different partners in the commodification of the city, such as the state, the Third Sector and the local and global private sectors. There are three important Israeli plans that inform official policies for Jerusalem. The most important is the 'Jerusalem 2000 Master Plan', also known as 'Jerusalem 2020', whose preparation was initiated by Olmert in 2000. The first version was launched by Lupolianski in 2004, and in 2009, Barkat submitted it for revisions after it had been processed by local planning committees. Also in 2009, the Ministry of the Interior blocked the Barkat version as it was considered too favourable to the Palestinians. Since then, the plan has never been ratified, despite being informally applied in the territory (Chiodelli, 2012). One of the objectives of 'Jerusalem 2020' is 'to maintain a solid Jewish majority in the city' by encouraging Jewish settlements in East Jerusalem and reducing negative migration by increasing the supply of affordable housing in existing Jewish neighbourhoods and in planned new ones. Even while acknowledging the lack of housing, adequate infrastructure and public services in Palestinian neighbourhoods, the master plan creates the false perception of treating all residents equally.

The project deals with such socio-spatial fractures as a beneficial 'self-segregation' of 'ethno-religious' groups – secular Jews, religious Jews and Palestinians – that allows for specific zoning for each quadrant of the city according to its racial identity (Arafeh, 2016d), reproducing the multicultural myth of Kollek's 'goulash'. While the housing issue for the Jewish population is expected to be addressed mostly by the construction of new settlements in East Jerusalem (64 per cent of the plan), more than half (55.7 per cent) of the growth in Palestinian housing is supposed to occur through densification in already existing areas on the edges of the city and not in the central region of the Old City, where the housing crisis is more severe but where the Palestinian presence is highly unwanted (Arafeh, 2020; Chiodelli, 2012). Among other discrepancies, the plan ends up allowing Jewish settler colonial expansion over Palestinian land and greater control over its population. Furthermore, the proposals are not materialized by the various bureaucratic restrictions imposed disproportionately on Palestinians to prevent them from building where even the plan allows, forcing them to resort to illegal self-construction as a way of dealing with the housing crisis. The plan also does not address the regulation of the thousands of informal buildings that populate Palestinian neighbourhoods and are permanently at risk of being destroyed by the authorities. At least 100,000 Palestinians, that is, about a third of the city's population, are at risk of being evicted and homeless due to incompatibility with the master plan (OCHA-OPT, 2019).

The least known of the plans is the Marom, drafted in 2004 by the national government and implemented by the Jerusalem Development Authority (JDA), whose unoriginal purpose is to make Jerusalem an 'international city, a leader in trade and quality of life in the public environment', with the support of Israeli civil society (Arafeh, 2016d). The most recent plan, from 2018, is 'Jerusalem 5800', also known as 'Jerusalem 2050', the result of the private initiative of Australian real estate entrepreneur Kevin Bermeister together with Udi Regunas, a businessman in the communication sector and former member of the ultranationalist settler movement Elad, the organization responsible for colonizing the Silwan neighbourhood through the City of

David archaeological-tourist enterprise (Arafeh, 2016d; Hasson, 2016). The plan includes several focused projects that can be independently implemented to make Jerusalem a 'global city, a major tourist, ecological, spiritual, and cultural centre of the world' and promote 'peace through economic prosperity' without supposedly addressing the city's political issues (Arafeh, 2016d). The plan also includes a chapter on the 'demographic problem' and aims to increase the Jewish share of the population by encouraging migration to the city.

The main objective of the plans is to make Jerusalem a Jewish and international city, a tourist, technological and educational destination to attract foreign capital and young Jews to live and work in the city, all in a way that brings together the settler colonial and economic objectives of the Israeli ruling classes (Arafeh, 2016d). Although the leading role for the high-tech industry and educational institutions is a novelty in the Jerusalem development project, an element common to all plans is the encouragement of the tourism industry with the aim of exploiting the historical, religious and archaeological aspects of the city. This vision has resulted in massive investments in urban and tourism infrastructure. In 2014 alone, the JDA announced an investment of 42 million shekels in the tourism sector as part of the Marom Plan. The tourism sector is central to Zionist aspirations in Jerusalem not only for its multiplier effect on the economy but also for its value as a political tool to control the narrative of a Jewish Jerusalem by erasing Palestinian history.

There is no set formula for neoliberal urbanism. Instead, there is an industry that supplies training for the global propagation of successful models and policies that can be replicated by urban managers who intend to improve their position in intercity competition and design a new vision of the future for their cities. During the Barkat administration, the application of urban policies was directly influenced by Harvard professor Michael Porter, responsible for the 'cluster' development model to attract capital and a skilled workforce (Keidar, 2018). In 2009, the Municipality of Jerusalem and Harvard University signed an official agreement for the development of policies to increase Jerusalem's competitiveness based on the tripartite alliance of culture and tourism, health and life sciences and (outsourced) medical and financial services. Thanks to StartUp Jerusalem, Barkat and Porter were introduced to one another via American and Israeli investors and entrepreneurs (Weisman, 2009).

In 2014, a complementary strategy became influential among Jerusalem authorities. This was urbanologist Richard Florida's 'creative class', which sees the concentration of creative talent in a culturally vibrant urban space that is open to ethnic, national, sexual and gender tolerance as the engine for entrepreneurial innovation and, consequently, economic development (Keidar, 2018). The adoption of the so-called creative script allowed state actors to work together with local NGOs, international philanthropists and Israeli corporations to align their economic agenda with their settler colonial ambition of growing the population of Zionist youth in the city. The main executor of the 'creative class' strategy in Jerusalem was the NGO New Spirit in collaboration with Jnext, a JDA body created in 2012 and responsible for investing in the city's technology sector, and the Leichtag Foundation, an American philanthropic institution involved in several projects aimed at developing 'human capital' among secular, ultra-Orthodox and Palestinian populations (Keidar, 2018; Leichtag Foundation, 2018).

In principle, the plan for attracting 'creative' individuals was to offer scholarships for young entrepreneurs to settle in less developed neighbourhoods in West Jerusalem for three years as a way for youth to respond directly to nationalist demands in the city (Keidar, 2018). Jnext offers a scholarship of 80,000 to 100,000 shekels for up to six years for every Jerusalemite hired by a high-tech company. After the failure of the initial strategy that limited the freedom of young people to 'make their mark' on the city in the way they wished – and not due to the interests of the authorities – state actors changed the approach to a more depoliticized one, which stopped explicitly appealing to a Zionist identity to encourage the target public to engage in entrepreneurship and settle in the city on the basis of a voluntary decision.

The depoliticization in the relationship between the Israeli state and Jewish citizens is seen as beneficial as it can transform Jewish citizens exclusively into entrepreneurs who can contribute to the economic development of the city and improve quality of life, while it is up to the state merely to provide training and market entry for a short period of time (Keidar, 2018). '[Our goal is] to increase market access for entrepreneurs in different conditions. Our only natural resource is human capital', explains Oded Barel-Sabag (personal communication, June 2019), head of Jnext, about its work in the city. Jnext also works with the private sector, the 'Third Sector' and universities to attract international and Israeli capital and professionals from the high-tech sector with the aim of making technology a central element in the construction of Jerusalem as a global city. In 2015, at the height of the Jerusalem Intifada, *Time* magazine selected Jerusalem as one of the top five emerging high-tech centres in the world. As the young activist-entrepreneur from Made in JLM, Roy Munin, observed at the time:

> People were saying Jerusalem was like a warzone. Underground there was a whole movement of people taking things into their own hands … . People were ashamed to say their start-up was in Jerusalem, but now it's a cool thing. (Quoted in Tress, 2015)

This strategy, therefore, marks a shift from the paradigm of expansion and consolidation of the Fordist Israeli settler colonial frontier based on organized planning, predictability, secure wages and a European-standard welfare state to a neoliberal adventure playground characterized by fragmentation, inconstancy and unpredictability. Settlers are no longer seen as citizens who have duties and rights in relation to the national project and the social welfare system built by settler colonial looting. They are now understood as selfish entrepreneurs responsible for seizing the opportunities offered by the state on the frontier. The frontier ceases to be a refuge of well-being provided by the state to ensure racial solidarity among Zionist Jews as a place of privilege and stability and becomes instead a space for individualized opportunities and risks. The responsibility for taking decisions that will allow them to seize the opportunities available in the market is transferred to entrepreneurial settlers. Encouraging collaboration between entrepreneurs who compete and are responsible for their own successes and failures becomes the preferred way of forging racial solidarity among neoliberal Zionists as they seek to protect their privileges and satisfy their material and subjective needs for a 'cooler' and more progressive Western lifestyle. Therefore, 'European-standard' labour continues to have a fundamental centrality for the Zionist settler colonial process to take place materially, but in neoliberalism it takes the unstable and volatile form of Western entrepreneurship.

Within this logic, Barkat was responsible for implementing several initiatives focused on tourism, culture and finance that transformed the social space of the city according to a market logic. The priority was the revitalization of the centre of West Jerusalem as a tourist and cultural destination for foreigners and young rich Jews (Alfasi and Ganan, 2015). Spatial reproduction in the Jerusalem of the 2010s seems to fulfil every requirement in the guidebooks for the construction of a market-friendly urban environment: the construction of urban infrastructure signed off by an internationally renowned architect; the construction of highways and railways for a quick connection with the international airport in Tel Aviv; the development of tram lines for fast and low-polluting transportation within the city; the construction of a financial business district at the entrance to West Jerusalem; the opening of international hotels close to business centres and tourist attractions; the promotion of cultural, sporting and business events of global importance, such as Formula 1 races, marathons and film festivals; the development of new shopping centres with international brand stores, such as the Mamila mall in the Old City; the opening of new boulevards, squares and green areas in the central region, such as Jaffa Street; the revitalization of the old Mahane Yehuda market so that it could house high-end restaurants, bars and nightclubs; the development of private, luxurious gated communities; and tax incentives and subsidies to attract new investments and entrepreneurs (Alfasi and Ganan, 2015; Braier and Yacobi, 2017; Keidar, 2018; Nolte and Yacobi, 2015; Shlay and Rosen, 2015; Yacobi, 2012a).

The most symbolic and contested undertaking was the construction of the light rail line connecting West Jerusalem to the settlement of Pisgat Ze'ev in East Jerusalem, on the border with the West Bank and next to the main settlement blocks that make up Greater Jerusalem. On the way, the vehicle passes the city's main sights, the town hall, the commercial and financial districts, middle-class Jewish settlements and two Palestinian neighbourhoods: Shuafat and Beit Hanina. The transport infrastructure is the first to connect Jewish and Palestinian neighbourhoods of the city and was portrayed as the representation of neoliberal integration between Israelis and Palestinians as preached by Barkat (Baumann, 2018). Its construction and administration by French corporations was the target of widespread rejection from Palestinians and international campaigning from the BDS movement.

Some researchers have identified the light rail infrastructure completed in 2011 as a form of settler colonial expansion and an extension of Israeli control over Palestinian neighbourhoods in East Jerusalem (Baumann, 2018; Nolte, 2016) although others disagree with this interpretation, pointing to its ability to foster 'inter-ethnic' encounters (Rokem and Vaughan, 2018). Baumann argues that the tram demonstrates how urban infrastructure is not only violent in its absence, as is the case in many areas of Jerusalem where infrastructure and public services are inadequate, but also when it is present, such as the rail lines and stations that pass through Palestinian neighbourhoods when it is well known that these very same neighbourhoods are historically lacking in infrastructure. However, the criticism of the political economy of the light rail has gone unnoticed by the facilitation of the growing flow of Palestinian workers from East Jerusalem and the West Bank who commute every day from their residences to their workplaces in West Jerusalem.

Contradictions of neoliberal apartheid and workers' revolts

The various infrastructure endeavours within the strategies of neoliberal urbanism in Jerusalem are among the main factors in the significant increase in the employment of Palestinian labour in the Israeli sectors of West Jerusalem after the Second Intifada. Another reason was the construction of the Wall in Jerusalem, which resulted in an important growth in the isolation of East Jerusalem from the rest of the West Bank, separated Palestinians from Palestinians, closed businesses, impoverished entire neighbourhoods and brought with it unemployment and homelessness, cornering Palestinian Jerusalemites faced with dispossession even more radically than before (Nasara, 2019; Shalhoub-Kevorkian, 2015; Shtern, 2018b). In 2003, unemployment affected 28 per cent of the Palestinian workforce in East Jerusalem (Khalidi, 2013: 22). In this context, working for Israeli capital has become one of the only possibilities for survival in Jerusalem in a safe way as opposed to the alternatives of illegal and informal work or running the risk of losing the right of residence by ceasing to have Jerusalem as 'the centre of your life' by seeking better living conditions.[2]

---

[2] After the construction of the Wall, completed in Jerusalem in 2005, Israel significantly increased the rate of revocation of residencies in East Jerusalem: in 2008 alone, 4,577 residencies were revoked. See btselem.org.

Working for the Israeli market is an attractive alternative due to higher salaries and free access without the need for a work visa.

Quickly, the number of Palestinian Jerusalemites working in West Jerusalem and other Israeli cities in the region grew to 47 per cent of the local workforce between 2010 and 2011, bringing unemployment down to 12 per cent (Khalidi, 2013; Shtern, 2017). Between 2014 and 2015, there was also 12 per cent growth in the number of East Jerusalem workers employed in West Jerusalem (Shtern, 2018b). In 2017, the unemployment rate in East Jerusalem was around 11.6 per cent thanks to the employment of Palestinian men in the Israeli market, which employed 40 per cent of the entire Palestinian workforce and represented the main source of income for 54 per cent of Palestinian residences in Jerusalem (Jafari et al., 2019). Palestinians, however, continue to be overrepresented in low-wage, high-risk and insecure sectors: despite constituting 28 per cent of the workforce in Jerusalem, they make up 71 per cent of workers in construction, 57 per cent in transport and 40 per cent in services (Shtern, 2017). However, a growth in the number of Palestinians in management and skilled labour positions in West Jerusalem from 8 per cent in 1980 to 27 per cent in 2010 may signal how the life of middle-class Jerusalemites has also turned to the Israeli sector. From being the centre of Palestinian society, Jerusalem after Oslo became an economically dependent and integrated part of the periphery of West Jerusalem (Shtern, 2018b). This transition can be seen in the decline in Jerusalem's contribution to the West Bank economy: from 14–15 per cent in 1987 to 8 per cent in 2000 and 7 per cent in 2010 (Khalidi, 2013: 12–13).

From an Israeli perspective, the increased employment of Palestinian workers and the day-to-day tolerance of their presence in public, work and consumption locations in West Jerusalem is not just the work of the invisible hand of the market but also part of an effort by the Barkat administration to reduce friction points with Palestinians and buy their consent through appeasement gestures, such as public meetings with Palestinian leaders and road repairs (Margalit, 2018). Above all, Barkat responded in a limited way to Palestinian demands for new permits to build housing, allowed community planning to proceed and slowed the pace of the destruction of Palestinian homes in contravention of the master plan. This process allowed, as of 2015, the number of permits for the construction of new housing to double from two hundred per year to four hundred but is still far from responding to the Palestinian urban crisis. However, as the social activist and founder of the NGO New Spirit, Yakir Segev, who at the time was an adviser close to Barkat, put it in 2010: 'We will not allow Palestinian residents to build as much as they wish ... we must monitor the demographic situation to ensure that within twenty years we do not wake up in a Palestinian city' (quoted in Margalit, 2018: 71).

Palestinian workers were seen as fundamental to the Israeli project of building Jerusalem as a global city, not only as cheap labour but also, based on a counterinsurgency strategy, as pacifying agents to dissuade more radical groups that could otherwise provoke violent destabilizations of the social order that would impact the flow of tourists and businesses in the city. Barkat wanted the neoliberal urbanism strategy to have the capacity to constitute a relationship of economic interdependence between Israelis and Palestinians that would ensure not peace but pacification (Margalit, 2018; Shtern, 2015). In accordance with traditional settler colonial counterinsurgency strategies, 'rational' workers would be used to prevent 'irrational' actors from carrying out mobilizations and attacks that would affect the stability of the social order and, consequently, their basic economic needs for social reproduction. There is a reorganization in the economy of settler colonial power, which seeks to become more inclusive and open to rule more by Palestinian consent than by coercion alone. Despite reversing the weight between the stick and the carrot to make the lives of Palestinians more useful to settler colonial aspirations, at no time was the construction of settlements and the removal of Palestinians stopped. Nor was poverty reduced among Palestinian Jerusalemites. On the contrary: between 2003 and 2015, the number of Palestinian families in East Jerusalem living below the poverty line rose from 64 to 79 per cent (Korach and Choshen, 2019).

Barkat's style of government sought to transform the degree of inclusive exclusion of Jerusalem's Palestinian residents, but the small change that was dropped on East Jerusalem fell mainly into the wallets of local elites who knew how to maintain the channel of communication with the Israelis, even if through hidden and indirect means (Margalit, 2018). Middle- and upper-class Palestinians were increasingly seen in luxury consumption centres and prestigious private schools in West Jerusalem (Shtern, 2016, 2018b). Presenting himself as a mayor who respected the human rights of Palestinians was central to Barkat's strategy of leveraging international economic and political capital for the development of Jerusalem at a time when the United States, Israel's main partner, was moving in that direction. In this way, the mayor aligned himself with the global progressive neoliberalism that was hegemonic when he took office in 2009: Obama had just occupied the White House in Washington, and the OECD was imposing a reduction of social inequality on Israel through the inclusion of Arab and Orthodox minorities in the national market (Margalit, 2018; Nasara, 2019).

Despite efforts to pacify the Palestinians with neoliberal tools, the first source of destabilization of the order with impacts on Barkat's plans for Jerusalem did not come from the Palestinians, but from the Israelis. In 2011, amid the popular protests of the Arab Spring, in the Middle East and in large metropolitan centres around the world against the effects of the great financial crisis of neoliberalism in 2007–8, Israel saw the biggest mass demonstration among its Jewish population in history. The protests mainly targeted high rents and the inability of younger Israelis to acquire private property, but they also demanded 'social justice' in the face of growing inequality, shrinking social benefits, the commodification of urban space and the precariousness of the labour market in Israel as a result of the neoliberal reforms imposed in the country since the late 1970s (Englert, 2017). The movement known as J-14, due to its having started on 14 July 2011 in a central square in Tel Aviv, gained the support of millions of Israelis across the country and spread to several cities, including West Jerusalem. The neoliberalization of Israel increased social polarization among Jews and disrupted the social foundations that had originally constituted the country and the settler colonial process. In Jerusalem, the predatory activity of the housing market and neoliberal capital can be seen in the proliferation of high-end gated communities and 'ghost neighbourhoods' owned by super-rich foreign Jews who buy second homes in the revitalized centre of West Jerusalem (Yacobi, 2012).

The sale of urban space in Jerusalem to the private sector predates the Barkat administration and goes back to the neoliberal reforms of the 1990s. Prior to then, almost all property in Israel was state-owned or belonged to proto-state organizations such as the Jewish National Fund, as it was originally Palestinian land that had been confiscated by the state. The privatization of residential property was one of the first neoliberal measures taken in the 1980s and is directly connected with the adoption of the Israeli right-wing strategy then in force to colonize the OPTs through the construction of suburbs for the secular working and middle classes. By benefiting its social-democratic middle-class social base in the short term, the Zionist left adopted the neoliberal privatization agenda in the 1990s that later came to harm it with the bursting of the housing bubble between 2008 and 2011 and the beginning of a process of super-gentrification by wealthy diaspora Jews (Gutwein, 2017; Yacobi, 2012b; Zaban, 2016).

Among the characteristics of the real estate privatization process are the promotion of tax incentives and subsidies for foreign Jewish businesspersons to acquire properties in Israel and continue to manage their businesses in their country of origin from the 'Promised Land', without prejudice to their activities (Yacobi, 2012). These incentives meant the development of numerous exclusive luxury gate communities for wealthy diaspora Jews as vacation or temporary homes in Jerusalem through foreign direct investment and with the participation of institutions that were supposed to care for the archaeological heritage of Jerusalem but were part of the coalitions behind these real estate developments (Alfasi and Ganan, 2015). It turns out that most of these residential complexes are empty during the year and end up reinforcing real estate speculation in the city. Thus, West Jerusalem has increasingly become a luxury tourist enclave for the transnational Zionist bourgeoisie, to the detriment of local working- and middle-class Israelis (Alfasi and Ganan, 2015; Yacobi, 2012a).

Yacobi (2012) notes that this phenomenon occurs more intensely in Jerusalem than in the rest of the country, due to its tourist, religious, spiritual and national characteristics. It is not just any Jerusalem that is sold to foreign investors, but the historic Jewish Jerusalem that appeals to the Orientalist imagination of architecture and the 'Jerusalem stone' that is characteristic of the Israeli built environment. This spatial identity, however, is part of the process whereby the settlers become new natives of the land by appropriating Palestinian ways of building (Yacobi, 2012).

Many of the 'ghost neighbourhoods' are in areas inhabited by poor Jewish immigrants who originally benefited from state-run regeneration programmes in the 1970s, such as Baka. The main attractions of these neighbourhoods for the luxury real estate market are the old Palestinian houses built for the emerging families of the 'New City' at the beginning of the twentieth century. Yacobi (2012) suggests that this structural interrelationship between neoliberal urbanism, settler colonialism and religious nationalism that is characteristic of contemporary neoliberal Zionist hegemony has reproduced internal borders within the already Judaized West Jerusalem, but now from a class cleavage that expropriates the settlers who are originally from the lower classes.

In a complementary way, Zaban (2016) demonstrates, in a study on the gentrification of Baka, how this internal border combines class and race identities. Baka was a Palestinian neighbourhood that was emptied during the Nakba and came to be populated mainly by Mizrahi Jews from countries like Morocco and Yemen. It was one of the centres of the Mizrahi 'black panthers' movement of the early 1970s that opposed oppression by Jews of European origin. Stigmatized as a poor and dangerous place by the white Jewish populations of Jerusalem, the neighbourhood underwent a government-led revitalization process in the 1980s that was initially not intended to alter its demographic composition (Zaban, 2016). The pioneers of gentrification were educated, middle-class Ashkenazi Jews on the left of the political spectrum. The advent of neoliberalism and the privatization of urban property promoted an even more extensive process of gentrification that brought white middle- and upper-class Jews to live in the neighbourhood on a large scale, with major participation of real estate agents in the transformation of Palestinian houses into apartments. Since the proliferation of luxury gated communities built by developers in the 1990s and 2000s, Baka has become home to British, American and French Jewish millionaires (Zaban, 2016).

In 1967 Mizrahi Jews made up practically 95 per cent of the neighbourhood's population; this number has since dropped to somewhere around 15–20 per cent. The super-rich make up approximately 30 per cent of the landowners, divided between Israelis and foreigners, while the rest are middle-class families and groups of youths who share the neighbourhood's expensive rents (Zaban, 2016). That is, in addition to the change in the class composition, there was a replacement in the racial characteristics of Baka, which was whitened as it was privatized. This process reinforces the racial component of neoliberalism and urban gentrifications that reproduce the logic of settler colonialism within West Jerusalem. A neoliberal apartheid in which race and class are socio-spatially combined in ways that differ from what was observed in East Jerusalem. An example of how the settler colonial nature of Zionism has also subjected Mizrahi Jews to domination by Ashkenazi Jews since the early twentieth century (Shohat, 1988).

The Barkat administration sought to reverse the gentrification of West Jerusalem, which pressured rent and property values. The mayor urged foreign owners to spend more time in the city or rent out their properties at below-market prices to local Jewish working families, which few did (Chiodelli, 2012). The 2011 protests, furthermore, did not herald greater social control over the real estate market or a reversal of the neoliberal reforms that are at the root of the social problems experienced by Israelis. The solution to the real estate and social crisis was the expansion of the expropriation of Palestinian territories in the West Bank, particularly in East Jerusalem. The high value of housing in Israel for the Jewish middle and working classes has united Israelis from across the political spectrum to respond to the 'settler fix' by accumulating land for Jewish settlement (Englert, 2017). The young leaders of the J-14 movement allied with the former leaders of the Yesha Council, the representative body for settlers in the West Bank, to make settlement in Palestinian lands the solution to the social crisis. In the Knesset, representatives of the Zionist Left and Right jointly formulated proposals to pressure Netanyahu to make settler colonization in the West Bank and East Jerusalem a response to the demands of Israeli protesters.

Likud MK (Member of the Knesset, the Israeli parliament) Ze'ev Elkin (quoted in Englert, 2017: 412) stated in 2011: 'I am sure our call will be a major part of the discussion on housing, and Judea and Samaria will be a solution to the problem, as it was during the previous housing crisis, in the early [19]90.' The year 2010 had seen the lowest number of new settlement constructions in the West Bank since 1986 because of a 'freeze' in expansion imposed by the Obama administration: only 741 buildings were built (Peace Now, 2020). From then on, this number grew annually, always remaining above a thousand per year, with almost three thousand new settlements in 2013. Between 2010 and 2014, the settler population in the West Bank, which includes the Greater Jerusalem blocs, grew from 311,100 to 370,700, jumping to 427,800 in 2018. In addition, the outposts, that is, the illegal settlements built by settler movements without formal authorization from the state, returned to occupy Palestinian land from 2012. In the jurisdiction of East Jerusalem, the number of settlers went from 193,000 in 2010 to 216,000 in 2017 (Korach and Choshen, 2019: 20). In 2018, Elkin, then Netanyahu's Likud party candidate for mayor of Jerusalem, made it his priority if he was elected to 'build, build, build' (Wootliff, 2018).

This renewal of the suburban settler colonial process through neoliberal urbanism to please the middle and working classes of settler society in a way that reinforces privilege and racial solidarity among Jews has increased the socio-economic pressure on the land and labour of Palestinians in East Jerusalem. The pacification imposed by Barkat failed to contain the violent Palestinian social uprising in 2014 as a consequence of the growing overlap of political, social and economic oppressions and dispossessions of the neoliberal apartheid regime. The deep dissatisfaction of Palestinians in East Jerusalem led to collective uprisings and individual attacks that took place in different parts of the city. Attacks on light rail stations located in Palestinian neighbourhoods in 2014 were a clear manifestation of rejection of renewed attempts at settler colonial domination over East Jerusalem, similarly to the events of the First Intifada (Baumann, 2018).

Despite the obvious pretext of resistance against racist settler violence, I argue that this spontaneous and organic popular uprising in East Jerusalem can be understood in the light of the accumulation of socio-economic deprivations imposed by the Israeli settler regime after Oslo and the Second Intifada that made the city susceptible to instability and vulnerability. The main Palestinian political parties and movements continue to have significant penetration in the neighbourhoods and have been informing Palestinian popular movements in the city, but the protests are more a reflection of tectonic movements in the structures of the colonial-neoliberal regime from below than part of a strategy orchestrated from above (Baumann, 2018). For example, more than half of the perpetrators of violent attacks against Israelis came from the neighbourhoods of Kfar Aqba and the Shuafat Refugee Camp, two neighbourhoods that are formally part of Jerusalem's municipal jurisdiction but have been excluded from the rest of East Jerusalem by construction of the Wall.

In recent years, these neighbourhoods have become havens for Jerusalemite and West Bank workers who want to escape social regulation by both Israel and the PA. They are located in a grey area that has allowed Palestinians greater freedom to live without the surveillance of Israeli and Palestinian security forces and inspectors, thus making the exclusion areas new peripheral centralities for Palestinian survival (Alkhalili, 2017; Baumann, 2016). They became a space for family union between Palestinians from Jerusalem and the West Bank who could not live together on the 'Israeli' side due to security restrictions, or live in areas under the PA without risking losing their right of residence.

Above all, they have served as a space for an informal solution to the urban crisis in Jerusalem, as Palestinian developers have illegally erected buildings with numbers of apartments far above the permitted level (Alkhalili, 2017; Baumann, 2016). Such a situation has served as an opportunity for exorbitant profits, for the rise of new local authorities involved in illegal businesses and as a shelter for radical groups unwanted by Israel and the PA. Despite its vitality, Kfar Aqba and the Shuafat Refugee Camp continue to be spaces that house thousands of young people and superfluous workers subjected to extremely precarious, undignified and dangerous conditions that feed daily dissatisfaction against the settler regime. During the first years of the Jerusalem Intifada, demonstrations also took place in the neighbourhoods of Shuafat, Yassiwa, Jabal al-Murkaber and Silwan, on the 'Israeli' side of the Wall.

The Israelis' most evident responses were violent repression of public riots and night-time police raids in Palestinian neighbourhoods that led to the arbitrary arrest of more than 2,500 youths, spreading fear and terror among Palestinian families (Margalit, 2018). Furthermore, the authorities reactivated punitive measures and daily harassment in Palestinian neighbourhoods, such as fines of 10,000 shekels and twenty years imprisonment for throwing stones, which is considered a terrorist act.[3] Faced with the growing fear in the settler society of the revolt led by the young Jerusalemites, groups of Israelis began to carry out violent racist attacks against individuals whom they thought were Palestinians, but ended up attacking Mizrahi Jews as well (Shtern, 2015). Barkat and the then Defence Minister Moshe Yalom encouraged Jerusalemite Jews to use their weapons against those they judged as terrorist suspects to

---

[3] The minimum age of imprisonment in Israel is fourteen, which means that many Palestinian teenagers are tried and imprisoned as adults with the aim of containing and punishing youth rebellion.

assist security forces (Hever, 2018), thereby reassuming the agency of settlers confronting natives at the borders.

At the beginning of the 2014 protests, one of the first measures taken by the Israeli authorities was the imposition of cement blocks at the entrances to Palestinian neighbourhoods, and metal ditches at public transport stations, inhibiting the movement of the entire native population inside Jerusalem in a way that had not occurred during the Second Intifada and that had been restricted to the rest of the West Bank (Margalit, 2018; Ravid, 2015). The dispute caused by these blockades revealed some important economic vulnerabilities of the Israeli settler regime due to its dependence on Palestinian workers who were prevented from accessing their workplaces.

Despite mass layoffs of Palestinian bus drivers and a strike by taxi drivers in the face of racist persecution of Palestinians in West Jerusalem during the uprising, the involvement of the organized Palestinian workers' movement was quite limited (Margalit, 2018). The involvement of a worker in the protests could lead to their being fired, as demanded by many Israeli groups, or having their residency revoked, their house demolished or being subject to some other form of punishment used by the settler regime. According to a Palestinian union leader who works in Jerusalem, many Palestinians pressured protesters to stop their revolt so that they could return to work normally (Mohamed, personal communication, July 2019). This movement exposed a split between the Palestinian precariat from East Jerusalem – the workers totally dependent on the settler regime and the unemployed youth – which functioned as a factor in the return to the status quo given the need for the oppressed and exploited to maintain their survival.

Nonetheless, the revolt, which was of an anti-colonial, rejectionist nature, managed to lay bare the efforts at normalization, integration and pacification that were being made in Jerusalem through strategies of neoliberal urbanism. Similarly to the First Intifada, they exposed the fragility of forms of government other than the use of overt force on the bodies and livelihoods of Palestinians. They also revealed the inability of the Israeli security and intelligence elites to predict and control large-scale mobilizations of Palestinians in Jerusalem, despite surveillance and control technologies, infiltration and recruitment of collaborators on the streets and networks that resulted in many, sometimes arbitrary, arrests (Hever, 2018). Also, transforming the Old City and its surroundings into a veritable panopticon with cameras, police and private security guards on every corner has not proven to be entirely effective in ensuring the safety of the settlers (Grassiani and Volinz, 2016). According to a prominent Palestinian community leader from Silwan, the revolt demonstrated the power of mobilization and the popular dissatisfaction of the Jerusalemites after a period of passivity and a deepening of their identity crisis after the Second Intifada (D. Ghoul, personal communication, July 2019).

Finally, the Jerusalem Intifada exposed an economic dependence on the part of Israeli capital on Palestinian labour that constitutes a fissure in Jerusalem's neoliberal apartheid. It was not only Palestinian workers who were harmed by the blockades and violent police repression, but also the Israeli capital that depends on these workers to sustain the economy that serves as a basis for allowing the reproduction of the very settler system that oppresses the Palestinian people. After a week, blockades in Palestinian neighbourhoods were lifted under pressure from Israeli businessmen who could not keep their businesses running without their Palestinian workforce and consumers (Margalit, 2018). The Israeli settler regime's historic efforts to reduce reliance on Palestinian labour since the First Intifada to lessen the demographic and economic 'threat' posed by the Palestinian working class has been undone by the contradictions inherent in the racial projects of settler colonialism and the demands of Israeli capitalists under neoliberalism.

The constitution and maintenance of the hegemony of neoliberal Israeli elites in relation to their social base and transnational capital from the dual dispossession of Palestinian land and labour has dialectically reproduced counterhegemonic forces that led to a crisis in the neoliberal apartheid in Jerusalem. However, the stabilizations and destabilizations of the social reproduction of Israelis and Palestinians under neoliberal settler colonialism are interdependent factors. Despite revealing cracks in the surface of the Israeli settler colonial shield, it also reinforced the racial foundation that sustains it.

Race and class divide at the root of neoliberal apartheid

In spite of the case made in this chapter about the centrality of labour to understand upheavals in Jerusalem in the 2010s, there are several limitations to the unity between Palestinian and Israeli workers in a cohesive multiracial/binational working-class organization seen, for example, in the Palestine Communist Party until 1948.[4] First, a large proportion of Palestinian workers are still unemployed, or 'making do' through informal/illegal activities as a survival strategy (Shalhoub-Kevorkian, 2015). Many of these people have formal or informal day jobs and work double shifts. It is common for adult Palestinian male drivers of all ages to use an often badly damaged private car as an illegal taxi to make up for the lack of legal public transport services for the Palestinian population of East Jerusalem. This type of activity, however, is not always tolerated by Israeli security forces, making these informal taxi drivers susceptible to harassment, arrest, having their car impounded or being blackmailed into becoming collaborators. In other words, settler colonial tricks and the overexploitation of informal workers prevent their mobilization with the rest of the colonized and exploited population.

The unionization of Palestinian workers in Jerusalem is quite low and fragmented for several reasons. Palestinians who get formal work with Israeli employers often end up accepting illegal or hyper-exploitative working conditions for fear of losing their jobs. Palestinian unions from the OPTs cannot operate in Israeli companies, and the new union movement of Palestinian workers who are citizens of Israel has very limited operations in East Jerusalem (Englert, 2017; Mohamed, personal communication, July 2019). In most cases, Palestinian workers are still required to join Histadrut, the traditional Zionist union, in order to gain access to labour rights (W. Salem, 2018). Some small Israeli unions, such as WAC-Maan and Kav LaOved, have managed to organize and secure rights for Palestinian workers in the Israeli industrial zones in East Jerusalem of Atarot and Mishor Adumin, but they have only had partial success (Wac-Maan, 2018).

The lack of unity between Palestinian workers in Israeli workplaces is also due to disputes between Jerusalemites and West Bankers for the same job vacancies. Since West Bank workers are in a situation of greater precariousness and vulnerability, they end up accepting conditions that are lower than those which Jerusalemites are usually willing to accept

---

[4] For more on the labour movement in Mandatory Palestine, see Lockman (1996).

(Siegman, 2018). Furthermore, Israeli companies that employ Palestinians, even supermarkets, can turn out to be very tightly securitized spaces of surveillance and control. Since all the Israeli employees will inevitably have served in either the armed forces or one of Israel's police forces, they bring their military and police techniques to the administration of the workplace (Siegman, 2018).

In Palestinian places of employment, the ability of native workers to organize is very small due to the fact that most Palestinian employers in Jerusalem are small family businesses that hire few staff, who are usually relatives hired on an informal basis (Jafari et al., 2019). Added to this is the fact that many businessmen and union leaders end up having a close relationship because of their nationality and their connections with the PA, reducing the ability of workers to organize and obtain their rights in accordance with Palestinian labour legislation. There are still the imperatives of the neoliberal rationale employed by the settler regime in Jerusalem as a way of provoking disunity and producing consent to the hegemonic order among the layers of the Palestinian working class through incentives to entrepreneurial activity, especially among Palestinian youth and women from East Jerusalem. In short, class divisions and socio-spatial fragmentations among the Palestinians, in addition to economic dependence on Israeli capital, prevent them from uniting and mobilizing further on labour and national issues.

On the other hand, union with exploited Israelis does not occur due to the dynamics of valorization and devaluation inherent to settler colonial racism. Precariously employed Jewish Israeli workers and the hegemonic Zionist trade union movement, despite being weakened by neoliberalism, usually reject unity and solidarity with Palestinian workers because of racist ideologies, and also because of competition in the labour market (Englert, 2017; Gutwein, 2017). The Jewish Israeli precariat tends to uphold the occupation and settler colonization not only by offering cheap housing on expropriated Palestinian land as mechanisms to compensate for the deterioration of the welfare state, but also by ensuring a series of formal and informal technologies that constitute a colour bar in the Israeli job market. This system common to apartheid regimes has been maintained in neoliberalism mainly through the Histadrut, which, despite having lost strength with the rise of neoliberal Zionism, serves as an enforcer in the defence of privileges for Israeli workers and in its constant direction of Palestinians towards exploitative, dangerous or unhealthy positions that pay low wages (Englert, 2020). Thus, exploited and oppressed Israelis, even in the face of the deterioration of neoliberal dispossession, remain part of the dominant historical bloc opposed to the Palestinians, who are also in precarious conditions and dispossessed.

Reality in Palestine reaffirms Fanon's (1963: 39) understanding of race and class relations in colonial contexts: 'In the colonies the economic substructure is also a superstructure. The cause is the consequence; you are rich because you are white, yon are white because you are rich.' That is, race structures class relations in colonial societies, as seen in the case of Palestine/Israel and Jerusalem. The racial division has structured all relations between Israelis and Palestinians in the territory to facilitate the Zionist hegemony over the territory from the destruction of the Palestinian nation and to prevent any possibilities of interracial solidarity that could lead to a path of decolonization. The strength of structural racism, despite the crises provoked by neoliberalism, was evident in the J-14 demonstrations in 2011, where there was no unity that overcame racial differences even among Jewish workers within Zionist society, nor a consensus on the Palestinian question (Englert, 2017). Englert notes how the claims of the J-14 movement demanded rewards for their adherence to the Zionist project. But the demands of the Mizrahim, marginalized within the settler society, as well as the activity of grassroots movements and the workers' union were simply ignored by the Ashkenazi leaders. Although the combination of neoliberal capitalism and settler colonialism has distinct and complementary effects on the Palestinian and Israeli working classes, their class identity is unable to forge broad, structural alliances beyond the divisions of nation, ethnicity, and race. Therefore, the conditions for the reproduction of a multiracial working-class movement in Jerusalem following the Second Intifada are compromised.

Crises, tensions and popular mobilizations against oppression and exploitation by the Israeli neoliberal ruling classes have become more frequent, but they do not seem to affect the settler colonial structure of neoliberal apartheid. Despite settler colonial racism being a cause of constant destabilization, due to its intrinsic violence that causes short-term disturbances in the accumulation process, it is also a solid basis in the long term by preventing the settler colonial regime and its neoliberal policies from having their core threatened by the fractures they cause in the exploited and oppressed population. Settler colonial racism stems the vulnerabilities produced by the contradictions of capitalism by fragmenting the struggle of subalterns and containing mass counterhegemonic movements that simultaneously target their settler colonial and neoliberal faces. Therefore, crises can end up being opportunities for the dominant classes to reproduce their forms of government that continue to promote the various divisions in society produced by the various combinations of race, class and space. One example is the enactment of Decision No. 3670 of 2018, which heralded the beginning of the largest Israeli investment cycle in East Jerusalem's history.

3

Neoliberal Israelization of East Jerusalem

How the Israeli plan for the neoliberal development of East Jerusalem does not serve the interests of the native population and adapts Palestinians to Israeli security and economic needs

The relationship between Palestinian Jerusalemites and the Israeli settler regime has changed over the 2010s, resulting in a greater integration of the native population into the Israeli system. More and more East Jerusalem Palestinians can now be seen in the job market, in commercial areas, in educational institutions, on public transport, in bureaucratic offices, in NGOs and in philanthropic foundations of West Jerusalem or in some way working in connection with the Israeli regime and Jewish settlements in East Jerusalem (Shtern, 2016, 2019; Shtern and Yacobi, 2019). The socio-spatial isolation and extreme vulnerability of Palestinians in East Jerusalem, which has seen a steady increase since the Oslo years, has driven natives closer to the settler colonial sphere of influence and away from the West Bank Palestinian community (W. Salem, 2018; Shalhoub-Kevorkian, 2012).

After decades of the State of Israel's profound wilful neglect of the Palestinian neighbourhoods of East Jerusalem, with the exception of the police, guards, soldiers and settlers who ensured settler colonial expansion, tax collection and the repression of native resistance, Israeli authorities announced for the first time in history – in June 2014, two days before the abduction of Mohammed Abu-Khdeir and the beginning of the Jerusalem Intifada – a plan to increase 'personal security and socio-economic development' in East Jerusalem. A budget of 200 million shekels was allocated for these purposes, to be invested by 2018 (Dagoni, 2019a). According to an analysis by the Comptroller of the

State of Israel, the plan suffered from profoundly inadequate preparation and poor execution, yielding neither socio-economic improvements for the Palestinians nor increased security for the residents of Jerusalem. The Israeli human rights NGO Ir Amin highlights that the only goals that were complied with were investment measures in policing and inspections targeting Palestinian individuals, their neighbourhoods, legal statuses and businesses (Dagoni, 2019a). In response to Israeli controllership, the persistence of Palestinian popular uprisings and to meet OECD requirements for the reduction of inequality in Israel, a more ambitious project was launched in 2018 that aims to invest approximately 2 billion shekels in East Jerusalem over five years. The project aims to 'bridge the gaps' between the Jerusalem of the Palestinians and that of the Jews (Hasson, 2018a).

Government Decision 3790 titled 'Narrowing Socio-economic Gaps and Economic Development in East Jerusalem' (Prime Minister Office, 2018) intends to reduce distrust and inequality between the Israeli and Palestinian populations and, at the same time, foster development and greater safety for all city residents. Most of the budget was originally earmarked to renovate the Palestinian educational system by imposing the Israeli curriculum in addition to other urban infrastructure projects, privately led economic development, the promotion of entrepreneurship – particularly among Palestinian women and youth – and official registration of Palestinian-owned private properties in Israeli planning committees (Prime Minister Office, 2018).

The decision looks to address both the long-established demands of Israeli human rights NGOs such as Ir Amin for the city, as well as the grievances of Palestinian leadership – such as Ramadan Tabash (personal communication, July 2019), a community leader from the Sur Baher neighbourhood – against the settler colonial neglect of public services and basic infrastructure for Palestinian neighbourhoods, which they point to as a direct affront to the rights of residents in terms of public health and education (N. Dagoni, personal communication, July 2019b). Despite not recognizing settler authority over the city, which historically has driven the native population to reject participation in Israeli politics, Palestinians are obligated to pay municipal taxes in order not to lose their right of residence and maintain access to other rights they cannot otherwise obtain – although Palestinians represent approximately 37 per cent of taxpayers, less than 10 per cent of the municipal budget was allocated to

Palestinian neighbourhoods in East Jerusalem on average historically (Jafari et al., 2019).

Given the alternatives at its disposal, settler colonial power appears to have opted for a strategy that inflicts the least of all possible evils on Palestinians. Despite considerable criticism, these projects for development and inclusion count many supporters among both Israelis and Palestinians. Evidence of this support can be noted in the launch of the urban revitalization project called 'Sillicon Wadi', which will reconfigure the Palestinian neighbourhood of Wadi Joz, immediately north of the Old City's Damascus Gate, near the West Jerusalem divide, to function as a new technology centre for the city's entrepreneurial ecosystem (The New Arab, 2020). The project represents yet another example of neoliberal urbanism strategies being adopted in Jerusalem, but which for the first time involve a Palestinian location as their supposed beneficiary. In the view of Jerusalem parliamentarian Laura Wharton (Boxerman, 2020), leader of the left-most Israeli-Zionist party on the political spectrum, Meretz, and active member of the support base for ultranationalist mayor Moseh Lion, in June 2020:

> The government finally woke up a few years ago and realized that leaving East Jerusalem in the state it is in is bad for everyone, and that the time has come for the government to get involved … . The thinking here [Wadi Joz] now is to develop high-tech and other industries that will allow people from East Jerusalem to find employment in Jerusalem. I've met many talented Palestinians who work in Ramallah and other places because there isn't a lot of high-tech in Jerusalem, and what exists is by and for [Jewish] Israelis. (Wharton quoted in Boxerman, 2020)

This urban reform will turn Wadi Joz – a Palestinian neighbourhood that, along with Bab A-Zahara and Musrara, make up the neglected and devalued Palestinian centre of East Jerusalem whose revitalization has been stalled for decades at municipal levels – into a neoliberal district comprised of corporate offices, technology teaching institutions, star-studded hotels and luxury shopping centres (Boxerman, 2020). The revitalization project will remove at least two hundred Palestinian commercial establishments where thousands of Palestinians work, including the only Palestinian-owned industrial zone in the city that houses Palestinian auto repair shops famous for being very popular with both settlers and natives.

The case of the Silicon Wadi project illustrates the counterinsurgency logic that is behind all the inclusion and development policies aimed by the State of Israel at Palestinian Jerusalemites in sectors that are not limited to the strictly economic, but are also valid for culture, education and other social areas that serve as 'non-conventional' forms of 'armed social work' against the natives. The objective is the fabrication of a stable and predictable new social order that enables the Israeli ruling classes in Jerusalem to accumulate capital. Palestinians in East Jerusalem would no longer be racialized and reproduced solely for their expulsion or overexploitation, as occurred in a hegemonic way throughout the settler colonial occupation of the city but would be trained and 'empowered' in order to become qualified workforce fit for consumption. Palestinians are less alienated to their adequacy to fulfil the demands of Israeli capital, but are not necessarily integrated into Israeli citizenship, that is, an 'inclusion without integration' (W. Salem, 2018). This process is referred to as Neoliberal Israelization, which is the expansion of Israeli rule over Palestinian life and territory in East Jerusalem without seeking their expulsion to Judaize the area or their assimilation into Israeli society. What we are witnessing is the reproduction of Israel's form of rule over East Jerusalem in accordance with the requirements imposed by global capital and Israeli demographic anxieties.

Furthermore, while it prioritizes high technology to advance Israeli economic interests, the plan does not provide incentives for the Palestinian tourism industry, nor does it seek to ease the restrictions that led to only 12 per cent of tourists who visited Jerusalem in 2013 to stay in hotels in East Jerusalem (Arafeh, 2016a) – a trend that persists to this day. Palestinian tour guides are marginalized, and native-owned establishments remain discriminated against, while licensing for new Palestinian hotels remains limited. These policies affect the main sector of the native economy on which 40 per cent of the population directly depends and from which thousands of other traders and service providers indirectly benefit (Arafeh, 2016a; R. Saadeh, personal communication, June 2019). The situation is particularly precarious among Old City shopkeepers who have been stifled by sky-high levels of taxation and indebtedness, leaving them more susceptible to dispossession by settler NGOs and Israeli authorities (Arafeh, 2016c; A. Dakkak, personal communication, August 2019).

Neoliberal Israelization can only be possible because of the historical de-development of economic sectors that are vital to Palestinian autonomy in East Jerusalem alongside the violent repression, overt surveillance, forced expulsion and suburban settlement. It is estimated that more than 250 Palestinian businesses closed their doors in the city between 1999 and 2015 directly due to settler restrictions on the native economy (Nasara, 2019: 9), while the economic losses caused by the construction of the Wall in Jerusalem were estimated by the UN in 2013 at more than US$1 billion, and its continuation would promote approximately US$200 million in lost opportunities for Palestinian Jerusalemites annually (Khalidi, 2013).

Fanon (1994) used the term 'technocratic paternalism' to describe the social welfare devices of the French government of Algeria in which colonial power is reorganized in a more gentle and fraudulent way so as to maintain a stable and productive order, allowing it to hide the racism that persists in the daily life of colonial occupation. In East Jerusalem, the Israeli neoliberal counterinsurgency employs the progressive agendas of diversity and inclusion to reform the system of government in order to permit the upward mobility of certain individuals without altering the settler colonial structure of subjugation, expulsion, and exploitation. Neoliberal Israelization creates new deception traps for the Palestinians.

The neoliberal Israelization paradigm

Literature dealing with the confluence between neoliberalism and Israelization in East Jerusalem has prioritized institutional and infrastructural aspects. Salem (2018), despite taking economic issues into account, addresses the issue of inclusion, development and Israelization of Palestinians in East Jerusalem from a mainly institutional point of view, such as the absence in the Palestinian public sphere due to the closure of the activities of the Orient House and other measures of the settler state. A portion of the literature addresses the issue of the inclusion of Palestinians through neoliberalism by examining aspects of public transport infrastructure, in particular the light train: while some see the venture as a way to advance settler colonial violence (Baumann, 2018; Nolte, 2016), others point to the possibilities of a multicultural encounter between Palestinians and Israelis beyond the settler colonial divide (Shtern, 2018a).

Broadening the lens of analysis, Shlomo (2016) notes how neoliberalization in East Jerusalem is contrasted and specific in relation to that of West Jerusalem due to the racial division in the city's socio-spatial relations. He argues that, through the privatization of the public transportation and education services that cater to Palestinians, the settler colonial power exploits the neglect suffered by Palestinian neighbourhoods to promote a 'subformalization' under the promise of bringing about an improvement. However, the Israeli settler regime would be resorting to private agents to assume, without direct connection, control of the softer technologies of government that deal with the conduct, security and well-being of Palestinians in East Jerusalem. That is, with their social reproduction. In a similar line of reasoning, Volinz (2018) demonstrates how the responsibility for Palestinians' state security arrangements has also been outsourced through the privatization of security and the inclusion of social actors in security assemblages, such as sewage and electricity companies, municipal bureaucracies for tax collection, environmental inspection and commercial regulation, as well as schools and health posts.

However, the literature also notes that the relations between Israeli settler colonization and the neoliberal market are not one-dimensional, that is, they do not always seem to favour the interests of the settler colonial project, but are constituted by several ambivalences. In analysing the growing presence of middle-class Palestinians in Israeli settlements in East Jerusalem, Yacobi and Pullan (2014) claim that there is a paradox in the relationship between settler colonial and market interests in East Jerusalem. While the state works to impose racial segregation in Jerusalem's socio-spatial relations by building settlements inhabited exclusively by Jews, the market would seem to enable middle-class Palestinians to subvert, even in a limited way, this historical logic by promoting a small 'fissure' in the efforts of the homogeneous Judaization of space through the acquisition of private property in Jewish settlements in East Jerusalem (Yacobi and Pullan, 2014).

Also on the supposed paradoxical relationship between neoliberalism and settler colonialism, Shtern (2018a) goes further by arguing that the neoliberal market allows for the creation of meeting places between Palestinians and Israeli Jews in residential settlements, workplaces, educational institutions and consumption centres that function, even if provisionally, as multicultural spaces and moments that can stimulate possibilities of decolonizing relations between Jews and Arabs in the city. In his view, the market would function as an agent of identities and social relations that form mixed spaces based on social class, globalization and neoliberal individualism that destabilize the racial segregation of colonialism (Shtern, 2018a).

Neoliberal counterinsurgency in Israel and the OPT

In Israeli neoliberal settler colonialism, we observe this hybridism in the proliferation of neoliberal rationality among the lower and middle strata of society in order to advance processes of depoliticization, dispossession and pacification through the work of international institutions and NGOs and their humanitarian aid and empowerment agendas across Palestine, including Israel and the OPT (Haddad, 2016; Hanieh, 2016; Samour, 2016; Shehadeh and Khalidi, 2014). Among their differences and similarities, we highlight the role of NGOs in conducting entrepreneurial training programmes, particularly focused on the technological area in Ramallah and Nazareth, and also cultural and educational activities promoting the construction of new neoliberal subjects who often ascend socially, adding to the formation of a middle class that collaborates in sustaining the human, and moral infrastructure necessary for the administration of neoliberal settler colonialism. High-tech entrepreneurship has served as a neoliberal carrot for the fraudulent development and pacification of the Palestinian urban middle classes across the territory under Israel's rule. These experiences of Israeli actors in the neoliberal counterinsurgency of Palestinians in the OPT and in Israel based on development policies and high-tech entrepreneurship have served as an important paradigm for the process that is underway in East Jerusalem.

This model was developed during the Obama administration (2009–16), which sought to make business collaboration, particularly in the technology area, a way to advance the political plan of its Secretary of State John Kerry in a re-edition of 'economic peace' (Rubin, 2018). Between 2014 and 2016, the United States promoted, through funding from USAID and the implementation of the Kaizen Company, a US company specializing in entrepreneurship-based development programmes in Third World nations, known as the SpaceX project, an initiative to promote cooperation in high-tech ventures between Israelis and Palestinians on both sides of the Green Line (The Kaizen Company, 2016). In the wake of this initiative, several Israeli NGOs, such as PIP (Palestinian Internship Programme) and the Peres Center for Peace and Innovation, saw the promotion of entrepreneurial and technological training programmes as a way to generate forms of technological, economic and, eventually, political collaboration – on many occasions, with US funding (Peres Center for Peace and US Department of State, 2020). Another American initiative during this period was the creation of a group of Palestinian and Israeli businessmen, many in the technology field, called Breaking the Impasse, which intended to facilitate political relations through economic exchanges. Although it failed to reach a political agreement, the group served as a business opportunity for several Israeli and Palestinian businessmen, particularly those in the high-tech field.

One of the fruits of this collaboration has been the formation of a still small but growing high-tech industry in Ramallah which, although portrayed as a way for natives to achieve national independence, is the result of investment and economic cooperation between Palestinian elites and Israeli capitalists (Dana, 2014b). The high-tech industry, however, has allowed the deepening of dependence and economic normalization between Israel and Palestinians. Most Palestinian technology companies provide outsourcing services in the development of software and hardware and also function as a 'back office' for foreign and Israeli corporations (Rubin, 2018). The outsourcing of services from Israeli companies to Palestinian companies as a way to meet the growing demand for services and workforce in the technology sector is supported by businessmen and diplomats as an opportunity for cooperation, development and political approximation between settlers and natives who are 'mutually interested' and 'rational' in matters of security and economy (Haddad, 2016; Peres Center for Peace and US Department of State, 2020). According to a Palestinian businessman in the high-tech sector, outsourcing is a 'win-win' situation and not a construction of economic dependence (Rubin, 2018).

Another case from the same period that sought to make the outsourcing of the Israeli economy into a form of cooperation with Palestinians was the construction of the industrial zones, a project shared by colonizers and colonized inaugurated in the OPT with investment by states and foreign capital to create 'market opportunities' to generate employment and poverty alleviation among Palestinians as well as 'peace dividends' (Dana, 2015). Direct investment by Israelis and international capital based on the recommendation of international institutions for the supposed development of Palestinians has allowed, in reality, the advance of globalized capitalism over the native territory for the production of export-oriented goods with free access to cheap Palestinian labour, the enrichment of economic-political elites and an opportunity for Israeli capital to break the blockades of the BDS campaigns in the Arab world. According to Dana (2015: 247), the 'experience in the West Bank has shown that the capitalist interaction between the colonizer and the colonised came to constitute a control mechanism that serves the colonial advance and pacification'. That is, the neoliberal management techniques of private corporations are vehicles that would presumably help build bottom-up economic conditions to promote top-level agreements, but serve, in the end, to pacify Palestinians and facilitate accumulation for the elites. Economic normalization, therefore, is simply the first step for political normalization (Dana, 2015; Haddad, 2016).

The 2018 Jerusalem development plan also comes on the heels of a series of projects to develop ethnic and religious 'minorities' in Israel – such as the Palestinian Arab population – as a way of meeting requirements to reduce poverty and unemployment and increase the GDP per capita as established by the OECD for Israel to remain in the category of developed nations (Shehadeh and Khalidi, 2014). The scenario in Israel is very similar to that of Jerusalem, where poverty is almost synonymous with being Palestinian, but the low socio-economic indices among the Orthodox Jewish population allow for inequality to be framed as a 'cultural' and social issue instead of a racial one.

Even after seven decades of living under liberal settler colonial sovereignty, the permanent socio-spatial segregation of the Palestinian citizens of Israel and the continuation of practices of alienation towards natives confirms the hypothesis of the exclusivism of Israeli settler colonialism (Shihade, 2012). Although Palestinians in Israel suffer from issues of identity and the practices of Israelization, a visit to a Palestinian village in Galilee, in northern Israel, demonstrates the non-occurrence of an assimilation of the Palestinian minority to the Jewish majority. Citizenship has always been approached by Israelis as a system of control and exclusion of Palestinians to allow for a stability of settler colonization throughout the country, while de-development functions as the main way to facilitate the dispossession, exploitation and pacification of the native population (S. N. Robinson, 2013; Shehadeh and Khalidi, 2014).

The alienation of Palestinians has been counterbalanced by government technologies that, to a limited extent, have promoted the inclusion of the native population for material and symbolic reasons that serve the interests of the Zionist project (Cohen, 2010; S. N. Robinson, 2013). At different stages of the historical process, for example, following a counterinsurgency strategy, the government implemented the Israelization of the school curriculum. Israeli leaders have tried to transform the identity of the indigenous population to produce the 'Israeli-Arab' subject: a docile, orderly and hardworking Arab citizen (Cohen, 2010). Alongside processes of socio-spatial segmentation reminiscent of the more traditional colonial strategies of divide and rule,[1] Israeli authorities forced the socio-economic de-development of Palestinians in Israel with the aim of deepening dependence on the Israeli labour market and the vulnerability of natives to patronage schemes. Their objective was to co-opt traditional elites and also ordinary citizens as informants in the formation of a middle class of collaborators who acted as native intermediaries representing settler colonial interests in the indirect government of the Palestinians (Cohen, 2010; S. N. Robinson, 2013; Shihade, 2012).

Although history is replete with well-intentioned speeches of 'modernization' of the Palestinians in close contact with the most economically developed segments of Israeli society, civilized according to the Western model after centuries of 'darkness' and 'backwardness' under the Ottoman Empire, at no time did settler authorities perceive the real socio-economic development and integration of the native population as a benefit to their settler colonial ambitions (Shehadeh and Khalidi, 2014). In any case, the external pressures of capital seem to have now forced the Israeli ruling classes to overcome the exclusive strategy of de-development of Palestinians in Israel as a form of pacification and super-exploitation in favour of a market-led development

---

[1] To create divisions among Palestinians, settler colonial rulers promoted the racialization of the Naqab Bedouins as 'good and loyal' Arabs, of Christians as exceptionally civilized as opposed to the Muslim majority, and of the Druze as a distinct non-Arab nationality for whom military conscription is mandatory. See Cohen (2010), Shihade (2012), Robinson (2013).

strategy that serves their more ambitious interests of integrating the global market from which the Palestinian economy in Israel has always been excluded, remaining local and underdeveloped (Shehadeh and Khalidi, 2014).

Until the early 2010s, the main effect of neoliberal reforms among Palestinians in Israel had been the growth of poverty due to drastic cuts in social benefits such as pensions and social security. But while the reduction of social inequality between Jews and Palestinians did not figure among the government's more incisive policies, it had been part of recommendations made by international organizations. In 2007, the Authority for the Economic Development of the Arab, Druze and Circassian sectors was established as a requirement for Israel to join the OECD. It was created to alleviate Palestinian poverty while maintaining control over their economic development with the goal of connecting them to Israel's development priorities. The large-scale economic inclusion of Palestinians came to be understood as beneficial and rational according to a cost–benefit assessment on the part of the Israelis, in addition to enabling a new economic normalization that would serve as a deterrent to feelings of hostility between different sectors of Palestinian society in Israel.

With an initial investment of approximately 15 billion shekels to be allocated over five years between 2017 and 2022, the project for the socio-economic development of Arab-Palestinians in Israel is focused on building a high-tech ecosystem and promoting entrepreneurial activity. Remarkably, entrepreneurship emerges not only as an objective and material practice but also as an activity capable of promoting a cultural transformation among Palestinians in Israel and eliminating what would be considered the 'last shackles' of Arab-Muslim conservatism, seen as responsible for the backwardness of the native economy and its inability to integrate into and keep up with the settler economy (Shehadeh and Khalidi, 2014).

In the opinion of Palestinian citizen of Israel and high-tech entrepreneur Ziyad Hanna, the main examples of this backwardness include a low participation of women in the workforce and the absence of *chutzpah*[2] necessary for entrepreneurial creativity:

---

[2] The term chutzpah is derived from the Hebrew and Idiche languages and means audacity. In the Israeli business community, the term has come to refer to the amount of bravery required to become a successful entrepreneur. Within the context of Israel's rise as a "start-up nation," chutzpah has become a term used to describe a specific trait of the Israeli entrepreneur that makes him or her a successful businessperson.

> I keep analysing [the] hi-tech [industry] in Israel, to try and understand what the secret sauce is. One element is *chutzpah*. In the Arab sector, we are a more conservative community. In hi-tech, it's fundamental to fail, and we fail to fail. This conservativeness exists mostly among the older generation. The new generation has changed a lot with more initiatives, more motivation and passion to change things … . Bringing hi-tech to the Arab community has a tremendous effect. It's not only about empowering engineers but also improving standards of living and improving the whole ecosystem. (Hanna cited in Halon, 2019)

Although the Palestinian elite blamed culture for a lack of greater native involvement in high-tech, racism has been driving Palestinian entrepreneurs and IT workers from Israel to Ramallah and abroad, where they could have more job opportunities, fleeing the colour barrier that exists in Israeli corporations. Such was the case for Saed Nashef, a Palestinian from Haifa, who became the founder of the largest Palestinian venture capital firm in Ramallah (Barrows-Friedman, 2012).

The high-tech industry in Nazareth, Israel's Palestinian capital, however, would be changing this process since 2016, when the State of Israel, through NGOs such as the Israeli IT Works, Al-Fanar and Tsofen, has invested millions of shekels annually in programmes for training, capacity-building, monitoring, granting scholarships and microcredit lines to encourage the formation of new high-tech workers and entrepreneurial initiatives, as well as in programmes to encourage the hiring of Palestinians in Israeli companies in the sector (Ziv, 2019). For example, Maof, an Israeli state agency that works as an accelerator for small and medium-sized businesses in Israel and is seen as instrumental in reducing inequality through entrepreneurship according to the OECD, has supported the NGO Hybrid in Nazareth since 2015 (Inter-Agency Task Force on Israeli Arab Issues, 2019). Hybrid is the main accelerator for high-tech start-ups in the city. The organization offers training workshops, professional monitoring programmes, microcredit lines and subsidies for those it considers to be the best entrepreneurs.

This process of neoliberal Israelization of Palestinian social spaces in Israel is marked by the growing presence of the Israeli Third Sector, funded by the state, private capital and Zionist philanthropy originally intended for the socio-economic assimilation of new settlers and the defence of Jewish privileges in the country (Tatour, 2016). Many of the NGOs involved in the direct implementation of policies for the socio-economic development of Palestinians in the Galilee are Israeli organizations with an Arab-Palestinian face that serve to build empathy and trust with the native population while keeping their Israeli roots as hidden as possible.

For example, JDC-Israel is the Israeli arm of the US-based JDC, which claims to be the largest Jewish philanthropic organization in the world and has been a supporter of Jewish communities since 1914, in particular settlers in Palestine. In line with neoliberal rationality, the objective of JDC-Israel is 'to contribute to the advancement of quality of life, equal opportunities and reduction of gaps in Israeli society' (JDC-Israel, 2020). In addition to contributing to the entrepreneurial training of Black, Mizrahi and haredim Jewish minorities, since 2007, the NGO has been promoting the Riyan programme, to help Arab, Druze and Bedouin populations in Israel find 'sustainable employment and pull themselves and their families out of poverty' (JDC-Israel, 2020). There are more than twenty-one Ryian Centres. These are operated by Israeli-Arab Al-Fanar, a third-party company created by JDC-Israel itself and jointly financed by the Ministry of Economy, the Prime Minister's Office and the Zionist Rothschild Foundation (Naftali et al., 2018).

The Ryian Centres function as locations for technical skills training in accordance with market demands in a voucher scheme for unemployed populations without high-level qualifications or access to state social benefits. All Ryian Centres contain Palestinian professionals who normally come from the community where the centres are located and act as 'community activists' with familiar ties to the local population which they use to recruit their target audience (Y. Hermetz, personal communication, July 2019; Naftali et al., 2018). Indigenous professionals also serve as role models and sources for the dissemination of information to promote 'changes in social attitudes' regarding the importance of employment, self-reliance, women's work and entrepreneurial education (JDC-Israel, 2020).

Based on the efforts of this neoliberal Israeli coalition, between 2008 and 2019, the number of Palestinian IT engineers in Israel rose from 350 to over 6,600 men and women, even though they represent only 4.5 per cent of the workforce in the Israeli high-tech industry (Ziv, 2019). The centre of Nazareth now contains incubators, accelerators and shared workspaces maintained by non-profit and state-funded organizations, as well as the outsourced offices of Israeli companies, Palestinian start-ups and multinational corporations. According to official data, in 2019 there were a total of fifty companies and 1,300 technology professionals in the city (Ziv, 2019). The rise of the high-tech scene and entrepreneurial activity is portrayed as a way of exploring the untapped economic reservoir to promote socio-economic well-being among the Palestinian community, meet the demand for skilled labour that exists in the Israeli high-tech industry and increase Israel's GDP, in addition to representing an important turning point for the modernization of native society. As Fawzi Shakur, the director of a Palestinian start-up in Nazareth, observes:

> The change has begun taking place among Arab mothers who instead of seeing their sons as lawyers, accountants, pharmacists, or doctors, realize they can also work in high-tech. I don't want to use the prime minister's nasty language, but Arabs are heading into high-tech in 'droves', [this] is starting to become acceptable. (Shakur quoted in Ziv, 2019)

Thus, entrepreneurial activity is presented as a form of inclusion through the market and as the creation of new Palestinian subjects. The existing neoliberal social relations within the high-tech market are portrayed as capable of applying to the rest of the native community and assisting in the movement of their position within Israeli society (Chronicle, 2019). Creating the conditions for this social ascension through the market can also be understood as a form of recognition of the capacity of the native youth that was being wasted as a result of the historical exclusion promoted by the State of Israel. The Palestinian director of Tsofen, Sami Saadi, hopes to build a 'great Arab-Jewish collaboration' for peace and development: 'The Arab community is so proud now. We opened the door for them', says Saadi (quoted in Stoll, 2019).

Decision 3790: The framework for neoliberal Israelization in East Jerusalem

Launched in 2018, the Decision 3790 'Narrowing Socio-economic Gaps and Promoting Economic Development in East Jerusalem' is the result of collaboration between the Ministry of Jerusalem Affairs and the municipality. The goal is to profoundly change the conditions of the city's Palestinian neighbourhoods through an investment of more than 2 billion shekels (over US$ 500 million) between 2019 and 2023 with a focus on improvements in education, urban infrastructure, employment and business activity. Institutionally, the project addresses two of Israel's official objectives: first, to meet the OECD demands for the reduction of socio-economic inequality, poverty and unemployment in Israel through targeted and temporary programmes aimed at training and market integration of national 'minorities' in Israel, from Arab-Palestinian-Israeli citizens to the ultra-Orthodox population; second, to strengthen Jerusalem as Israel's single and indivisible capital, that is, as a modern and economically vibrant Zionist city that contains entrepreneurial urbanism strategies and a high-tech creative economy capable of attracting tourists, foreign capital and more Jews to live in it.

Therefore, by seeking to narrow five decades of socio-economic inequality in just five years, the investment project would provide an answer to the strategy for the neoliberal settler colonization of East Jerusalem, in which Palestinians are gathered as resources for capital through institutional marketing and the selling of Jerusalem. The governmental decision responds to old claims of sectors of the local Palestinian society and also of the Israeli left, such as human rights NGOs who have criticized the evident imbalance between the contribution made by natives to the municipal budget and the amount of public services that were provided in return (Dagoni, 2019a). It is worth noting that the project, in essence, represents a recognition of the demands of parts of the Palestinian Jerusalemite society that has always sought to maintain an open dialogue with the Israelis, despite disagreements over national issues, and has historically demanded an improvement of public services in a city governed by the settler power. It can be seen as the fruits of a history of long-sought rational and pragmatic action by a portion of the Palestinians. However, settler colonial recognition of native demands always comes with an underlying political intent.

It is common to hear from Israeli bureaucrats involved in the implementation of the project that the complete negligence of the government in relation to natives residing in East Jerusalem occurred because it would not make sense to invest in a place that was not guaranteed to remain under Israeli sovereignty after an agreement with the Palestinians (Y. Issar, personal communication, June 2019; Y. Toren, personal communication, July 2019). This justification is not new. 'We avoided investing in areas that would not ultimately fall under Israeli sovereignty', said the former mayor and former prime minister Ehud Olmert in 2012 (quoted in International Crisis Group, 2019).

With that in mind, it would be irrational, from a settler point of view, to promote a policy that did not signify a Judaization of the city, affect the demographic balance and expand direct control of the territory in favour of the Israelis. The stalling of political negotiations between Israel and Palestinians and the Trump government's official recognition of Jerusalem as the capital of Israel allowing the transfer of the US embassy to the city in 2017, however, did change the status quo for Israeli authorities. The US president's decision was a green light for the Israeli ruling classes' plans and economic ambitions in East Jerusalem even before the consolidation of the larger project for the entire West Bank, which came to be presented in the 2020 unilateral 'Deal of the Century'.[3] In an interview, senior referent of strategy and governance in the municipality's strategic planning and policy division, Yaron Toren, spoke plainly:

> Since the failure of Oslo, there was uncertainty about the solution for Jerusalem as it might not be ours so we should not be responsible for its development. So, we just provided the basic services. Why bother solving problems if East Jerusalem is not ours? There is now an understanding that all of Jerusalem is part of Israel. East Jerusalem is ours. (Toren, 2019)

Hence, the correlation between the change in the form of governing the Palestinians from solely de-development and alienation to also neoliberal development and integration, precisely when Israeli elites advance in the annexation of West Bank territories where a few thousand Palestinians still live, is no accident. The architect of Decision 3790 – former minister for Jerusalem affairs and losing candidate in the 2018 municipal election, Ze'ev Elkin, a far-right, religious, ultranationalist politician and long-time advocate of city partition for the expansion of the Jewish majority – already had in

---

[3] After both Trump and Netanyahu were ousted from their positions in 2021, the 'Deal of the Century' was buried. Nevertheless, the annexation of parts of the West Bank has been advanced since the return of Netanyahu to the prime minister office in December 2022.

2018, so to speak, laboratorial understanding of the new Israeli policy for the Palestinian population of the city. Elkin said in September 2018, a few months after the plan was launched:

> Today's Jerusalem represents the demographic DNA of Israel in twenty years .... We must develop models for handling the challenges in Jerusalem that will help us handle future challenges in Israel. (Elkin quoted in International Crisis Group, 2019: 24)

The argument of seeing East Jerusalem's development as a testing laboratory for the management of the West Bank territories that will come to be annexed was used by Elkin to convince the small but strong lobby of settler NGOs Elad, Ateret Cohanim and Israel Land Fund among the elected representatives in the Jerusalem City Council (International Crisis Group, 2019), who were against allocating public resources to the integration and development of Palestinians in East Jerusalem; they instead favoured the Judaization of the city. Councilman Arieh King, leader of the Israel Land Fund and a resident of the Maale Ha-Zeitim settlement in Silwan, is one of the strongmen of conservative mayor Moshe Leon. At the same time, Leon has been praised for the dialogue he has maintained with local Palestinian leaders in order to facilitate the implementation of socio-economic development policies, presented as mutually beneficial to both parties (Hasson, 2020a). However, 2019, the first full year of Leon's government, which saw the implementation of Decision 3790, was also the year in which a record number of Palestinian home demolitions and abusive police actions occurred in East Jerusalem (Ir Amin, 2020). The recognition by the settlers of the native's historic demands for quality-of-life improvements did not signify the end of settler colonization, destruction or repression, but rather a deepening thereof. Instead, there is a reorganization of the carrots and sticks available to the ruling classes to govern the spaces and lives of Palestinians.

The counterinsurgent logic of projects for the development and inclusion of Palestinians was quite evident in the plan launched in 2014 by the Israeli authorities. In it, investments in the policing and surveillance of East Jerusalem to increase the 'sense of security' were explicitly linked to socio-economic mitigation policies that were exclusively aimed at Jerusalemites (Dagoni, 2019). The project intended to create a new social order within the parameters of the national 'City without Violence' programme, which allocates resources for surveillance and policing in several cities in Israel. Decision 3790, however, takes an even deeper and more comprehensive approach to replicating the Palestinian pacification process without breaking with the structural logic that was implemented in the city since the early days of the occupation.

The most evident trace can be found in the security–development nexus that permeates all Israeli policies towards the Palestinians throughout the territory and serves as an explicit justification for Decision 3790, elaborated also considering the 2014–17 Jerusalem Intifada. Indeed, according to bureaucrat Toren (2019), it would be unwise to draw explicit ties between Palestinian uprisings and development programmes. This would encourage the view according to which 'the more you throw stones at us, the more money we give' (Y. Toren, personal communication, July 2019). For this reason, security policies were excluded from the recent development plan, which kept only the policies at the socio-economic level. This does not, however, prevent the interconnection between security and development.

The security–development nexus also involves the direct participation of military and security agents in areas that go beyond their immediate remit, such as education, culture and economic development. For example, the office located in the centre of West Jerusalem shared between the Ministry for Jerusalem Affairs, responsible for planning and overall coordination of Decision 3790, and the East Jerusalem Development Company, a state-owned company in charge of projects designed to encourage tourism in the Jewish Quarter of the Old City and now responsible for the development of the economic infrastructure of Palestinian neighbourhoods, was populated in 2019 by at least seventeen former members of the Shin-Bet (Hasson, 2019a). The Shin-Bet is the Israeli secret service responsible for surveillance operations, recruitment of collaborators, sabotage and murder of internal enemies, that is, Palestinians.

During the field research in 2019, Arik Brabbing, the former director of the Shin-Bet in the District of Jerusalem, assumed the head of the East Jerusalem Development Company and made a point of being present for part of the interview with a Palestinian member of the company responsible for a revitalization programme of commercial streets in Palestinian neighbourhoods, Mohamad Nijam (personal communication, July 2019).

Brabbing's predecessor, Ofer Or was one of the architects of the plan for the socio-economic development of East Jerusalem Palestinians. Or became one of the pioneers of the idea of promoting entrepreneurial training programmes for Palestinian residents after having served as the director of the Shin-Bet in the aftermath of the Second Intifada (Ramon, 2021). In other words, the socio-economic well-being of Palestinians is always perceived through the rationality of security, and Israeli projects that were designed for this population have only ever made it through the state bureaucracy to meet this goal.

The large presence of the Shin-Bet is seen as contrary to both the settler colonial expansion interests of the far right and those of Israelis pursuing a conciliation with Palestinian residents (Hasson, 2019a). According to a Palestinian leader in East Jerusalem, Shin-Bet agents prevent the development of relationships that could be mutually beneficial.

> You have to bring people who understand engineering and master plans, not how to prevent a terror attack. They act as if they were still in the Shin Bet, using sticks rather than carrots. (Quoted in Hasson, 2019a)

The development company led by ex-Shin-Bet agents is also responsible for facilitating relations with the native population to enable the enforcement of Decision 3790. For example, when it is necessary to pave a street or expropriate a lot, agents contact landowners and local leaders, known in some regions as *mukhtars*, to facilitate dialogues. *Mukhtar* was a post held by the patriarchs of important families in ancient Palestinian villages who acted somewhat like a mayor and whose political function during the Ottoman period was to mediate the relationship between the people and the imperial bureaucracy. Although this structure was formally abolished, the term continues to be applied to generically designate a local leader who can be responsible for representing residents and arbitrating internal conflicts, often in conjunction with other local powers such as Palestinian political parties and Israeli policy.

The figure of the *mukhtar*, however, has been conveniently used by occupying colonial forces, first the British and then the Israelis, to enable forms of indirectly governing the native population. The way *mukhtars* function is by recruiting collaborators who act as representatives of the colonizing power's interests, as opposed to other political organizations that are often forced to operate underground to escape Israeli persecution and surveillance.

Former mayor Teddy Kollek maintained his relations with the Palestinian population mainly through these figures, who were abolished by Olmert and later resurrected in new forms by Barkat (Margalit, 2018). Furthermore, the preservation of old tribal structures conveniently serves the Israelis' orientalist claims of abolishing the social and political organization of the Palestinians to adapt them to the neoliberal globalization in which they would be refusing to participate.

Toren sees in the state's actions an effort to transform native society and remove it from the backwardness of the organization of the *hamula*, a term in Arabic – no longer in use today – that designates ancient Palestinian villages to which natives were historically confined, so as to bring them to the wonderful world of globalized perks, which are enjoyed and delivered by the Jewish settler community.

> The entire *hamula* tribe structure, patriarchal, traditional, and conservative, is falling apart everywhere because of increased economic freedom … . In East Jerusalem, there are two central [economic] problems: the women do not work enough, and the men work mostly in blue-collar labour. Then, when they reach the age 45 and 55, they have a giant problem. We say they 'break their back', you know, becoming too old for hard work. We must and we want to change this reality. We want men to work in both blue-collar and more sophisticated jobs … . In East Jerusalem, which is shifting from conservatism to something we don't even know what to call yet, many people are getting hurt along the way. For example, young women may see a great new world through social media, but their fathers still want them to adhere to old customs. Before, there was only the patriarchal and conservative *hamula* way of life. Now there is a collision between the modern world and the old values. And getting stuck in the middle [of that process] as a young Palestinian woman is not a good place to be. Some of these young women are being sent by their fathers and mothers to the most expensive schools in the Arab world, Western Europe or America. We try to get as many of these people to enter the Israeli system, because we tell them this is what will give them the best chances of dignified career, a dignified life in Jerusalem. Now, do I expect all these people to earn a master's degree? No. But I want a normal pyramid. (Y. Toren, personal communication, July 2019)

Orientalism still reveals itself as a central tool in Toren's discourse. The discourse of 'protecting' Muslim women from the prevailing religious conservatism of Palestinian society, which remains a common expression of contemporary imperialism and orientalism, says more about how colonizers still see themselves as the providers of a neoliberal modernity – inevitable because of its supposed material and moral superiority – that would 'liberate' women, than it does about the actual existing material conditions of Palestinian women. Palestinian women are represented in Israeli development discourses as unproductive and defenceless creatures that need to be protected from the 'barbarity' of conservative native society and freed to work. However, women's productivity is not understood because of their agency, but as a result of settler colonial projects grounded in a neoliberal rationality. The discourse of liberation and empowerment serves only to help Israelis submit Palestinian women to the rule of capital.

This kind of rationality has been criticized by post-colonial and feminist interventions in the field of development studies. Women are historically excluded from development policies, and their experiences of resistance are invisible in colonial discourses. When they appear, women are represented as helpless, people who need to be rescued from their 'backward' societies and from 'their' men (Wilson, 2012). As Spivak puts it: 'White men saving brown women from brown men' (Spivak, 2010). In neoliberalism, freedom and empowerment are ways of encouraging new strategies for the individual survival of poor women, seen as a more reliable source of productive work and as potential entrepreneurs whose workload must be intensified. Hence, microfinance models with an emphasis on women emerge to solve poverty and gender inequality to integrate them into the circuits of global capital (Wilson, 2012).

It is also evident in Toren's paternalistic neoliberal discourse that East Jerusalem's economic development hinges on an Israeli attempt to alter the social stratification of the Palestinians, which involves new modes of government and exploitation. Israelis no longer only want to overexploit the highly precarious 'blue collar' Palestinian male workforce in civil construction and agriculture, which is reproduced autonomously, with very low material resources and little colonial control in the face of development policies aimed at the de-Arabization and Judaization of Jerusalem. The neoliberal transformations of the infrastructure of the Jewish economy in Israel and the future ambitions of the ruling classes demand a reproduction of the capacities of the Palestinian population that make it newly available to capital, which involves a mastery both of Hebrew and of the technology qualifications of 'white collar' professionals. In this way, Israelis can access the native wealth that is destined for investments abroad while carrying out a reproduction of the 'economic peace' logic on a local scale in which the absence of national freedom is rewarded by limited material benefits.

The formation of this Palestinian middle class advocated by Toren to build a 'normal pyramid' serves both the economic purposes of adapting the population to the needs of transnational capital, as well as the formation of an intermediate class of qualified and capable Palestinian individuals to assist in the counterinsurgent efforts of building a new order that is at once pacified, predictable and productive. Instead of managing the settler colonial order through *mukhtars*, a tolerable amount of native autonomy and the imposition of economic de-development, neoliberal Israelization promotes what is presented as an objective and necessary modernization that seeks to dispute not just the labour force of the Palestinians but also their hearts and minds. Neoliberal carrots do not only serve as an economic counterpart for the surface-level stabilization of a new order, but also create new subjects that make up a new class and, ultimately, a new community of Palestinians in East Jerusalem based on the destruction of the former 'primitive, tribal and conservative' native society in the long run. Israeli leaders make no secret of their intention to reshape the identity of Palestinian Jerusalemites into 'the Arabs of Jerusalem' (International Crisis Group, 2019).

The counterinsurgent character of these development policies that aim to create new Arab-Israeli subjects, not new Arab-Israeli citizens,[4] is evident in the vision of David Koren, the settler bureaucrat responsible for imposing the

---

[4] During this period of increasing isolation and Israelization of East Jerusalem, a growth in the number of Palestinian applications for Israeli citizenship can be observed since 2009. However, in addition to the Ministry of the Interior maintaining a series of bureaucratic restrictions that prevent applications for citizenships by Jerusalemites, the number of rejections increases alongside the number of applications: in 2019 there were 1,200 grants and 1,361 rejections of citizenships for Palestinian Jerusalemites (Hasson, 2020b). In any case, in 2019, 95 per cent of Palestinians still only had a permanent residency status (Hasson, 2020b). The Israeli naturalization process requires a minimal proximity to 'Israeliness', such as knowledge of Hebrew and an oath of loyalty to Israel. Helplessness is such and so widespread that dependence on the scarce social benefits provided by the state, such as the public health system, is reason enough to warrant an application for Israeli citizenship given the permanent threat of physical expulsion or revocation of residence. See Salem (2018).

new Israeli curriculum on Palestinian schools in East Jerusalem. He claims that the 'struggle for sovereignty' in Jerusalem has gone from being waged 'from above', in international diplomatic summits, to occurring 'from below', in the city's everyday life (Koren, 2017). The disputes surrounding urban spaces and their sociability stop being the responsibility of diplomats and state officials to become that of street sweepers, inspectors, urban planners, teachers, police officers and social workers.

For Koren, Israelization signifies the 'end of the intermediate era for East Jerusalem' as a social space located between Israeli and Palestinian authorities, in which the Palestinians of Jerusalem are no longer seen as a surplus population and become an integral part of Israeli society. He endorses the current course of advancing civil and soft administrative measures to reach a greater number of Palestinian residents on issues of education, social welfare, infrastructure and labour to increase their sense of belonging to the city (Koren, 2017). Koren sees the 'diffusion of satisfaction' as central to social stability, productivity and gratification beyond the formal recognition of citizenship.

Furthermore, the absence of citizenship and lack of construction of new homes for the native population, considered by the Palestinians as the main limitations to their socio-economic well-being in East Jerusalem (Korach and Gavrieli 2019), reinforce the persistence of settler anxiety with regard to the demographic question as a criterion that informs Israeli developmental policy. Inclusion of Palestinian Jerusalemites to 'neoliberal Israeliness' provides Israeli settlers with the best of both worlds: the ensured reproduction of natives according to their economic needs without having to integrate them into the demographic composition of Israeli citizens. Israeli diplomat and former politician of the Likud Tzipi Hotovely understands Israelization as a transitional stage from the naturalization of Palestinians in Jerusalem to a definitive status within the paradigms of Israeli citizenship and sociability, but certainly not for all residents.

> We must bear in mind that this [Palestinian population] is a hostile entity and it is impossible to turn them into citizens overnight. There is an intermediate phase of residency that can serve as a sort of candidacy period for citizenship. The drastic step of immediate citizenship for a million and a half Palestinians would be irresponsible. (Quoted in International Crisis Group, 2019: 25)

This type of reasoning is in line with the settler colonial view that those indigenous people who fail to claim a political difference and do not present a stark contrast to settler society can become eligible for recognition and integration policies (Simpson, 2017). However, recognition, inclusion and pacification – everything – become mediated by the neoliberal market and no longer by a citizenry that has been globally dispossessed through neoliberal reforms.

De-development of Palestinian economy, capacity-building and industrial zones

High taxes, overt inspection, a drop in the number of Palestinian consumers due to the city's isolation and the construction of walls, as well as a reduced number of tourists due to direct restrictions on guides, hotels and other segments of the Palestinian industry, have caused the entire Palestinian local economy, particularly tourism and trade, to suffer a steep decline in recent decades (Arafeh and Khalidi, 2017; Jafari et al., 2019). Settler colonial policies have a direct impact on the business environment in the city, which becomes unsustainable, leading to a lack of security not only for investments by Arab and Palestinian capitalists but also for small local craft industries. In the name of 'national security', Israeli authorities have restricted, targeted and limited all native nationalist initiatives that support the resistance to neoliberal Israelization. It is also important to remember that Israelis have a monopoly over the control of the use of police and military force, civil legal institutions, monetary and fiscal policies, water, sewage, communication and electricity infrastructure, land, borders and of the transit of people and goods, which for Palestinians is restricted in every way (Hanieh, 2016).

All the Palestinian businessmen, community leaders, representatives of trade associations and directors of independent NGOs interviewed over the course of the field research declared they had not been consulted to partake in the elaboration or implementation of Decision 3790. Therefore, Israeli actions represent only Israeli objectives: they silence native demands for well-being, add to the continued de-development of the autonomous Palestinian economy and strengthen sectors dependent on settler capital. De-development, on the one hand, and neoliberal Israelization, on the other, have served to fabricate a dynamic of market competition that allows Israeli authorities to break down the 'soft borders' that materially and ideologically sustain Palestinian resistance.

For example, the traditional Arab Chamber of Commerce and Industry in Jerusalem, with ties to the Palestinian bourgeoisie in the West Bank, has existed since 1936 and was one of the Palestinian institutions that was closed at the beginning of the Second Intifada, alongside the Orient House. Since then, the chamber has operated clandestinely in the city with the aim of helping traders and businessmen with the few resources at its disposal, stemming mainly from donations by European development institutions, Turkey and the Palestinian nationalist bourgeoisie in the territory and from the diaspora (L. Al-Husseini, personal communication, June 2019; A. Dakkak, personal communication, August 2019). Its directors, however, suffer persistent harassment, having been arrested on several occasions, and their operations are conducted in a way that avoids attracting attention so as not to experience retaliations from the settler regime.

Consequently, the activities of the chamber hardly manage to reach less organized sectors of Jerusalemite society or those outside the traditional Palestinian social and political institutions. But even when it manages to reach its target audience with training courses, microcredit lines and financial subsidies, it cannot compete with those offered by Israeli-backed organizations. The chamber's initiative to encourage microentrepreneurs and small businesses, called StepUp, has failed to compete with the material aid offered by Israeli programmes aimed at the Palestinian public (Noura, personal communication, July 2019). According to the StepUp employee responsible for recruiting new participants, not even the nationalist argument has worked to attract local entrepreneurs. 'It's very tempting', says the employee in reference to the superiority of resources offered by the Israelis to facilitate access to the Israeli market.

From the point of view of Israeli interlocutors from the public and private sectors working in East Jerusalem, the case of Mati corresponds to the biggest success story of Israeli initiative in the native territory. After a few years of working informally with Palestinian Jerusalemites by government incentive, in October 2015 the NGO opened an East Jerusalem office in the building of the Anwar College, a vocational school maintained by the Israeli Ministry of Economy in the centre of East Jerusalem (Arafeh and Khalidi, 2017; G. Tobi, personal communication, July 2019). Mati entered the formal East Jerusalem market as part of the development plan launched by the state in 2014 that sought to replicate with Palestinian Jerusalemites the experience and methodology that had been used to promote entrepreneurship among Israeli Jews, in particular among new immigrant and *haredim* settlers, as a way of integrating these minorities into the Israeli market and society (Naftali et al., 2018).

The NGO works together with the East Jerusalem Development Company, Maof and Israeli community centres located in Palestinian neighbourhoods to conduct courses and provide grants and loans to those who wish to start new ventures or expand existing businesses. The training programmes are either free of charge or based on voucher model and offer a range of topics such as Israeli export and import legislation, tax exemption possibilities, digital marketing techniques and Hebrew classes. The NGO also offers free advice on the preparation and execution of business plans and seeks to create business opportunities in the Arab and Jewish sectors of the Israeli market (Arafeh and Khalidi, 2017). Mati offers more than 600,000 shekels annually in subsidies, plus interest-free loans for those who participate in its training programme, which can vary from a few thousand shekels for the purchase of a stove or refrigerator, to millions of shekels for business expansions. In addition to being funded by state grants, the NGO receives donations from Zionist philanthropists in the United States.

Mati professionals report that the first years of activity in East Jerusalem were limited by a difficulty in building trust with their target audience (Arafeh and Khalidi, 2017). According to Mati's Israeli CEO, Golan Tobi (personal communication, July 2019), public dissatisfaction with their work (expressed both by some Israelis and by the PA) has led the NGO to avoid publicity in order to reduce political pressure. On the other hand, Mati fills the void left by a lack of Palestinian institutions that could offer support to Palestinian entrepreneurs, and the reasons for its success reside precisely in their capacity to form a team comprised exclusively of Palestinian Jerusalemites who know the community and are responsible for building bridges and designing programmes according to the needs of native entrepreneurs (Arafeh and Khalidi, 2017; G. Tobi, personal communication, July 2019). According to the director of the East Jerusalem branch, Riham Jaber, Mati's presence has helped build acceptance among Palestinians regarding the possibility of doing business with Israelis (Arafeh and Khalidi, 2017).

Tobi sees this increase in trust as a form of recognition of Mati's depoliticized work to build bridges between businessmen and Jewish and Arab workers, enabling the development of the city. It is a fact that there is not a single boycott led by the Palestinian leadership against Mati. This shows that the NGO is accepted as a service that, despite possibly containing an underlying political agenda, can contribute to the social well-being of Palestinians in East Jerusalem. Riham and other Palestinians working for Israeli initiatives in East Jerusalem normally see their work as a way to contribute to the Palestinian resistance economy in the city by providing the material means that enable Jerusalemites to keep their businesses open and prosper economically without ceasing to have Jerusalem at the centre of their lives (Arafeh and Khalidi, 2017). It is a form of assistance that helps Palestinians adapt to the conditions imposed by the settler colonial occupation without crossing any normalizing lines. Tobi (2019) sees Mati's work in East Jerusalem as an integral part of efforts to build a new multicultural sociability that is mediated by the market.

> They [the Palestinians] see that we came without a political agenda, only to help people create new businesses and new jobs and to help boost the East Jerusalem economy … . The potential in East Jerusalem is huge. And because of them [their failure to cease the opportunity], the city is very poor. But something happened in the past few years: they want to be part of West Jerusalem. They no longer want to be a part of Ramallah and the Palestinian Authority … . But there are a lot of gaps to be filled: most of the women don't speak Hebrew, so they cannot find work in West Jerusalem. Most of them don't know how to look for a job … . The potential for business and employment in East Jerusalem is one of the biggest potentials for Jerusalem in the next few years … . Now we have the opportunity to invest and help them become part of the West Jerusalem business and employment sectors. I believe that when people have something to lose, such as a job and a business, they will concentrate more on living their lives and less on security problems [riots] … . We need to give them the tools to become part of this society. The challenge is to integrate the secular, *haredi* and Arab economies … . People from East Jerusalem want to be part … want to do business with West Jerusalem, but

they're afraid. West Jerusalem business owners are also still afraid to do business with East Jerusalem. (G. Tobi, personal communication, July 2019)

Tobi attributes pacifying properties to Palestinian entrepreneurship, and his words betray a technocratic paternalism that sees his work as a benevolent form of assistance and protection that serves an 'incapable' Palestinian population that is too inept to actively participate in the developed and globalized economy of West Jerusalem, particularly in the case of Palestinian women. In 2017, Mati implemented 'Empowering Women through Business', a programme to assist Palestinian women, most of them housewives. Training programmes and microcredit lines were designed to help them in their search for job stability, financial autonomy and increased participation in the family economy (Arafeh and Khalidi, 2017). Mati is also active in licensing day-care centres in private homes to meet the high demand for institutions that care for young children of women who are at work (Naftali et al., 2018). Sixty-five per cent of those who applied for assistance and support at Mati in East Jerusalem were women, 71 per cent of which started new businesses.

In terms of the younger population, and in collaboration with Anwar College, Mati aids students seeking to establish new businesses. Both these institutions are examples of vocational training programmes that are directly or indirectly subsidized by the state, specifically to help young Jerusalemites improve their performance in the city's labour and entrepreneurial markets, mainly in the Jewish sector[5] (Naftali et al., 2018). Most vocational programmes offer training and contribute financially to the formation of professionals and companies in traditional Palestinian sectors, such as beauty salons, day-care centres, schools and other small businesses, but which are now integrated into the Israeli financial system and market. As part of a government initiative, Anwar and Mati began to offer training and incentives specifically designed for the high-tech market (Anwar College, 2020).

The Leichtag Foundation, a US Zionist philanthropic foundation, contributes both to Mati's programme for the promotion of female and youth entrepreneurship in East Jerusalem and to Israeli NGO New Spirit's quality-of-life improvement and technological empowerment initiatives

---

[5] In 2017, there were twenty-one colleges specialized in professional training for young adults in East Jerusalem though not all were recognized by the State of Israel.

for the secular Jewish, ultra-Orthodox and Palestinian populations in Jerusalem. Since 2016, the foundation has been overseeing a project called the Jerusalem Model. Launched in response to the Jerusalem Intifada, the project provides financial support for more than two hundred social entrepreneurs from the 'four tribes'[6] of Jerusalem through social activism projects aimed at creating market opportunities that promote a shared use of the city and a strengthening of Jerusalem civil society in order to increase the city's competitiveness (A. Markose, personal communication, July 2019). In these initiatives, it is possible to see how the integration of Palestinians into the Israeli labor market and the encouragement of entrepreneurship became central components of Israel's counterinsurgency strategy, to the point where they were directly funded by US Zionist philanthropy in addition to the Israeli government. Inclusion of Palestinians as one of Israel's "four tribes" is part of the process of depoliticizing the Palestinian question: from a settler colonial question to be solved through radical decolonization to a liberal question to be resolved through the incorporation of Palestinians into Israeli multicultural society.

Mati also carries out joint entrepreneurial training in computing and technology with Jest, a Palestinian NGO founded through a direct initiative of the Israeli government's development unit to encourage entrepreneurship in East Jerusalem. It was the first socio-economic measure taken by the settler state for its Palestinian subjects in the city, in 2013 (Ramon, 2021). According to Hani Alami (personal communication, August 2019), a Palestinian businessman in the high-tech sector, founder of Jest and adviser to Mati: 'What Mati is doing is part of the Israelis' new strategy … . There is a change in the way Israelis view East Jerusalem. We will be seeing more and more entrepreneurship.'

Another important Israeli policy to foster Palestinian entrepreneurship is a plan for industrial zones in East Jerusalem. These spaces are classified as areas designed to attract capital and generate native development, driven by the training and financing programmes described above. Decision 3790 foresees the opening of four industrial zones in East Jerusalem: one in the centre of

---

[6] The Israelis see their population comprised of 'four tribes': Secular, Religious and Orthodox Jews, and the Arabs.

East Jerusalem, the 'Sillicon Wadi' technology park in Wadi Joz, and three additional ones in peripheral regions: Issawiye, A-Tur and Sur Baher.

The person in charge of the implementation for the peripheral industrial zones is the director of the public infrastructure planning and development unit of the East Jerusalem Development Company, Ya'ara Issar. According to her, the entire plan for the economic progress of East Jerusalem was drawn up and executed based on old municipal plans that had never been implemented and were adapted to fit the current context: 'We have our vision of how it should be, which has been in development for years', she emphasized (Y. Issar, personal communication, June 2019).

The goal is to create and strengthen new economic hubs in peripheral Palestinian neighbourhoods, sparing residents long commutes to West Jerusalem or other localities in Israel for work, business, shopping and accessing public services such as health clinics. Despite being located on the outskirts of the city, due to the difficulty of finding available areas for construction in East Jerusalem – a central problem that Decision 3790 does not address – the industrial zones are planned in connection with projects for road infrastructure, particularly the 'American Road'. Also known as 'Apartheid Road', the highway connects Palestinian neighbourhoods with Jewish settlements inside and outside of East Jerusalem. Its northern stretch will be financed by the budget allocated for the development of Palestinian East Jerusalem (Dagoni, 2019a).

The industrial zones are depicted by Issar as another Israeli policy to Westernize East Jerusalem in sharp contrast to conservative Palestinian subjectivities associated with their religion or their agrarian past.

> East Jerusalem will cease being a rural zone; it is no longer fit for agriculture, like it used to be [in the villages]. It's not rural Jerusalem; it's urban Jerusalem. And I think this change is very hard on the community, but I think it is something global that could happen anyway and anywhere. Housing is the main problem, but I can't promote housing now because of the political situation. Of course, I think it's best to focus on economic development. I think it will make a huge change in quality of life and in so many aspects in East Jerusalem … . The industrial zones will be open to Palestinians from East Jerusalem and Jewish Israelis that want to invest their money here. I want the son of a garage owner to be able to open an architecture office

in its place. It is possible to keep the basic characteristics of the villages, but also bring them to a different level. Transform the rural village to become an urban neighbourhood in Jerusalem .... I want to see much more Western urban development. This is a process that already happens in East Jerusalem, it is not something new; it is not a revolution. It is just a process of empowering the process that is already happening over there. I hope to see economical change, more city taxes, more employees, and of course, empower the people who are already small business entrepreneurs in East Jerusalem. I want everything to be on a much larger scale. (Issar, 2019)

As Issar remarks, some peripheral neighbourhoods of East Jerusalem, such as Beit Hanina and Shuafat, have been flourishing because of an increase in investments by Palestinian Jerusalemite businessmen in Palestinian private properties. According to Samer Nuseibeh (personal communication, June 2019), an entrepreneur in the real estate sector, these are places where Israeli authorities have relaxed restrictions for new urban developments, such as the construction of Western-style residential condominiums, shopping centres and supermarkets. However, the high costs of developments, resulting from an artificial valuation of Palestinian property made available for construction because of Israeli zoning, taxes and the value of labour, have kept this small real estate boom to the north of East Jerusalem, exclusive to middle- and upper-class Jerusalemites. The result is a gentrification of Palestinian workers who are often forced to relocate to neighbourhoods on the other side of the Wall, like Kfar Aqba. As Issar notes, she can't 'promote housing now because of the political situation', that is, because of settler anxiety over demography and disputes over Palestinian land for Jewish settlement.

Unlike the development being led by local native elites in Beit Hanina and Shuafat, the new industrial zones that are planned by the settler government, whose project and confiscation negotiations are being intermediated by Palestinian community leaders and urban planners, will not be controlled by the native owners of these territories. There is nothing to prevent Palestinian entrepreneurs from enjoying practically the same rights they already possess in the industrial settlement of Atarot, in northern East Jerusalem and a few kilometres from Ramallah, where many Palestinian businesses have migrated so as not to leave the city (Farah, 2019). Nor is there anything to prevent Palestinian workers from being restricted to the same 'blue collar' positions within Israeli corporations, while Jews assume, as usual, the higher 'white collar' positions. In other words, Jewish privilege persists. No protections will be provided for Palestinian entrepreneurs beyond the already existing training programmes, microcredit loans and subsidies. Thus, they are a new way of using urbanism strategies for Israeli settler colonization.

On the other hand, Bab a-Zahara, home to the city's main Palestinian shopping streets, is suffering from long neglect and de-development. The centre of East Jerusalem has a wide range of stores, hotels, markets, restaurants and office buildings that house NGOs, political institutions, unions and schools that function as an extension of the *suq* in the Old City's Muslim Quarter. Palestinian tourism and commerce are a permanent fixture of Jerusalem's indigenous way of life and history. They embody the Palestinian narrative of settler colonial history. The Palestinian economy of Bab a-Zahara functions as a line of defence against the pressures of Judaization and Israelization and to preserve a Palestinian identity within the native space and population. However, the neighbourhood has become increasingly empty, devalued and abandoned in recent years as a result of the various settler colonial policies aimed at de-developing the native resistance economy, hitting small family businesses and the tourism industry that sustain the bourgeoisie and petite bourgeoisie of nationalist Jerusalemites (Arafeh and Khalidi, 2017).

Shopkeepers reveal the growing difficulty of keeping their businesses open due to the various restrictions that strangle native commercial life. These limitations range from banning parking around the Damascus Gate and preventing West Bank Palestinians from going to prayer at the al-Aqsa Mosque, to the boycott by Israeli agents and tour guides of Palestinian establishments that do not pay them bribes. Although the Old City is the most densely populated and visited place in Jerusalem, entire Palestinian shopping streets have become virtually deserted after having their businesses shuttered. Abu Zahra (personal communication, July 2019), a Palestinian businessman and a nationalist militant who owns a market just outside the Old City, compares the plight of Palestinian street commerce under Israeli restrictions to a 'military siege'. Settler colonial pressures have made him and other merchants move their businesses to locations on the outskirts of the city, where it is easier for people to circulate freely without police harassment, cars are fined less, permits to open new businesses are easily obtained, taxes are lower and settler inspections are less blatant (M. A. Zahra, personal communication, July 2019). Even Abu Zahra's market in the city's centre have gone from selling wholesale to the city and the rest of the country, to selling retail to a few passers-by.

Palestinian tourism remains absent from Israeli plans for the development of East Jerusalem, even though it represents approximately 40 per cent of the entire native economy in Jerusalem, mobilizes other sectors such as commerce and transport and is the main material reason that supports a continued Palestinian presence in the Old City after more than five decades of dispossession and economic restrictions. The entire Old City region and the Zahra and Salahadin shopping streets, the most traditional in the city, were also excluded from Decision 3790. The housing issue is not mentioned in Israeli budgets or in the 'Sillicon Wadi' project, although it appears in the Palestinian Bab a-Zahara revitalization plan (The New Arab, 2020).

The Palestinian technology industry in East Jerusalem does not justify an Israeli investment the size of 'Sillicon Wadi'. As in Nazareth and Ramallah, East Jerusalem high-tech companies are deeply dependent on the settler sector for outsourcing and hiring, while very few native start-ups manage to prosper (H. Alami, personal communication, August 2019; A. Husseini, personal communication, July 2019; H. Khattab, personal communication, August 2019). Indeed, there is no evidence that Palestinian capital can compete with Israeli and transnational capital. Building a project like 'Sillicon Wadi' in the heart of this resistance economy would deliver a heavy blow to Palestinian presence in East Jerusalem in the long term. It poses a threat not only through the direct forced eviction but also by way of unfair competition which targets Palestinian businesses and employment opportunities in the region. At worst, a weakened independent resistance economy is replaced by an economy that is completely dependent and subordinate to Israeli and transnational capital.

We observe a correlation among all Israeli projects for new industrial zones in East Jerusalem: while the "Sillicon Wadi" project reinforces the gentrification and expulsion of the native population and businesses in the city's centre where there is great interest from transnational capital and settler organizations, the outskirts are subjected to a reinforcement of the socio-economic marginalization of natives in their hometown. In fact, all of the recent native economic advances that have occurred in the neighbourhood of Beit Hanina are already the result of settler colonial pressures in the central region of East Jerusalem that have forced Palestinian businesses, companies, institutions and NGOs to relocate to the city's margins (Arafeh and Khalidi, 2017). Israeli restrictions have already caused many Palestinian business owners to close up shops and move to the OPT or abroad in search of less racially discriminatory market conditions. Others migrate to West Jerusalem and other settlements so as to keep the city at the centre of their lives and avoid having their right to residence revoked by the settler regime (Arafeh and Khalidi, 2017; Farah, 2019; S. Nuseibeh, personal communication, June 2019). In the end, a new cycle of dispossession and marginalization of Palestinians in East Jerusalem forges ahead.

Completing neoliberal Israelization: Culture, education and police

The neoliberal Israelization strategy – carried out through unfair market competition, the proliferation of the entrepreneurial rationality and the suffocation of independent Palestinian institutions that resist settler power – goes beyond the realm of the economy alone. Counterinsurgent politics penetrate the entire Palestinian sociability, including the culture and education sectors, adapting the Palestinian population to Israeli demands for work, consumption and, ultimately, social stability. We observe a replication of the same modus operandi seen in the cases of Mati and Jest which relies on an Arab façade, a triangulation between the Third Sector, the market and the government, and the employment of Arab-Palestinians as recruiters and trainers of a 'target audience' to help the Israeli authorities design and execute their policies with greater efficiency. Many of the collaborations involving organizations that may appear to be Palestinian are purposely concealed to keep any link between these initiatives and state resources under wraps. This is one way the 'neutral' civilian population can be won over, as part of a strategy to pacify local society according to a neoliberal *politique des races*.

City Hall cultural centres, spread across the city, are an important instrument for the counterinsurgency strategy. According to Ariella (personal communication, July 2019), who is a City Hall cabinet member handling leisure, culture and youth initiatives, her department alone carries out more than a thousand activities a year with Palestinian artists and youth in Israeli community centres located in Palestinian neighbourhoods, often, she adds, with the support of other Palestinian NGOs and associations that adhere to the programme. The municipality operates discretely and without publicity in order to avoid boycotts. 'The important part is to help the community', she says. Her work focuses on extracurricular activities for young people and women during off-hours, with the aim of contributing to social stability and the socio-economic development of individuals and their communities. Many of these programmes are part of the 'informal education' chapter of Decision 3790, which includes the technological and vocational training programmes geared towards the 'empowerment' of 'human capital' (Dagoni, 2019). Once again, we see the security–development logic informing the actions of well-intentioned Israeli bureaucrats:

> Everyone agrees that if you have more sports and extracurricular activities, young [Palestinian] people will be more proactive and less involved in political and criminal activities, reducing the feeling of neglect, of having nothing to lose. This is good for everyone as it involves [them in] positive activities for the community and the city … . Different people with different agendas have found shared reasons [to cooperate] in East Jerusalem. (Ariella, personal communication, July 2019)

Community centres are local representations of the Israeli municipal power throughout the city and are usually led by local NGOs responsible for coordinating and carrying out various activities, such as planning, leisure and culture, in addition to serving as a representative and deliberative body for residents themselves. Due to their intermediary position, community centres have always lacked credibility among the Palestinian population and have never had much presence historically in the native neighbourhoods of East Jerusalem. In some Palestinian neighbourhoods, its members are even excluded from local political circles, while Palestinians usually keep away from the centres to avoid being ostracized. According to a Palestinian militant, the leaders embedded in community centres do not have any legitimacy in the eyes of the community and serve only to mediate Israeli policies (D. Ghoul, personal communication, July 2019).

Faced with the opening of new centres in neighbourhoods that lacked any settler representation over the last decade, City Hall members have transferred more responsibilities to the centres, such as projects for female empowerment or youth movements for children and adolescents, as a way to increase their ability to build trust with local residents (Ariella, personal communication, July 2019; Y. Toren, personal communication, July 2019). Community centres have also hosted courses by Mati and Riyan and are responsible for coordinating all the development initiatives pertaining to street revitalization, the creation of industrial zones and urban zoning under Decision 3790. According to David Koren (2017), who worked for eight years in the Barkat administration as the city's head of 'Arab affairs', the main front of the struggle lies precisely in the 'inner world' of Palestinian youth, who are split between the educational and cultural attractions offered by Israelis and Palestinians. Approximately eighteen thousand Palestinian children have participated in leisure and youth leadership programmes promoted by the state in community centres and schools that have adopted the Israeli curriculum (Dagoni and Wegner, 2022).

This strengthening of community centres, however, occurs in conjunction with the persecution of traditional Palestinian social clubs that exist in all of the city's neighbourhoods. These clubs have historically functioned as places for socializing, sports and cultural activities for Palestinian youth and, mainly, as spaces for political formation, where different parties still tend to exert an important influence in maintaining a Palestinian sociability in the city (S. Nuseibeh, personal communication, June 2019). Part of the space belonging to the social club of Ras al-Amoud, for example, was confiscated for the construction of the settlement of Maale Ha-Zevitm. The club suffers frequent attacks by settlers and is under the constant supervision of cameras, private security guards and Israeli police. In addition, Israel systematically arrests Jerusalem Palestinian cultural leaders, such as Rania Elias, director of the Yabous Cultural Centre, under the false suspicion of financing or having connections to terrorism (Memo, 2020).

In this dispute for the spaces of power in East Jerusalem, new actors emerge to interpose themselves within the new configurations of government. Ramadan Tabash, the director of the Sur Baher community centre, home to some forty thousand Palestinians, is a man of great political aspirations. He was a member of the Likud party and relied on Israeli support to be the only Palestinian Jerusalemite to run for a city council post in the 2018 elections, after other Palestinians left the race under political pressures (Hasson, 2018b).

In 2018, Tabash led a campaign in which he did not challenge Israeli claims of sovereignty over East Jerusalem and called for greater state investment in Palestinian neighbourhoods. After losing the election, Tabash ran, also unsuccessfully, for the position of municipal adviser for Arab affairs in East Jerusalem, a position that has never been occupied by a Palestinian (R. Tabash, personal communication, July 2019). As a way of increasing his political capital both among Israeli authorities and among the local Palestinian population, he has allowed the implementation of the most varied initiatives that the settler regime wants to carry out in East Jerusalem, always under the development–security nexus.

> I said to the Israelis: 'Give me money and I'll solve your security problem' … . We don't need to be friends [with Israelis], but let's work together to help the population with the respect of my brothers in Fatah and the PA. If they want to be leaders, they need to provide leadership … . Everyone fights in their own way. I don't just talk, I do. I only care about the population; I don't care where the money comes from. (Tabash, 2019)

Based on this pragmatic approach of building bridges for dialogue and exchanges with the Israelis, Tabash treats Sur Baher as a kind of laboratory of East Jerusalem integration initiatives where the counterinsurgency strategy inherent in the neoliberal Israelization project seems to come full circle. According to the community leader, among the many initiatives tested by Israeli public authorities in his district, such as a project to revitalize commercial streets in peripheral neighbourhoods to complement the new industrial zones, the only one that was imposed against his will was the creation of a community police, fire and ambulance corps subsidized by the Ministry of Security (R. Tabash, personal communication, July 2019). Tabash explains that the corps would be composed of Palestinian citizens of Israel with experience in these activities, while a civilian corps of volunteers made up of neighbourhood residents would work in plain clothes to help police forces build ties with the community. 'I told the population that this [the creation of the police force] would facilitate access to other public services', he justifies. He even highlighted the experimental nature of the unprecedented presence of Israeli-Palestinian security forces in East Jerusalem neighbourhoods for the creation of a model to be applied in the rest of the city in conjunction with the socio-economic development plan.

Although native community policing reinforces the construction of a neoliberal counterinsurgency in East Jerusalem, Tabash and several other interlocutors agree unanimously that the main area attracting the interest of the settler regime to build a new pacified social order in the city is basic education (R. Tabash, personal communication, July 2019; Y. Toren, personal communication, July 2019). Education investments in East Jerusalem amount to 445 million shekels to be allocated for improvements in public elementary and secondary schools, but with one important condition: only those institutions that accept to adopt the Israeli curriculum adapted to Arab schools will receive funding (Dagoni, 2019). Many of the school principals responsible for implementing the new curricula are Palestinian citizens of Israel with no connection to the local community, but partial to the Israeli education model aimed at their Arab subjects.

On some occasions, despite their limited knowledge of the community, school directors act as intermediaries between the government and the native population, overseeing projects that bear no direct relation to education, as they are subjects who end up having more legitimacy with the social base of neighbourhoods than the directors of community centres and *mukhtars* (Y. Toren, personal communication, July 2019). Another advantage school principals perceive in adopting the official curriculum is that salaries offered in Israeli schools are far higher than those offered in Palestinian schools, a clear incentive for attracting some of the best native teachers, says Sawsan (personal communication, July 2019), a Palestinian principal working in a school managed by the Waqf. The government has set aside 68.7 million shekels for curriculum implementation, in addition to 54.7 million for infrastructure reforms, 67 million for rent payments and 15 million for teaching Hebrew, strictly for schools that adopt the new curriculum that prepares its students for the *Bagrut*, the Israeli post-high school exam (Dagoni, 2019a). The priority for reforming the education system would be to enable greater integration of Palestinians into higher education and, of course, to the demands of the Israeli labour market.

The implementation of the Israeli curriculum in Palestinian schools has been happening quietly since 2011. In most cases, this change occurs due to the demands of parents who see an early adaptation to Hebrew and to the values and skills required by Israelis as a way to facilitate admission to higher education and the labour market (Sawsan, personal communication, July 2019). This life trajectory would allow their children to achieve a higher quality of life without having to leave Jerusalem. An estimated 10 per cent of East Jerusalem schools used the Israeli curriculum in 2018, reaching a total of seven thousand students (Koren, 2017). Family members, education professionals and community leaders justify adapting to restrictions imposed by the settler government as a form of resistance. However, upon receiving a strategic dimension with Decision 3790, the Israelization of school education became the target of public condemnation by the Islamic Waqf[7] (International Crisis Group, 2019).

The Israeli curriculum is criticized by Palestinians primarily for interfering in the construction of a national Palestinian identification among young Jerusalemites. The Israeli curriculum imposes a Zionist narrative on the historical process of the Israeli-Zionist settler colonization of Palestine and censors references to Arab and Palestinian nationalism in textbooks.[8] Aref Husseini (personal communication, July 2019), a Palestinian businessman in the high-tech sector involved in technology education initiatives for Palestinian youth, called native autonomy surrounding basic education the 'last frontier' that maintains East Jerusalem as part of the Palestinian national struggle for liberation, alongside the tourism industry and social clubs.

David Koren (2017), who is responsible for the imposition of the Israeli curriculum in East Jerusalem, understands the situation as a struggle for the control of East Jerusalem between agents outsourced by Israel and the PA, such as the private schools. At stake is the loyalty of local residents in areas such as basic education, where the position of parent associations is critical for the school to either adopt the Israeli curriculum or retain the Palestinian one. Koren (2018) concedes that the imposition of an Israeli curriculum aims to 'neutralize the incitement to violence' that is supposedly present in the Palestinian curriculum in order to instil, from an early age, an adaptation of

---

[7] In addition to being responsible for managing the Muslim holy sites in the city, such as the Esplanade of the Mosques, as well as Palestinian private schools that teach the PA curriculum, the Waqf functions as one of the last remaining public leaders of Palestinian society in East Jerusalem that are still allowed by the settler colonial authorities. The Islamic institution, as well as its Christian counterpart, is fundamental for publicizing measures that would bridge the gap between an inevitable adaptation to the material conditions of colonial occupation and the avoidable normalization of relations with the Israelis who must be boycotted.

[8] Peled-Elhanan (2019) demonstrates how Palestinians, Arabs and Muslims have historically been portrayed as 'enemies', 'threats' and 'dangers' in Israeli school textbooks that function as a propaganda tool for the 'indigenization' of Jews as the true natives of Palestine. Israeli curricula still erase the history of colonization, massacres and other crimes committed by Israelis.

Arab-Palestinian youth to the values of Israeli society and the skills needed to meet the demands of the Israeli market. Koren (2018), who was already a member of the National Security Council and served for many years in the Military Intelligence unit of the Israeli Defence Forces, thinks the subjective and objective transformations of young Palestinians, who were the main articulators of mass movements during the Jerusalem Intifada, are equally fundamental for the 'Israelization' of Palestinian education and society. Koren (2018) understands education as an instrument of counterinsurgency to attract the supposedly 'neutral' native population that craves survival and a better quality of life, to protect them from the 'threats' of Islamic fundamentalists.

> 110,000 students study according to a curriculum that does not make any positive mention of the existence of the State of Israel and includes incitement to violence against Jews and Israel. Although censorship of the curriculum carried out by the Municipality monitors inciteful content, it does not have much effect on what is learned in the classroom or on what a teacher discusses with his pupils. Therefore, the transition to an Israeli curriculum in Arabic, which includes positive material about the State of Israel and its institutions, will have an important influence in terms of education, culture and security … . Public discussions about the curriculum should not emphasize the Israeli component (which would give it a political nature), but rather the access that Israeli matriculation provides to higher education and high-level employment … . After many hours of discussion with Arab high school students in Jerusalem, I am certain that attending the Hebrew University is one of their main aspirations. The [Israeli] model seeks to create a framework of common discourse with educational figures in eastern Jerusalem in order to formulate a curriculum that will be acceptable to both sides. The 'Jerusalem matriculation' will neutralize the incitement to violence and will include the components of religion, history and culture, which are important to Arabs in eastern Jerusalem. (Koren, 2018)

The Israeli curriculum is also a product of what Laval (2019) calls 'educational neoliberalism', in which, under pressure from global capital and international institutions such as the WB and the OECD, schools are now managed like companies, with goals and targets for teachers and students to mould children from an early age in accordance with the needs of contemporary capitalism. The elaboration of curricula based on the values of 'innovation' and 'efficiency' which are sold as modernizing leads to the adoption of measures such as standardized tests, ideas such as human capital, and the technological and entrepreneurial development of skills that lend themselves more to market interests than to the well-rounded formation and emancipation of students (Laval, 2019).

The technological and entrepreneurial aspects of the curricula are precisely what Koren (2018) believes to be the most efficient for the advancement of a depoliticized Israelization, as merely an adaptation to the technical principles of globalization. That is, what is seen as advanced, Western and technological is directly linked to Israeli values, morals and capacities. The bureaucrat highlights that the curriculum should not be merely imposed, as is the wish of many Israeli politicians, but that infrastructure improvements, faculty training, the promotion of emotional needs and the facilitation of access to the Israeli labour market should be sufficient to attract Palestinian students and their families. However, its deeply political nature and pacifying ambitions are so evident that they end up consolidating the rejection of the Palestinians in the name of preserving their national autonomy and identity, which has delayed the Israelization of education in East Jerusalem for the first two years of its implementation[9] (Hasson, 2020a). In any case, the Ministry of Education opened thirteen new schools with the Israeli curriculum for Palestinians in the city as part of Decision 3790, in addition to converting twenty-seven institutions that followed the PA's educational model to following the Israeli one. Growing steadily since 2017, the number of Palestinian youths in the Israeli curriculum was between 12 and 17 per cent in 2021. Despite investments, there was still a deficit of 2,840 classrooms in East Jerusalem in 2021 (Dagoni and Wegner, 2022).

Other educational initiatives that are also part of neoliberal Israelization manage to be better accepted among Palestinian youth. Since 2014, the NGO World ORT, a London-based Jewish philanthropic institution with an international focus on promoting entrepreneurial and technology teaching programmes, opened a technology education centre for Palestinian girls in Beit Hanina (Israel21c, 2016). In the same neighbourhood, in 2016, the Jerusalem

---

[9] There are still schools that adopt both the Israeli and Palestinian curricula, in an attempt to keep receiving resources intended for those who cooperate while not upsetting parents and more nationalistic students who prefer the curriculum of the PA (R. Tabash, personal communication, July 2019).

Municipality and the Ministry of Education opened the School of Technology exclusively for Palestinian boys with courses in software engineering, electronics and computing, as well as lessons in advanced Hebrew. Both high school technology institutions are run by Palestinians, leaving many residents unaware of the fact that they are funded by the Israeli government.

Another novelty in the cycle of neoliberal Israelization has been the growing presence of Palestinian Jerusalemites in colleges in West Jerusalem, a consequence of an inclusion policy for higher education institutions that predates Decision 3790. Since 2017, the traditional Hebrew University of Jerusalem has started accepting the *tawjihi*, the Palestinian post-high school exam. Several Israeli universities have opened preparatory programmes called *Sadarah/Kidma* for the integration of Palestinian Jerusalemites who wish to enter higher education without taking the Israeli exam (Hasson, 2017). These courses offer classes in Hebrew, Israeli studies and computer science based on the programme model originally designed for the assimilation of new foreign settlers who migrate to Israel. Women make up the majority of participants and have a higher average level of education than men in East Jerusalem, but they often select courses that provide some form of technical training for the labour market, such as pedagogy, pharmaceuticals and nursing (M. K. Kassabri, personal communication, July 2019). The adoption by educational institutions of the state's diversity programmes has allowed the Israeli universities to access to public resources and fill vacancies resulting from a lack of demand from Jewish students for higher education courses. The university's first Arab dean, Professor Mona Khuri Kassabri, a Palestinian from Haifa, is responsible for overseeing the inclusion and diversity programmes of the institution. Once again, the development–security nexus underlies the explanation for the Israeli inclusion policies.

> Some people say maybe that studying at the Hebrew University is partaking in normalisation. On the other hand, in my opinion, people should be free to study wherever they want. When people have an education, they can do whatever they want .... People from Jerusalem are expected to work in East and West Jerusalem. We should help them access this market. Otherwise, poverty will never decrease .... I'm not sure if they [Jerusalemites] are more open-minded, but they know this is the only way they can get an education and a decent job. And the parents have also come to support them more.

> A couple of years ago, this was unthinkable … . The more students come to the University, the easier it is for other families to accept it. People have started to understand that the population needs the education, even if it is in an Israeli institution … . It is naive to say that Israelis just want to help the people of East Jerusalem. That is not the reason. For sure, it's political issue. If people are educated, they have fewer problems. The Israeli government came to the understanding that people who have had an education negotiate differently (Kassabri, 2019)

Settler colonial racist discrimination, however, is still present in the Hebrew University, despite integration efforts. Palestinian students, particularly Muslim religious women, suffer racist discrimination from their colleagues and teachers, in addition to being exposed to the constant presence of uniformed and armed students doing their military service (Hasson, 2019b). Nevertheless, coexistence at the university and in other parts of Jerusalem is understood by Fuad Abu Hamed, a Sur Baher resident, businessman, former student and professor at the Hebrew University, as a possibility of building a new harmonious and peaceful sociability. Abu Hamed believes that the microcosm of the university can spill over to the rest of the city and, eventually, to the entire country, promoting a process of reconciliation from below that will substitute attempts at diplomatic agreements between political elites.

> A diplomatic solution becomes more unlikely with each passing day. This is an Israelisation process that we willingly adopt, but when you consider people and their problems, you realize that this won't make the problem of East Jerusalem go away. Perhaps in the next stage people will grow closer to Israelis and these graduates will want to go live in Jewish neighbourhoods such as Armon Hanatziv and French Hill. This will change Jerusalem. (Abu Hamed quoted in Hasson, 2019b)

The contradictions and ambivalences of a government built on the intersections of settler colonialism and neoliberalism produce illusions that are present not only in the literature (Shtern, 2018a) but also in the agents and actors that engage in this process, such as Professor Abu Hamed. This interpretation of reality even makes it possible to classify adaptation to neoliberal Israelization as a form of resistance. However, the presence of Palestinians in universities, industrial zones and residential settlements that were originally built for the exclusive purpose of Jewish settlement, rather than signifying a paradox between the settler colonial and the neoliberal or a form of decolonization through the market, represents a normalization of the market-based settler colonial relationship and of the contact of the colonized population with institutions that were previously exclusive to settlers. These are cases in which the consumption of a commodity – an apartment, a university tuition or an industrial lot – would allow Palestinians to adapt and survive in their hometown with a minimum of dignity in the face of restrictions. Rather than signifying a regression of the settler colonial process, these encounters and exchanges between Palestinians and Israelis through market relations produce a convenient image of a neoliberal multiculturalism, one that is blind to racism and welcomes the inclusion of Palestinians with greater capital – both human and economic – to live among Israelis, despite the preservation of a racial hierarchy. In this way, the market would allow settlers to camouflage racism and use native integration as an opportunity for capital accumulation.

4

Neoliberal anti-colonialism in the Palestinian resistance

How different Palestinian resistance initiatives have resorted to different modalities of entrepreneurship to reform Israeli modes of government or pave the way to national liberation

Many Palestinians, for a variety of reasons, have become engaged in Israeli integration and development policies in East Jerusalem. This movement is not new to Palestinian Jerusalemites, but rather characteristic of the inherent contradictions specific to their social and spatial situation in a territory disputed by the Israeli regime and Palestinian institutions. While many Jerusalemites have always pragmatically favoured keeping an open channel with Israelis – some outright preferring to join Israeli citizenship – there are others who have historically rejected relations with the settler regime and prefer to remain connected to Palestinian West Bank society and the PA (Cohen, 2011; W. Salem, 2018). This divergence is interpreted as a choice between pursuing a better quality of life or remaining faithful to the Palestinian national struggle. In other words, there is an incompatibility between seeking better material living conditions – which requires greater involvement with the Israelis and therefore risks being seen as a normalization of settler colonial relations – and perseverance in the struggle for national liberation, based on the ethic of the *sumud*[1] and the anti-normalizing

---

[1] An Arabic term that translates as steadfastness, *sumud* expresses the Palestinian people's practice and mentality of resistance that has enabled them to continue living in their land and fighting for national liberation despite enduring centuries of foreign colonial domination, not only by the Israelis but also by the British, Ottomans and other imperial and imperialist powers.

rejection of the settler regime, which requires material sacrifices. Sahr Baidoun (personal communication, June 2019), a militant from Silwan, summarized this daily struggle: 'Every step we take must be carefully calculated.'

Settler colonial racism pervades the homes and minds of Palestinians producing a double material and subjective suffering that transforms the longing for emancipation into a struggle that goes beyond economic and institutional materiality. It also affects the subjectivity of the recognition, humanization and dignity of the colonized subjects. The contradictions of the Israeli settler colonial situation would force Palestinian Jerusalemites to choose to confront one of these forms of oppression in detriment of the others. In practice, however, there is no such thing as an absolute ethical differentiation between a better quality of life and national struggle. In fact, there are many ways of striking a balance between these two variables that Palestinian Jerusalemites must negotiate daily in relation to the settler regime. Jerusalemites are dependent on Israeli civil authorities for basic day-to-day necessities such as home-building or passport issuance (Salem, 2018).[2] The lines that determine what Jerusalemites identify as normalization are somewhat flexible, but there are a few 'red lines'. Basic education, which is understood as a form of deconstructing the Palestinian identity of younger generations, is seen as a red line.

This situation is made worse by the absence of legitimate and wide-reaching public leadership, a result of the de-development policies and methodical repressions directed at the political representations of Palestinians. In the event of a legitimate leader's rise to prominence, their capacities are steadfastly neutralized: due to the persecution of the settler regime, they are forced to operate through clandestine channels. Furthermore, there is a general sense

---

[2] According to Salem (2018), adaptation to the objective conditions of the hegemonic order, an enduring humiliation suffered by many Palestinians, takes on four different forms. Forced adaptation takes place in workplaces, healthcare and unions, such as Histradut, where Palestinians are forced to join in order not to lose their jobs. Voluntary adaptation incurs direct involvement in Israeli institutions, such as universities and state institutions, and participation in municipal elections. There is also the form of adaptation that seeks to avoid the downside of elimination policies, such as registering an NGO under Israeli law so that it can continue to operate in the city or pay fines for having built a house illegally to prevent its demolition. Finally, Salem classifies 'adaptation by rejection' as a form that can take place both as an ostensible rejection of the settler regime, such as in the confrontations of the Jerusalem Intifada, or as a silent rejection, such as the construction of houses without permission that allows one to continue living 'illegally' in one's hometown under Israeli law or maintain an official address in East Jerusalem while living elsewhere to avoid identity confiscation.

of disillusionment among the Palestinian population – particularly among the younger generations – with institutional politics and traditional political parties, whose diplomatic negotiations have produced outcomes that leave much to be desired in the struggle to improve practical daily life and expand the horizon of national liberation. Consequently, Palestinian responses to neoliberal settler colonialism have become increasingly spontaneous, scattered and uncoordinated (W. Salem, 2018). Often, these responses are driven by despair, such as the individual attacks by young Palestinians armed with knives or vehicles against Israeli police or military in the Jerusalem Intifada. In other words, these are young individuals armed with the limited means at their disposal who act alone outside of a larger coordinated strategy. One can easily glimpse the neoliberal do-it-yourself rationality behind these lonely and uncoordinated attacks by despondent youth who lack an emancipatory political horizon.

In the minefield that is the political life of a Palestinian in East Jerusalem, neoliberalism and market relations offer the possibility of pursuing both material well-being and subjective dignity without sacrificing national ethics or normalizing relations with the Israelis. Despite open criticism from many local Palestinian leaders and the PA being levelled at Israel's neoliberal plans for East Jerusalem, thousands of Palestinians have engaged with these initiatives over the past decade without having their conduct become the target of public reprimands or coordinated boycotts. For this group, many areas of the settler colonial project (such as incentives for entrepreneurship, employment and access to a higher education) are understood as relatively depoliticized initiatives that can bring greater socio-economic well-being without compromising the process of national liberation. In consequence, the vocabulary and practices of progressive neoliberalism are becoming an engine for different forms of Palestinian *(r)existence*, whether they aim at national liberation, seek to reform the settler regime from within or do not assume a specific political agenda.

Given the daily contradictions that surround Palestinian (r)existence in East Jerusalem, the impact of neoliberalism on these various forms of (r)existence in the city under the neoliberal Israelization process merits further investigation. The process of pacification through neoliberalism operates simultaneously from below and from above among Palestinians, generating many challenges for local resistance and survival. Interstices appear in this reliance on the economy as a form of resistance through which it is possible to verify how alternative modes of Palestinian economy have been co-opted by neoliberalism and, ultimately, by settler colonialism.

Entrepreneurship can function as a neoliberal ambush leading Palestinians of all social classes towards labour precarization and the falsification of active forms of resistance. The protagonists of this process can be called activist-entrepreneurs: Palestinian Jerusalemites, usually well educated in local or foreign institutions, who use entrepreneurship as a form of activism that functions through the market, understood as a neutral and depoliticized space where racism does not operate, at least not with the same intensity or exclusively in the interest of Palestinian dispossession. The goal of these actors is to placate and possibly overcome the severe material and subjective sufferings to which the Palestinian population of East Jerusalem has been subjected.

Neoliberal anti-colonialism and the resistance economy paradigm

In East Jerusalem, the construction of a neoliberal hegemony occurs through the imposition, on both the PA and the State of Israel, of 'good practices' recommended in the 'guidelines' of international institutions (OECD and WB). Due to their somewhat elusive nature, these neoliberal processes also seem to occur from the ground up, by way of NGOs, grassroots social movements and other transnational civil society organizations. At first glance, these actors may not seem connected to any upper echelons of power, but they are usually linked to larger neoliberal projects. Furthermore, neoliberalization in East Jerusalem is also shaped by the clash between Israeli neoliberalism on the Western 'front' and Palestinian Fayadism[3] on the Eastern 'front'. Thus, neoliberalism produces a complex social fabric that comprises a mixture of divergent political positions that are nonetheless structured by the same

---

[3] Fayadism is the name given to the economic agenda that Palestinian politician Salam Fayyad promoted during his period as prime minister of the PA (2007–13), when there was an accentuation of economic austerity and other neoliberal measures sponsored by international financial institutions to the building of the State of Palestine.

neoliberal reason. This new sociability even allows the inclusion of Palestinian anti-colonial sentiment, though only expressed in its entrepreneurial form, which placates the native rejection of settler colonial hegemony. Consequently, this results in fragmentations not only between the adopters of neoliberalism and those who reject it, but also among different blocs of activist-entrepreneurs.

On the one hand, there are activist-entrepreneurs who take part in what we call the *local agenda*. These wish to create an internal rift in the settler system by seizing the opportunities offered by neoliberal Israelization to reform the hegemonic order. Their aim is to facilitate the ascension of the oppressed layers of native society to foster a (neo)liberal multiculturalism in Jerusalem without directly attacking settler privileges. This strategy involves combining the interests of natives with the goals of a more tolerant and open part of Israeli society to advance depoliticized urban reforms according to a win-win frame of mind. On the other hand, there are those who, aware of the impossibility of real reforms or real integration of Palestinians to the Israeli order, seek to circumvent the Israeli system by directly accessing the international market through the channels that were made available by the Oslo Accords. This includes PA bureaucrats and the nationalist Palestinian bourgeoisie in the OPTs. Members of the *national agenda* aim to create, by way of a Fayadist neoliberal strategy, a socio-economic development that can contribute to the fight over the hearts and minds of the Jerusalem population – the youth in particular – and against the seductions of neoliberal Israelization. In this way, they aspire to build the foundations for the future of an independent Palestinian State with East Jerusalem as its capital.

Divergences between these agendas lead the actors of these blocs to operate separately and even to see themselves as competitors, although overlaps between the groups are inevitable since it is impossible for two separate Palestinian economies to exist simultaneously in the city. However, the quality of these initiatives in response to the immediate material demands of the Palestinians, to their continued existence in the city and right to dignity, does not preclude them from falling prey to settler colonial pitfalls. The frauds inherent in progressive neoliberalism help perpetuate two settler colonial stratagems that impede Palestinian emancipation. On the one hand, the farce of Israelization and its promise of seamless integration into the Israeli system; on the other hand, the fraud of the two-state solution, according to which East

Jerusalem should be ceded by the Israelis for the formation of an independent Palestinian State, as determined by international law and the consensus of nations. However, this possibility has proven increasingly unrealistic, despite the diplomatic and financial efforts of several nations and of Palestinian elites to keep this paradigm alive. On both fronts, neoliberal entrepreneurship is presented, either through the human face of a well-intended settler or through the human face of soft imperialism, as an alternative of peaceful and rational struggle that will bring about transformations and an access to civil rights in the case of the local agenda, or human rights in the case of the national agenda.

According to some of these actors, neoliberal capitalism and racial settler colonialism are distinct economic and political phenomena. For them, while settler colonialism and neoliberalism may converge at some point, they can also oppose each other if they become instrumentalized correctly by Palestinian actors through market relations, where they begin to represent the interests of the oppressed rather than those of the oppressors. Based on this approach, entrepreneurship is understood as a depoliticized technical activity capable of solving problems and promoting the necessary social change to address the objective and subjective demands of Palestinian subjects.

However, by combining the soft settler colonialism of neoliberal Israelization and the soft imperialism of international institutions, the ruling classes manage to ensnare the native population in a trap: a consensus is formed through a voluntary adherence to neoliberal hegemony in which entrepreneurship is seen as a tactical ally and the only form of struggle that is rationally viable. Entrepreneurship is not merely understood by these actors as a way of accessing and distributing material gains to Palestinians, but also as a means of autonomously pursuing and achieving the type of social ascension that could fulfil their ambitions of dignity and deconstruct the racist and orientalist images that confine them to an ontological place of backwardness, animalization, hatred and violence because of their national, ethnic and religious identity. Palestinian revolutionary militants would thus be transformed into neoliberal entrepreneurs and human rights activists trained in rational dialogue, guided by mutual material interests and defenders of liberal institutions.

As a consequence of the neoliberalization of Palestinian anti-colonialism, the Palestinian population has become increasingly individualistic and guided by values of meritocracy, consumption, entrepreneurship and competition for the fulfilment of individual and nationalist ambitions (Samour, 2016). As part of this process, externally financed NGOs have become protagonists in the Palestinian movement, engaging as actors for the socio-economic development and promotion of the Israeli strategy of 'economic peace' with Israel (Dana, 2019; Haddad, 2016). If, on the one hand, the middle class and elites co-opted by the neoliberal agenda have become dependent on the stability of the post-Oslo settler colonial order, on the other hand, the working class has become more vulnerable and fragmented through the weakening of unions and privatizations resulting from structural reforms (Hilal, 2015; Ross, 2019). The result is the rupturing of solidarity and collective demobilization.

Some Palestinian critics of the post-Oslo regime in the OPT classify the work of the PA as an 'invisible occupation' that, by obeying the Fayadist paradigms of neoliberal development, ends up domesticating the Palestinian national movement, putting an end to the Palestinian anti-colonial imaginary beyond neoliberal notions of economics and politics (Hanieh, 2016; Seidel, 2019). The confinement of the Palestinian struggle for liberation to the paradigms of the nation state and neoliberal development has led the economic factor to become separated from the political in the orientation of the anti-colonial praxis, thereby allowing it to be co-opted by the neoliberal counterrevolution. Faced with an entrenchment of the neoliberal order in the political imaginary, a question is posed as to whether the construction of a resistance economy would signify the construction of a project that in fact contributes to help Palestinians in their struggle for self-determination, freedom and return (Haddad, 2015). These are questions that were posed by Palestinian intellectuals in the OPT before Oslo, with the practices of the first Intifada as historical reference, when Palestinians became involved in several grassroots collaborative economic initiatives with the objective of rejecting the occupation and reducing their economic dependence on Israelis (Arafeh, 2018).

After Oslo, the authors involved in the elaboration of a new resistance economy propose revisiting the idea of forming an active *sumud*[4] that may

---

[4] In the 1980s, many Palestinian intellectuals began to discuss models for transforming the resistance practices of the native population linked to the idea of *sumud* into more active practices. The 1970s *sumud* strategy of steadfastness against expulsion came to be understood as static and reactionary. Alternatively, they began to defend cooperative economic practices that would make it possible to

undo the subordination of the PA's institutional policy to the neoliberal economy. In their view, a resistance economy involves the subordination of the economy to politics to forge a new sociability of solidarity and cooperation from a grassroots movement that enables the construction of a new anti-colonial imaginary free from the shackles of state nationalism and the neoliberal developmental model. Across Palestine, small grassroots initiatives have emerged to challenge the paradigms of the neoliberal state by building a resistance economy founded on basic fundamental rights. Based on other international experiments, the literature identifies sectors such as tourism, community banks, agriculture, heritage preservation projects and renewable energy as additional activities that could contribute to a Palestinian resistance economy.

An important experiment is the agricultural cooperative that aims for food sovereignty and sustainable self-sufficiency, while at the same time protecting indigenous land and population from territorial dispossession. Agriculture is the main arena of any resistance economy. In addition to being a means of conquering food sovereignty, it also provides a native alternative to the settler products that flood Palestinian markets. It is the 'last frontier' of the indigenous society against settler colonization. Seidel (2019), however, points out that the practices and vocabulary of a resistance economy are in danger of being captured by progressive neoliberalism, when 'sustainable development' appropriates agricultural resistance practices.

The case of Rawabi, a new Palestinian city built on the outskirts of Ramallah that aims to become a model for the free and neoliberal Palestine of the future and is home to high-tech companies and the new globalized Palestinian classes, is illustrative of the traps set by neoliberal settler colonialism. Based on the examination of Rawabi, Roy (2016) calls this model of neoliberal anti-colonial resistance an example of 'post-*sumud*', meaning that it rests on the pretence of reproducing the traditional native toughness, but transforms resistance into a business opportunity that is also convenient for the settler colonial power. As

---

reduce dependence on the settler labour and consumption markets. This would be a first step towards economic development that meant strengthening native self-sufficiency to build the foundations for a future Palestinian state within the 1967 borders. The First Intifada would be recognized as the moment when economic cooperation would be put into practice in a more efficient way for political emancipation (Arafeh 2018).

a materialization of the hegemony of progressive neoliberalism in the West Bank, the project is a contribution to the political effort that aims to 'eliminate radicals on both sides', as stated in the propaganda for the inauguration of the Palestinian city in 2015 (Grandinetti, 2015). Rawabi is the first planned urban centre in Palestinian history and was built with funding from Qatar that was raised at an international conference for investors held in Bethlehem in 2008 as part of the PA's 'Palestine Is Open for Business' campaign (Grandinetti, 2015; Khalidi and Samour, 2011). The initiative was endorsed by sectors of Israeli society, such as former prime minister Shimon Peres, who saw Rawabi as a way to advance the agenda of 'economic peace' and generate profits for both the settler and native bourgeoisies. Nevertheless, it suffered from legal difficulties and delays because of the limitations imposed by the Israeli occupation, such as a lack of access to the water and sewage network controlled by the settler bureaucracy. In other words, even the Palestinian elites do not have it easy under Israeli settler colonization.

The project's initiator is the Palestinian Bashar al-Masri, a businessman with investments in several sectors and a member of one of the most traditional families in Hebron and Palestine,[5] who sees Rawabi as a 'national success story' that advances the Palestinian cause in new ways that are more modern and better adapted to the global order (Ross, 2019: 225). The construction of Rawabi wants to be seen as a form of resistance and *sumud* that allows Palestinians to continue living on their land with dignity by providing the material conditions for business activity, employment for thousands of Palestinians and other opportunities for a greater quality of life under occupation. It attempts to change the image of Palestine from a place of conflict and backwardness to one of modernity and business (Grandinetti, 2015). As a gated community guarded by cameras and private security companies, the city is also home to a financial, commercial and business district known as the Rawabi Tech Hub, which includes Palestinian banks, hotels, a luxury mall, an amphitheatre and high-tech corporations that work

---

[5] The patriarch Munib al-Masri is an engineering entrepreneur with businesses throughout the Middle East and the founder of PADICO, a company that emerged out of investments from Oslo. Munib is part of a group of businessmen who, together with the PA, have tried to maintain their political and economic influence and support in East Jerusalem, which led to him being arrested by the Israelis at a secret meeting held in the city in 2018. See www.timesofisrael.com/israel-shutters-pa-backed-conference-in-east-jerusalem-top-businessman-arrested.

directly with businesses in Gaza, Israel and abroad. The technological project also includes a training centre, a philanthropic institution and a business accelerator to promote entrepreneurial training, community strengthening, leadership formation, social diversity and the success of Palestinian start-ups (Rawabi, 2020). By looking to be the epicentre of the Palestinian technological ecosystem, Rawabi has also become the locus for cooperation between Israeli and Palestinian capital investment in the high-tech industry in the West Bank – several Israeli corporations have offices in the city for outsourcing purposes (Rubin, 2018).

Roy (2016) also sees Rawabi as an example of neoliberalism operating in favour of Israeli settler colonialism in which a reimagination of the land according to neoliberal urbanism mirrors the advancement of Israeli settler colonialism. Indeed, the urban development of Rawabi and the practices of Israeli settler colonial urbanism share much in common. Rawabi received more than three thousand pine trees from the Jewish National Fund, and Masri consulted with Israeli architects and urban planners for the city's development, including Moshed Safdie, the architect responsible for the elaboration of Modi'in, a settlement in Greater Jerusalem (Ross, 2019; Roy, 2016). Many Palestinians mock the city's architecture and topographical location by calling Rawabi a 'Palestinian settlement'. In addition, by accommodating middle-class Palestinians from other parts of the country where they are no longer welcomed by Israeli settler colonialism, such as East Jerusalem, 'projects like Rawabi inadvertently contribute to accelerating the Judaization of parts of Israel/Palestine that have yet to succumb to this fate' (Ross, 2019: 386).

Roy (2016) also argues that Rawabi represents a learning process by which, as a result of working and living in close contact with Zionism, Palestinians end up adopting the tools of the colonizers to resist settler colonization, thus forging the 'post-*sumud*'. In treating the neoliberal market as an ally, even if merely tactical and pragmatic, to pursue its objective of building a national state in the OPT, neoliberal entrepreneurs like Masri end up tightening the screw of neoliberal anti-colonialism instead of loosening it with their goal of transforming the *sumud* into an active practice. The adoption of neoliberal reason as a guiding principle of Palestinian anti-colonial praxis is a form of fetishism since the illusion of entrepreneurship ensnares them in a colonial trap. Through a Fanonian lens, this process could be read as the representation of the pathologies that lead the native to a phantasmagorical mimicry of the settler in an attempt to escape the depreciation to which they are subjected by racism. This fetishistic use of entrepreneurship is evident in various sectors of the Palestinian economy in East Jerusalem.

Neoliberal urbanism, the right to housing and Palestinian urban planners

The illusion of a separation between economy and politics and between settler colonialism and neoliberalism prevalent in East Jerusalem can be further examined in the question of Palestinian land, private property and housing. The issues of housing and land are central to the practices of settler colonialism in general and to its Israeli form in particular. The control of land consolidates the expansion of the social space of Judaization through the instrumentalization of urban planning. Dialectically, housing and the preservation of land constitute two central aspects of Palestinian (r)existence. In East Jerusalem, a lack of housing for Palestinians is artificially produced as a way of directly and indirectly expelling the native population to alter the demographic composition and occupation of space in the city, thereby making it increasingly Jewish and Zionist. However, control over land use does not contain an exclusively ethnic-racial dimension, but mainly an economic one. Israelis have historically denied native landowners in East Jerusalem the full enjoyment of their property rights. Suffice it to say that their land titles are not formally registered in settler institutions. Consequently, limitations on the use of property affects the demographic and spatial presence of natives in the city and compromises their capacity to prosper by using their land as an asset for commercial exchanges or obtaining bank credits.

The supposed paradox between economic and political goals reveals itself in two aspects. First, the lack of land registration has ironically helped Palestinian landowners to continue living in their homeland despite Israeli pressures. Israeli settler colonization is quite concerned with conferring a legal legitimacy to the process of native expulsion and settlement through urban planning. Lack of access to native property titles prevents settlers from finding intricacies in the law that would permit legal forms of dispossession.[6] This is because, although the mapping, fencing and registration of native land ownership has been widely used throughout history as a colonial expedient, the land market in Palestine was not regulated by the European colonizers but by the Ottoman Empire (Bhandar, 2018). The creation of the private ownership of land occurred during the decline of the Ottoman Empire, which enabled the Zionist movement to purchase the land where the first Jewish settlements in Palestine were built. Additionally, following land reform, property titles were conceded to the native population, including in the Jerusalem region, which followed Western standards and were therefore legible to colonizers. However, due to their liberal political orientations, neither of the colonial occupants of the territory, first the British and then the Israelis, have sought to carry out new property mapping or registrations in Jerusalem. From 1948 to 1967, when the city was under Jordanian rule, regularization of Palestinian property rights resumed. The violation of private property titles would constitute an ostensibly illiberal act, whereas the non-registration of Palestinian property not so much.

This point leads to the second aspect of an apparent paradox between settler colonialism and capitalism. Studies show that the economy of Jerusalem suffers an annual loss of at least 2 billion shekels due to the absence of formal registration of native property (Nesher, 2018). Approximately 90 per cent of Palestinian properties are not formally registered. Therefore, the registration of Palestinian titles provided in Decision 3790 that aimed to regularize all properties by 2025, is in line with the neoliberal doctrine that understands land regularization as a means of promoting entrepreneurship for the masses and the integration of the lower classes into the financial market. Private land ownership allows entrepreneurs to access bank credits that boost the private financial economy, promotes increased tax collection by the state, heats up the consumer market and encourages competition among entrepreneurs themselves (Bhandar, 2018; Davis, 2006). As it happens, the Israeli government

---

[6] Settler movements have relied on alternatives such as offering prices far above market value for Palestinian properties situated on the colonial frontiers of the Old City, Silwan or Sheikh Jarrah. Another tactic employed by settlers is the acquisition of large properties on the outskirts of the city, places such as Sur Baher and Beit Hanina, which they then offer in exchange for small properties in the Old City. These exchanges are often brokered by collaborating Palestinians.

branch responsible for land registration in East Jerusalem is the Ministry of Finance (Dagoni, 2019a). However, over the course of the field research, the issue of land registration proved to be the most nebulous item of the plan, lacking any blueprint for implementation, and widely considered to be one of the red lines of neoliberal Israelization.

According to Samira (personal communication, July 2019), a Palestinian Jerusalemite urban planner with ties to several Israeli institutions and directly involved in the East Jerusalem development projects and the drafting of Decision 3790, state bureaucrats are inflexible when it comes to alternatives that would allow the use of economic rights and an adherence to the zoning plan without disclosing the identity of the title holders. These so-called shadow registrations would be entrusted to a third party that recognizes the owner's papers and allows the holder to make use of their property without disclosing their identity to public authorities. This would be the only alternative that would respect the political and economic interests of Palestinians. But, according to Samira, Israelis are willing to push for the formalization of land registration according to their own criteria 'whether Palestinians like it or not'.

Like many other Palestinian urban planners and native professionals who collaborate in Israeli initiatives for East Jerusalem, Samira sees her work as a form of lesser evil that helps Palestinians make the most of the opportunities and gaps in the settler regime's bureaucracy to extract short-term material gains. Her immediate goal is to enable Palestinians to enjoy a modicum of dignity under settler colonial occupation, while her greater ambition is to reform Israeli power structures for the benefit the native population. For this reason, urban planning has become an important instrument of resistance for Palestinians who have historically been involved in the development of several community zoning plans, often in collaboration with Israeli NGOs and activists.

However, in resorting to the Israeli legal framework for the regularization of illegal construction, obtaining permits for new residences or blocking settler colonial developments in their neighbourhoods, Palestinian grassroots initiatives have been historically frustrated by settler colonial restrictions. Such was the case for the residents of Wadi Hilweh, who unsuccessfully organized to stop the construction of the City of David settlement. And also for the residents of Beit Safafa, whose legal actions against the construction of a settlement road that would split their neighbourhood in half were obstructed by Israeli justice (Cohen-Bar and Kronish, 2013). Given the obstacles faced by Palestinian residents seeking to navigate Israeli institutions to exercise their legal rights and the apparent colonial-neoliberal contradiction pertaining to the land issue, Palestinian urban planners have sought to instrumentalize Israeli economic and political policies by embedding a few Palestinian interests in them.

Samira was hired by the community centre of a Palestinian neighbourhood but had to abandon her position because the centre's employees are often suspected to be collaborating with the occupation. To regain the community's trust, she began to work as a freelancer in different urban projects for Israeli authorities and Palestinian communities. Despite the tarnished image of the Israeli administration's plans for the development of East Jerusalem, Samira does not rule out working with Israelis to implement her innovative urban renewal projects if it benefits Palestinians. 'It is not a small amount of money, it is our right as residents of Jerusalem, it is part of our right to the city … . According to international law, we have a right as an occupied population. We do not have too many options, we need to work with the municipality,' she says.

This rationale is not purely ideological but shaped from a complex combination of factors that includes the absence of a possible short-term alternative, a strong identity of belonging to the city and the struggle for the fulfilment of the rights of the Palestinian people, both as legal residents of Israel and as a native population under international occupation. Samira is critical of the boundaries of what would constitute 'normalization' and committed to pragmatically explore all the opportunities available. 'We need people who talk less and do more', she says.

> In Jerusalem, everything is 'grey'. It is necessary to work with the system to improve living conditions … . If you want to make a difference, you must have this short-term vision … . What is the difference between these types of integration? People work with Israelis but are not friends with them. They study at the Hebrew University, but they are against normalisation … . They don't see the academic as normalisation, but they see the cultural as normalisation. This discussion causes fragmentation; it doesn't bring people

together ... . Political cooperation is normalisation. And developing living conditions is important and essential. (Samira, 2019)

As Palestinians feared from the beginning, East Jerusalem land regularization has been used to formalize the legal and covert confiscation of native lands. In May 2021, social movements in Jerusalem discovered that the state had completed the registration of properties in Umm Haroun, in the Palestinian neighbourhood of Sheikh Jarrah, on behalf of Jewish owners prior to 1948. A total of forty-five families in forty buildings are having their possessions expropriated without any prior notification. According to a report published by the Ministry of Jerusalem in 2022, 158 blocks of land are being regularized in Sheikh Jarrah and Mount of Olives (Palestinian neighbourhoods under constant attacks by Israeli settlers); at Neve Yaakov, French Hill and Ramot (existing Jewish settlements built on confiscated Palestinian property); and Atarot, Givat Hashaked and Givat Hamatos (areas designated for the construction of large Jewish settlements in the near future) (Dagoni and Wegner, 2022).

In other words, the Judaization of East Jerusalem has advanced under the cloak of neoliberal Israelization, with or without the collaboration of Palestinian residents. These practices that have occurred in the absence of any transparency are added to the ostensible actions of settler movements, such as Elad and Ateret Cohanim, which have seized Palestinian homes by force in the Sheikh Jarrah and Batan al-Hawa neighbourhoods of Silwan. Also in May 2021, the resistance of the El-Kurd family against the confiscation of their residence by Jewish settlers drew global attention.

The only reason the contradiction between settler colonial and neoliberal objectives is apparent is because Israelis are willing to lose money if it means expelling Palestinians from their lands. The regularization of Palestinian land use to promote popular entrepreneurship in a manner that contributes to the economic growth of the city advocated by neoliberal thinkers is not a real possibility for the Israeli settler colonial framework. Neoliberal measures only serve to advance Israeli colonial settler objectives, such as the expulsion and subjugation of the Palestinians. In the gaps of this apparent contradiction, concessions to the Palestinians serve only to facilitate a better pacification also through consent.

Entrepreneurship, indebtedness and proletarianization of Palestinian women

Another contradictory feature of the ideological separation between settler colonialism and neoliberalism observed in the Palestinian entrepreneurial praxis is the awareness of settler colonial racism. Fanon (1963) observes that the recognition of racism can change the 'way of life' of colonized subjects, but not their life itself, as the structure of domination can reproduce itself and take on new features in which the position of the colonized subject assumes a new relative position but remains subaltern. As with Samira, a similar attitude can be observed in other female Palestinian Jerusalemite entrepreneurs, such as Rana Quteineh (personal communication, June 2019), the director of Jest.

According to Quteineh, Jest's objective is to act as an intermediary between entrepreneurs and corporations to enable the strengthening of the Palestinian economy as well as a greater integration of Palestinians into the Israeli entrepreneurial ecosystem. She sees entrepreneurship as a depoliticized instrument that is essential to promote social change, not only for Palestinians but also for all of Jerusalem. For this reason, she is willing to work with all those who can contribute to making the life of native Jerusalemites more materially tolerable so that they can continue living in the city. In 2020, QueenB, an Israeli NGO specializing in computing for young women, and Jest held a workshop on programming for Palestinian youth from Jerusalem at the Palestinian NGO's headquarters in East Jerusalem. The partnership was brokered traditional by the Jerusalem Foundation as part of Decision 3790 (M. Mahfouz, personal communication, August 2019).

Quteineh also believes entrepreneurship is a way to fight the 'brain drain' and helplessness affecting East Jerusalem youth. Like Israeli counterparts examined in Chapter 3, she also understands this kind activity through the security–development nexus.

> People need something more to keep living in East Jerusalem. Entrepreneurship can bring opportunities for everyone, and we believe it is the right thing to do. When people throw stones, it is because they have nothing to do. Our main goal is to [reduce] poverty, but changing the environment is also a way to improve life … . What we are doing is creating opportunities for people to forget about politics and change their

situation. The government has a 'minority' policy that tries to make things better, but it's not enough … . Certainly, our goal is to change politics, but putting institutional policy aside can create a different politics. We see entrepreneurship as a political engine, as a form of grassroots mobilisation. It is necessary to create the conditions that allow people to stay in the city. With good brains, good ideas and good opportunities, you create a reason to live and fight the brain drain affecting the Palestinian side. (Quteineh, 2019)

Despite her openness to forge business partnerships with Israelis, Quteineh is aware of the traps that may be set in her path. Jest and its founder, high-tech entrepreneur Hani Alami, have already been targets of anti-normalization campaigns by Palestinians. Quteineh has also turned down invitations to participate in events in the West Jerusalem High-Tech scene due to concerns that her image as an observant Muslim woman could be used as a representation of diversity in the Jerusalem 'ecosystem', something that does not exist in practice.

Nevertheless, it is common to hear from Palestinian entrepreneurs that the transformative potential of entrepreneurship and high technology can generate political change and of overcoming the physical obstacles that obstruct everything from the movement of natives through the territory to better Internet connections, limiting economic productivity. Successful Jerusalemite entrepreneur Amani Abu Tair sees high-tech entrepreneurship as a way for Palestinians to do 'business without borders', bypassing Israeli checkpoints (DW, 2019). Abu Tair has already received financial support from USAID and Israeli venture capital firm Jerusalem Jumpspeed Partners – belonging to Israeli entrepreneur Ben Wiener – for the development of a technology to help blind children read, as well as for an educational application software in Arabic that facilitates communication between members of the school community. With this grant, Abu Tair was able to study at prestigious Israeli institutions, intern at tech corporations, become president of her own company Wazza.Inc and receive numerous awards for her innovative abilities.

> There is no limit to innovation. We believe the world is a small village and we can reach anybody online … . We entrepreneurs from Palestine are working hard to create our future … . In the digital world, there are no borders for me to cross. (Abu Tair quoted in DW 2019)

Abu Tair, Quteineh and Samira can be classified as examples of how social mobility and economic integration of Palestinian women is possible, particularly in the technology sector, and despite structural inequalities of race, gender and class. Their cases could be understood as examples of individual effort and of making the most of the opportunities that are available in the market for women who are driven by entrepreneurial reason, allowing them to bypass the obstacles imposed on Palestinian women and, in the end, 'to create a different politics' in which economic well-being and technical skill supersede gender, religious and national identities.

Low participation in the Israeli labour market, especially among women, is identified as one of the main reasons for the high rate of poverty, as well as the depth of poverty, affecting the native population of East Jerusalem (Dagoni and Wegner 2020). This is highlighted in Decision 3790. In 2017, only 27 per cent of Palestinian women of working age (25–64 years), compared to 81 per cent of Palestinian men, participated in the labour market, while 80 per cent of Jewish women and 75 per cent of Jewish men constituted the workforce in Jerusalem (Dagoni and Wegner, 2020).[7] In 2018, around 24.5 per cent of Palestinian women active in the labour market were employed (Dagoni and Wegner, 2020) – the rest probably held informal jobs. As Shalhoub-Kevorian and Busbridge (2014) note, occupation is particularly harmful to Palestinian women, who live in a situation of extreme vulnerability and de-development in a context where settler colonization only exacerbates the oppressions of patriarchy.

Decision 3790 aims to increase the employment rate among women to approximately 30 per cent by 2023. A study estimated that if the number of Palestinian women earning a minimum wage of 5,300 shekels in Jerusalem were to reach 35 per cent, this would result in a contribution of 457 million shekels to the city's economy (Sadeh, 2018). To achieve this goal, every initiative aimed at increasing employment and entrepreneurship among the Palestinian population of East Jerusalem has prioritized the female population. For example, the Riyan Center aimed to have at least 70 per cent of women among the participants in its economic empowerment programmes (Dagoni and

---

[7] The rate is lower among men than among women because of the low participation of ultra-Orthodox men in the labour market.

Wegner, 2020). Women accounted for 72 per cent of all active participants in the first half of 2019. The plan's priority is to adapt Palestinian women to Israeli work requirements such as mastering Hebrew and acquiring skills for positions in the job market such as engineering courses and data-driven programming. The Ministry of Labour, Social Affairs and Social Services distributes vouchers to participants that give them the right to choose a vocational course, but, at the same time, options are restricted to the alternatives that are available on the market and recognized by the state. Responsibility for these choices is therefore transferred to the subjects before training even begins.

The range of courses offered by Riyan, for example, is criticized by participants for not being broad enough (Naftali et al., 2018). Training programmes are not organized according to the demands of workers, but of employers. Vouchers never subsidize 100 per cent of the cost of courses, but their values vary according to market demand for certain specializations. When women are the target audience, NGO employees purposely create barriers to participation in the training areas most sought after by the female population, such as pedagogy, in order to channel them toward professions with a greater market demand such as cooks, computer technicians, dental assistants, photography and digital animation (Y. Hermetz, personal communication, July 2019).

These efforts are added to Mati's programmes seen in Chapter 3 that had already been promoting entrepreneurship as a form of female empowerment (Arafeh and Khalidi, 2017). To sustain this economic integration of the female population, the state's plan called for the construction of 44 day care centres in thirteen locations throughout East Jerusalem between 2019 and 2023, but their implementation was rather slow: by 2021, only one day care centre had been built in the neighbourhood of Shuafat, while construction was pending for another ten; it is estimated that East Jerusalem has a deficit of 242 day cares and nurseries. Of the approximately forty thousand children under the age of four living in East Jerusalem in 2019, only 2 per cent had access to day care enrolment, compared to 24 per cent in Israel (Dagoni and Wegner, 2020).

Due to the numerous obstacles that burden the lives of Palestinian women, professional training and entrepreneurship are understood both among Israelis and Palestinians as important instruments for material and subjective improvement (Y. Issar, personal communication, June 2019). In addition to Mati, several Palestinian grassroots associations with no connection to

Israelis also offer professional training programmes, such as the Wadi Hilweh Community Centre in Silwan. Entrepreneurship is understood by Israeli bureaucrat Yara Issar as a flexible form of empowerment that allows women to seek financial independence without having to integrate the Israeli labour market, leave their homes and children, or commute across the city to work. Many Palestinian women are afraid to leave their homes to work since the experience of crossing a checkpoint and using public transportation, even within Jerusalem, can be particularly humiliating and dangerous (Shalhoub-Kerkovian and Busbridge, 2014). Therefore, as Issar (personal communication, June 2019) understands it, entrepreneurship would be a way to deviate from 'cultural' issues and the conservative attitudes that prevent women from providing for their families, especially once men's salaries are no longer enough to cover the rising costs of living in Jerusalem. Once again, it is possible to observe an orientalist neoliberal paternalism in Issar's outlook:

> Many [women] prefer to stay at home and do not have the capacity and familiarity required of the Israeli market, there is no all-day school system where they can leave their children while they are at work, there is a lack of education also, a lack of nurseries. Change will come from within, inside the villages. By providing industrial zones on the outskirts of East Jerusalem, it won't be necessary to go far and [women] will be able to work close to home and contribute to supporting their families without having to go against traditional norms … . You have to see the change happening. Increasing employment would require a giant system. This process has been successful with Haredi women, why not with Arab women? (Y. Issar, personal communication, June 2019)

Socio-economic development policies for Palestinian women, however, do not address the structural problems that have historically produced underdevelopment in the first place. As in the case of land regularization discussed above, the promotion of entrepreneurship and the integration of Palestinian women into the labour market is not primarily aimed at generating wealth and lifting them out of poverty. The real intention of these practices is to serve as a neoliberal tool of counterinsurgency. At no time, do Israelis seek to associate these temporary training programmes with more unorthodox measures advocated even by international financial institutions, such as cash transfer programmes that would allow the population the minimum necessary means to ensure its survival. There is also no fight against the precarization and informalization of Palestinians in Israeli workplaces, which allows a continuation of the overexploitation of labour and the devaluation of the workforce, enabling an increase in the profits of Israeli capital. The growing adherence of Palestinian women to the job market since 2014 has not resulted in greater empowerment, but further precarization (Dagoni and Wegner, 2020).

Even before Decision 3790, female participation in the labour market had grown significantly, from 22 per cent in 2016 to 27 per cent in 2017, while the number of employed women grew from 20 to 24.5 per cent (Dagoni and Wegner, 2020). Nevertheless, the increase in the employment rate was not accompanied with a decrease in the poverty rate. According to official information, the opposite occurred: the rate of people living in poverty was 74.95 per cent in 2016 and 77.5 per cent in 2017, and it has kept rising ever since, as the integration of Palestinian men and women also increases. In other words, even though women are employed and active, they are poorer than before, most likely because they are employed in low-wage and part-time positions, often in precarious working conditions and with no potential to advance or ascend economically. For example, out of all the women who got a job through the Riyan Centre, 62 per cent earn a minimum wage or less, while only 0.66 per cent obtained a job with a salary approaching the average wage in Israel – 7,500 shekels. While most of the men who have found employment through Riyan also earn the minimum wage (40 per cent), approximately 5 per cent earn over 7,500 – more than five times the number of women. Therefore, the minimum wage is, in practice, the maximum wage for Palestinian women in East Jerusalem.

The cases of some of these women entrepreneurs are indicative of the tragic reality of life under neoliberal settler colonization. For example, Amuhammad (personal communication, August 2019) is a middle-aged Jerusalemite woman with an incomplete primary education who used to cook hot meals in her home for workers in East Jerusalem. After paying for a training programme at Mati and receiving financial assistance from the NGO, she purchased professional equipment to open a restaurant in Bab a-Zahara. Following Mati's directions and with the free assistance of a local design company run by a Palestinian woman, she set up a Facebook page, designed a new logo, distributed flyers and changed the name of the establishment. Two years later, however, Amuhammad is still working to pay off the debts she incurred to cover the cost of employees, taxes, rent and suppliers – on the day of the interview, she only had two customers. 'I am proud of my work, I learned to cook by myself. [The restaurant] is my baby, I don't want to close it,' says Amuhammad, who supports her family alone because her husband is sick and does not receive any assistance from the Israeli government. She is looking for additional financial aid but has found it difficult to obtain a new contribution from Mati. In Ramallah, she says she cannot get support because her business is located in Jerusalem, outside the area of interest of donors.

Meanwhile, Elhan (personal communication, August 2019) is an entrepreneur in the health and beauty industry who also learned the trade on her own. In her own home and with the support of her entire family, a middle-class household, she manufactures soaps, skin care products and essences that she informally sells to Palestinian women at fairs. She wants to expand her business to open a beauty clinic where she can provide services and sell her products but has found that her options in the labour market as a Palestinian woman from Jerusalem are limited, leaving her at a dead end.

> I don't trust Israeli banks … . At Mati, I had to pay for the training to apply for a scholarship, but they were teaching something I already know. I ended up taking the classes at Mati, but they didn't want to help me because I don't want to open my business in Jerusalem, even though the Jerusalem market is bad. (Elhan, 2019)

Elhan does not want to enter the Israeli market because she is not comfortable and wants to avoid normalization. Due to her interest in expanding activities in Ramallah, where the consumer market for her products is much larger, Israeli initiatives for Jerusalem have closed its doors. At Jest, Elhan felt uncomfortable because she did not speak English and could not understand the purpose of the training: '[Classes] in digital marketing were very difficult for me, with big words for large companies.' At the Arab Chamber of Commerce and Industry in Jerusalem, she encountered limitations as she was required to legalize her business under Israeli or Palestinian regulations to formally trade. 'I cannot afford the costs', she says (Elhan, personal communication, August 2019). As for funding opportunities in Ramallah, she says she finds it difficult because she is from Jerusalem and does not have good connections within the PA.

As we can see, what has been happening, in practice, in East Jerusalem is a process of proletarianization of Palestinian women, whether through formal or informal work, or the indebtedness resulting from entrepreneurship and self-employment. Instead of truly 'empowered' Palestinian women, they have become, for the most part, workers at the mercy of exploitation by capital, either through direct exploitation or through indebtedness. There is no effort on the part of Israeli authorities to integrate these women into positions with fair wages and decent working conditions, nor to monitor the subjective suffering involved in this process and put an end to the various oppressive practices of settler colonial occupation that reinforce patriarchy, such as the demolitions that destroy the spaces whence women's identities and relationships as mother and wife are structured and carried out (Shalhoub-Kerkovian and Busbridge, 2014). According to Shalhoub-Kevorkian and Busbridge (2014), the destruction of the home signifies the destruction of the defining component of women socially, whereupon the system of patriarchal control is reinforced leaving homeless women particularly vulnerable and limited in their life options. They are proof that settler colonial policies reinforce the structural inequality between native men and women, deepening the de-development, dependency and vulnerability of Palestinian women and rendering their knowledge and experience unsuitable for participation in the labour market.

Unlike the settlers' initiatives, the Wadi Hilweh Community Centre provides professional training for women in Silwan along with different types of psychosocial therapies to bring relief and dignity, as well as physical exercise, group activities, awareness of women's rights, recognition of women's agency and legal support if necessary (S. Baidoun, personal communication, June 2019). Additionally, it promotes the involvement of women in community activities, such as a summer camp for children, and in neighbourhood political issues, such as resistance to the dispossession of residents from their homes by the movement of settlers and the City of David settlement. According to the centre's director, Sahr Baidoun:

> Every woman who leaves her house is a victory, it is a change, the first step leads to the second, which can empower her. Socializing is the first step towards

change, there are now more than 200 women working at the centre … . We never achieved a victory against the settlers. Our main victory is with women, with young people, in the formation of new leaders in the neighbourhood. (Baidoun, 2019)

In other words, the economic empowerment of Palestinian women is tied to their subjective, cultural, educational, community and political empowerment; as Palestinian women emancipated within the context of resistance to Israeli settler colonization, not as another self-employed worker rendered vulnerable to spoliation while attempting to deflect neoliberal settler colonialism by resorting to the market. Settler colonial domination is inseparable from the economic dynamics of global capitalism: the limitations on Amuhammad and Elhan's undertakings occur not only because of their choices in the Jerusalem free market, but because of racist policies that have historically provoked the de-development of Palestinian women in the city. As self-employed entrepreneurs, Palestinian women are made to assume all the risks and responsibilities pertaining to their successes or failures despite the extreme vulnerability and precariousness of their condition. Decades of oppression will not be ended by the targeted and temporary policies of the occupying forces. Palestinian women continue to face daily humiliation, mobility restrictions, difficulty in accessing education, fears of having their house demolished and other oppressions as they seek to find the daily means to survive, resist and possibly even prosper *despite* the Israeli settler colonial matrix of control.

Palestinian youth, tech entrepreneurship and Israeli neoliberal mask

The limitations that affect the integration of Palestinian women can be identified in a similar way among Palestinian youth vying for a spot in the rich Israeli high-tech industry. The shortage of skilled workers in the high-tech industry has led Israelis to facilitate visas for workers from Eastern Europe, Asia, the United States and the West Bank (Blum, 2020). In this case, Arab-Muslim culture is also seen as an obstacle to the integration of young Palestinians into the Israeli technological economy. For example, according to one of Jest's founders, Yazeed Ghandour, there is a 'lack of motivation' among young Palestinians in East Jerusalem to opt for riskier careers such as in the high-tech sector.

Youth tend to prefer safer options such as family businesses and public employment that bring greater stability to the family. Many Palestinians who have sought to participate in the Israeli high-tech market report a difficulty in adapting to the increasingly specific technical requirements of companies that prove incompatible with their Palestinian education. In addition to education, there are other difficulties such as travelling very long distances to the workplace as a result of Israeli restrictions and the racism that often functions as an impediment before the first interview even takes place (Saps, 2019). Indeed, even for the few Palestinians who seem to overcome these restrictions, Israeli racism is revealed as the real obstacle to their professional ambitions.

In Jerusalem, the educational institutions, NGOs and corporations that make up the Israeli technological ecosystem have sought to recruit young Palestinians that may serve as examples of 'good Arabs' involved in the multicultural local industry. This is the case of Ameen, an East Jerusalem computer engineering student at the Hebrew University. Ameen was born into an upper-middle-class family in Beit Safafa, originally a Palestinian village that was split in two in 1948 and saw its residents divided between citizens and non-citizens. Since 1967, Beit Safafa has been reunited and became a prosperous and well-integrated suburb of West Jerusalem. After attending a middle school that followed the PA curriculum, Ameen (personal communication, July 2019) completed high school at an Israeli private school: 'It was the best decision of my life, it gave me a future.'

Given the possibility of moving freely between the territories of the West Bank and Israel and his fluency in both Arab and Hebrew, Ameen's identity was not built around Palestinian nationalism or its Israeli counterpart. He recognizes himself only as an Arab from Jerusalem. His command of Hebrew and his fluidity in the Israeli sociability of West Jerusalem, however, have not prevented him from experiencing first hand the racism that confines him to a condition of subordination and Palestinian identity to which he did not wish to be linked. Both at university and at work, Ameen reports the perception of being sealed off from integration by a 'wall' or being instrumentalized for political objectives from which he is alienated.

> I was just trying to be honest, but they wanted to use me to showcase their policies … . I know I'll never be part of them, they talk about their time in the army, and they don't smoke. The companies clearly say that they will hire us even though we aren't so good, just because we are Arabs, because they want to present a diversity that is not real but invented … . I don't even identify as a Palestinian but as an Arab. I feel the difference in how they treat me just because I'm Arab. And I won't let them use me. (Ameen, personal communication, July 2019)

Despite corresponding to all the settler colonial assumptions that should safely grant him entry into the neoliberal hegemonic system, the racism that has been historically produced by Israeli settler colonialism confines Ameen to a position of exclusion and structural subalternity. It is a position he has had to submit to against his will and to which the market has not been blind. The impossibility of enjoying true social, political and economic freedom under the settler colonial regime is, in his view, what makes exile in another country the only way of escaping the humiliations and dispossessions imposed by racism in his city of birth.

It is precisely this silent indirect expulsion, the 'brain drain' and the dispute over the 'hearts and minds' of Palestinian youth that Palestinian social entrepreneurs involved in the technology sector seek to reverse. This dispute can be illustrated on the one hand by the initiatives of entrepreneur Hani Alami, one of the founders of Jest, and, on the other hand, by the initiatives of entrepreneur Aref Husseini, one of the creators of Al-Nayzak. In addition to serving as an example for entrepreneurial activism in a high-tech industry that seeks to provide an alternative for young people like Ameen, Alami and Husseini illustrate the dispute between actors who use entrepreneurship to pursue both the local and national agendas.

Both are Jerusalemite businessmen who made their careers in the Israeli and international high-tech industry before becoming activists. To this end, they opened several non-profit NGOs as part of their social responsibility as entrepreneurs toward their community. While Alami and Jest prefer a strategy of rapprochement with the Israelis without rejecting strategic partnerships with Ramallah, Husseini and Al-Nayzak take a more rejectionist stance in the name of the nationalist project of making East Jerusalem the capital of an independent Palestinian state within the Green Line.

However, like all Jerusalemites, Husseini is also forced to adapt to some limitations imposed by the Israelis to continue working in East Jerusalem – for years he has been developing the Jerusalem Innovation Park project to be the city's largest Palestinian centre for training and research in science, technology and engineering. Husseini understands that the relationship with the Israelis in Jerusalem leads to an economic normalization that excludes the possibility of establishing an independent Palestinian State. It would signify an integration with the settler economy and its international circuits that would lead to the boycott of the native population, further deepening the divide between Palestinians in Jerusalem and Palestinians in the West Bank.

Al-Nayzak is a non-profit organization that is also present in Ramallah, Nablus and Gaza and intends to promote a form of 'rational' development in Palestine (Al-Nayzak, 2020). In East Jerusalem, the NGO mainly promotes technology education as well as an incubator for new start-ups. According to Husseini, between ten and fifteen ideas are generated per year within Al-Nayzak, but none have yet been successful in advancing their enterprise. The NGO's projects are financed by Palestinian companies such as Jawal and Bank of Palestine, branches of the PA, Palestinian philanthropic foundations such as the Jerusalemite Faisal Husseini and the transnational Taawon, and international support from the EU and the UN.

In East Jerusalem, Al-Nayzak's main objective is to serve as reinforcement to the last native 'lines of defence' against the city's Israeli initiatives both in education and in the economy. The intent is to ensure the preservation of a Palestinian identity among Jerusalem's youth and the existence of a resistance economy in the city. Faced with the impossibility of real competition with the Israeli ecosystem, Husseini (personal communication, July 2019) favours an affiliation to foreign markets as a way 'outside of' the settler regime that enables a strengthening of the native high-tech industry. He wants to offer a Palestinian alternative that can compete on material economic terms with the settlers for the hearts, minds and skills of the Jerusalemite youth.

> We think that we are so smart that we can take their money and remain Palestinian. Once you are connected to that money, the entire Palestinian community, including the business community, will boycott you and international money will start pouring in because of you joined the Israelis.... All the answers are about improving our daily lives but in the long term,

our chances of one day having an independent Palestinian State are diminishing .... If you are part of the inclusion [Israelization], to create jobs for Palestinians, raise money, promote civil rights, then the Israelis are perfect. You can try to be smarter than the State, but you can never be more powerful than the state, right? They can play around [do business] with you all you like but they can also close your start-up the next day .... The only way is to build an alternative to this system, but we can't really prevent the new generations from falling into this trap .... We need to ensure and maintain the resilience of East Jerusalem and work with the younger generations, with skills for the future to keep hoping, surviving for the future of Palestine. You have to play the materialistic game and not just the symbolic one. (Husseini, 2019)

Alami (personal communication, August 2019) also aims to collaborate with the technological ecosystem in East Jerusalem, to give Palestinian youth a reason to continue living in the city, but without assuming an anti-Israelization position. Specifically, he intends to be the bridge between Palestinian talent and Israeli capital to create opportunities seen as 'small steps that can change the future'. Through Jest, Alami wants to create a network between Israelis and Palestinians who wish to collaborate economically to generate mutual technological development. Through this approach, he desires to make Jerusalem the 'great junction' between Tel Aviv and Ramallah, as well as between the Western and Eastern global markets, from Europe to Dubai. Alami understands that his position causes discomfort on both sides, but he continues to believe that digital entrepreneurship is the best way to overcome the political restrictions imposed by borders, walls and checkpoints to achieve economic development. His aim is to sow seeds that may grow into new start-ups and transform into hope for the oppressed.

> We [the co-founders of Jest] met in Jerusalem and decided to work with the Palestinians who are still in the city to make entrepreneurship a form of change .... We don't just want to develop big companies, with big ideas and high technology, but also small start-ups where you can create four or five new job positions. That's already a big step for Jerusalem .... What we are doing is growing seeds for hope in Jerusalem. We need to resolve the economic issue and provide dignity before talking about the peace process. We need to regain the hope of living in the city .... We want the Palestinians to have a fair opportunity to succeed in the city .... Every time we try to

make a change here in the city, you run the risk of being attacked by both Palestinians and Israelis. But you have two options: either you leave the city or stay and change things. I suffered BDS attacks because I connected a young Palestinian girl with Intel-Israel, but BDS did not offer an alternative for that person. Her roots are in Jerusalem; she wants to stay in the city … . The rifts today are wider between Israelis and Israelis, and Palestinians and Palestinians, no longer between Israelis and Palestinians. So, there's a greater possibility of finding common ground between Israelis and Palestinians … . The two sides of the Israelis' project for East Jerusalem, security and development, represent the two sides of Israeli society. We see ourselves as part of this struggle for society and for budgets … . Normal people want to live peacefully; they don't care about religion, security, where you come from, where you're going. (Alami, 2019)

It is clear that Husseini functions politically as a representation of the PA's Fayadism in East Jerusalem, while Alami's actions are more in line with neoliberal Israelization. However, beyond the divergences in their agendas, both Husseini and Al-Nayzak, like Alami and Jest, are complementary components of the small Palestinian technological entrepreneurial ecosystem in East Jerusalem that obeys the neoliberal development rationality. The restrictions imposed by Israeli settler colonization prevent Palestinian actors who see themselves as competitors from truly operating in two distinct and isolated spheres. There is a very strong network of connections between individuals, NGOs and corporations operating in the local high-tech market, but it is always somehow tied to the West Bank, Israel or other transnational processes.

For example, in 2019, the World Economic Forum launched the Jerusalem chapters – West and East – of its programme to promote technological entrepreneurship and leadership formation. The Global Shapers Community provides funding for the creation of collaborative networks of young entrepreneurs under the age of thirty so they can craft solutions to local and global problems that 'challenge the status quo' (WEF, 2020). Representatives from more than 369 urban areas in 171 countries participate annually in the Forum meetings in Davos. In East Jerusalem, the programme aims to connect Palestinian leaders who, together with the hub in West Jerusalem, may promote 'regional and universal peace with dignity and access to opportunity for all'.

Global Shapers also contributes to the creation of an entrepreneurial ecosystem to integrate Palestinians from the OPT. In 2019, Global Shapers' hubs in East Jerusalem, Ramallah, Nablus and Gaza, in cooperation with the PA's Ministry of Entrepreneurship and Empowerment (created in 2019) and the WB, held the first 'Palestinian International Entrepreneurship Conference: Empowering the Entrepreneurial Ecosystem' in Bethlehem (PNN, 2019). The event brought together Palestinian entrepreneurs along with more than two hundred representatives from the European technology market, a delegation from the World Economic Forum and emissaries from technology corporations such as Dell and Orange. Jerusalemite entrepreneur Amany Abu Tair, a member of the Global Shapers network, was one of the organizers and speakers at the event. 'We feel that the voices of start-ups in Palestine are not heard, and we rarely have important investors and technology companies paying attention to Palestine', said Abu Tair (Quoted in PNN, 2019). In a nutshell, the WEF promotes, through the same program, initiatives that are complementary in their vision – the union of Israeli and Palestinian entrepreneurs in Jerusalem for the promotion of peace and the strengthening of the Palestinian entrepreneurial ecosystem in the West Bank - but which, in the view of Palestinian activist-entrepreneurs from East Jerusalem, would represent divergent agendas – local and national, respectively. Abu Thair herself is active on both fronts.

As we can see, the neoliberal entrepreneurial rationality transcends divergences between agendas and anti-normalization movements. In other words, a hegemony of progressive neoliberalism prevails when addressing cultural, political and economic issues originally produced by Israeli settler colonialism, but which, faced with deep socio-spatial fragmentation, gives rise to localized versions of actors who see technological entrepreneurship as a way of building an Arab-Palestinian economy and generate social transformation. Different agendas for strategic action converge in their quest to contribute to the empowerment and social ascension of the lower classes of the native population through professional training programmes, the exaltation of the entrepreneurial approach and the creation of market opportunities. East Jerusalem is a place where different neoliberal streams meet in a game of smoke and mirrors that reinforces neoliberal reason as the only possibility of (r)existence for Palestinians.

On the one hand, it is understandable that digital technology and entrepreneurship have been fetishized by the Palestinian middle and upper classes as solutions to their problems. The Internet and other digital technological innovations allow Palestinians divided by the settler colonial occupation to communicate easily and cooperate in initiatives that bring material benefits to the base level of society. In addition, proximity to the technological and abundant wealth of the Israeli 'start-up nation' next door, coupled with incentives from capital and international institutions such as the WEF, OECD and WB, make technological entrepreneurship not only a pragmatic and supposedly rational choice for Palestinians within an otherwise limited field of options, but something to be desired to overcome the condition of being colonized.

In the digital world, circumventing and bypassing the soldiers and checkpoints appears to be a realistic possibility. Examples of development, seen in the streets, offices, clothes and gadgets that are proudly displayed in the neighbourhoods, bodies and hands of Israelis seem within reach of those savvy enough to exploit the right market 'opportunities'. Faced with the 'solutionist' aura disseminated by the marketing campaigns of entrepreneurs in Silicon Valley of California and the 'Sillicon Wadi' of Tel Aviv, in which technology is presented as a panacea for everything from neoliberal austerity to failing democracy, institutional bureaucracies and practically every sector of the economy, 'peace' and national liberation seem easily within the reach of the brilliant, innovative and rebellious minds of high-tech entrepreneurs. Why would Palestinian entrepreneurs not be able to 'hack' their way out of the settler regime?

These ideals of innovation, disruption and technical solutionism inherent to technological entrepreneurship have created the illusion of a more intelligent, humanitarian and sustainable capitalism. According to Morozov (2018), this in fact constitutes a reactionary mystification that, at best, provides what he calls a 'predatory emancipation'. That is, an extremely limited form of freedom that is restricted by the terms of capital, which, in the end, signifies even greater slavery. Emancipation, as long as it is conducted on terms established by Silicon Valley, is a never-ending process because every act of emancipation creates several new types of dependencies. And the reason why a bunch of information services is seen as a path towards emancipation itself has to do with the reframing of what it means to be free in the twenty-first century: by and large, this is a freedom to choose in the global marketplace rather than freedom to offend and provoke those in power (Morozov, 2018: 207–8).

In East Jerusalem, technological entrepreneurship is used as form of contestation that avoids direct confrontation by circumventing or adapting to the restrictions imposed by settler colonialism. Despite their efforts to discern between the Israeli and the international market, Palestinian actors cannot change the course of settler colonization, interrupt it or transform it. Nor would these efforts be able to reinforce the preservation of a Palestinian identity and economy against the advance of neoliberal Israelization in East Jerusalem. Palestinian and Israeli 'entrepreneurial ecosystems' are highly connected in a relationship of dependence that reproduces settler colonial hierarchies. In addition to being economically dependent on Israeli high-tech investments, Palestinians also depend on cabling and satellite infrastructure, leaving them vulnerable to the digital surveillance techniques and technologies that are increasingly present in the networks and streets of Jerusalem (Hever, 2018). This would explain why radical Palestinian militants have limited themselves to the offline world.

The occupation of East Jerusalem reinforces the neoliberal hegemony by imposing a series of restrictions that require Palestinian actors to operate under the radar to receive market investment without disturbing the settler colonial powers. Jest and Al-Nayzak, as well as other Palestinian technology companies in the city, must often keep their political agendas and Palestinian identities hidden from their public images, on social media and from their offices. As with the individual case of Ameen, adaptation imposes these Palestinians to wear a supposedly apolitical neoliberal mask to survive the constraints of settler colonialism and obtain recognition from capital. Because of the settler colonial racism, neoliberal means Israeli in East Jerusalem. The Israeli racist regime prevents the material gains obtained through entrepreneurship from removing Palestinians from their position of subalternity. The material and subjective transformations brought by neoliberal anti-colonialism end up boosting the structures of domination without altering the hierarchy between settlers and natives.

Elites, tourism and the commodification of Palestinian identity

Tourism in the Holy Land is key to sustaining a resistance economy in East Jerusalem. Of vital importance to Palestinians, it provides support for many other economic sectors, such as the small family businesses in the central region and enables a disruption of the Zionist hegemonic narrative about the city's history and contemporary affairs. However, the Palestinian tourism sector has shrunk due to the growing isolation suffered by the city since 2000 and has become increasingly dependent on the Israelis. In recent years, Palestinian travel agencies have been forced to copy Israeli itineraries, merchants have migrated their businesses to Israeli shopping centres, and hotels have had to adapt to restrictions imposed by the settler industry to stay open (R. Saadeh, personal communication, June 2019).

Because of constraints on the freedom of movement of Palestinians from the West Bank, business travel and commercial and religious tourism have dropped dramatically. Meanwhile, Ramallah and Bethlehem have become destinations for leisure and trade at a lower cost for local and foreign tourists due to the lower value of labour, taxes and private property (R. Saadeh, personal communication, June 2019). It is estimated that around 60 per cent of Palestinian hotels and 30 per cent of commercial establishments in central East Jerusalem have closed in recent years due to various restrictions (Jafari et al., 2019). The city's main tourist sites, such as the Old City, the Dome of the Rock and the Church of the Nativity, are controlled and populated by Palestinians. However, natives have not been able to circumvent Israeli domination to transform these assets into a lucrative business or a contribution to social welfare. According to the director of the Jerusalem Arab Chamber of Commerce, Louay al-Husseini (personal communication, July 2019), 'tourism would be the only real way for Palestinians [Jerusalemites] to be able to compete economically with the Israelis'. Unlike agriculture, where incentives from the State of Israel, legal confiscation of land and the free granting of land to settler producers result in unfair competition, in tourism Palestinians retain control of the main attractions in Jerusalem, Bethlehem and Nazareth.

With financial support from the European Union and in cooperation with the Arab Chamber of Commerce in Jerusalem, the Jerusalem Tourism Cluster (JTC) has developed initiatives to strengthen the identity of the city, including incentives for Muslim tourism from countries with which Israel maintains diplomatic relations and projects that preserve and highlight its cultural heritage (native artisanship, architecture and historic trails) (R. Saadeh, personal communication, June 2019). One of the principal concerns of these initiatives is to reach the edges of Palestinian society to engage them in a network of tourism and business that undoes the settler colonial borders that fragment the territory. In this way, Palestinian tourist itineraries decolonize the image of the country that is presented to visitors: they surpass the socio-spatial limitations imposed by the occupying forces to rescue a universal understanding of the national territory of historic Palestine (Boer, 2016). Foreign tourists, unlike the millions of Palestinian non-citizens in the OPT, are allowed freedom of movement throughout the country and, therefore, the privilege of visiting places that are off-limits to the native population. One example is the Massar Ibrahim pilgrim trail, which cuts across the territory of the occupied West Bank, past walls, fences and checkpoints, connecting several small Palestinian communities seldom explored by traditional tourism (R. Saadeh, personal communication, June 2019).

Recent initiatives from JTC and Grassroots Jerusalem have sought to reposition Jerusalem's image and help emphasize the native narrative of its history by providing political tours of the city. In 2019, Grassroots Jerusalem launched a new edition of its travel guide, Wujood, which recommends Palestinian hotels, establishments, cultural centres and activities, in addition to presenting the city's history from the native point of view. The political tours of East Jerusalem challenge the legitimacy of the narrative that supports settler activities in the city, both the historical-religious justifications for the City of David, as well as the repressive surveillance measures and dispossessions that come with restrictive urban planning. In addition, they collaborate to strengthen small family businesses in central East Jerusalem, particularly shopkeepers in the Old City, against the onslaught of settler movements. Palestinian guides who conduct political tours typically lack formal authorization from Israeli authorities and are forced to operate on the fringes to avoid surveillance and policing. Therefore, they operate illegally, representing a danger to the agents directly involved. For example, Daoud Ghoul, a Ras al-Amoud activist and political guide, has been arrested twice by Israeli authorities (Wafa, 2020).

Trade associations, philanthropic institutions, NGOs and individuals from the Palestinian upper classes, such as the Holy Land Incoming Tour Operators Association and the Arab Hotels Association, in addition to the Chamber and the JTC, are among the actors that have sought to forge cooperation between different initiatives to support a resistance economy. The Chamber has a project called Atic that funds Palestinian initiatives that promote the resurgence of traditional industries such as leather and other handicraft productions. Through this cooperation, they intend to preserve the physical presence, cultural heritage and native popular economy in East Jerusalem (L. Al-Husseini, personal communication, June 2019). Since 2016, the city's tourist associations, with the support of other civil society organizations such as Al-Nayzak, have been organizing the Nablus Road Open Days festival, which hosts outdoor cultural activities, political debates and trade fairs in the city's centre, bringing together Palestinian entrepreneurs, artists and intellectuals, particularly women. The main objective is to attract foreign tourists to Palestinian spaces, providing leisure and business opportunities for local residents (R. Saadeh, personal communication, June 2019).

These actors aim to transform the Palestinian identity into a differentiator that will attract more tourists, consumers and investors to East Jerusalem. For this reason, Palestinian entrepreneurs from the tourism sector have reclaimed both Palestinian identity and indigeneity. Rather than relying solely on religious pilgrimage, Palestinian tourism entrepreneurs want to attract visitors who are interested in the cultural richness and multiculturalism of its present, thereby increasing the diversity and quantity of tourists. According to Raed Saadeh, owner of the traditional Jerusalem Hotel and director of the JTC, the combination of tourism and culture is the only way to strengthen the economy, both to resist Israeli settler colonization and to transform East Jerusalem into an 'independent city'.

Saadeh (2015) emphasizes the ethnic diversity of the city, a 'mosaic' composed of individuals of Gypsy, Moroccan, Afghan, Syrian, Copt, Ethiopian, Armenian and Greek origins, in addition to Arabs and Jews. He believes these groups constitute a singularity that is 'waiting to be explored' (Saadeh, 2015). Palestinian entrepreneurs see identity and culture as elements that can be used to create a 'unique experience' for visitors of East Jerusalem who will be able to consume local traditional dance, music and goods and improve the image that is sold by native Jerusalem marketing campaigns (R. Saadeh, personal communication, June 2019). For example, Palestinian hotels, such as the traditional Ambassador Hotel, have highlighted their Arab-Palestinian identity by reintroducing arabesques in their decor. According to Saadeh (2015: 82):

> Our competitive capacity can be reinforced in new packages and offers for different visitors. Jerusalem needs a host of new products to challenge the oppressive seasonality that affects tourism. Competitiveness is about differentiation. It is about a Palestinian product that can only be found in the city. It is about how the Jerusalem community is able to use its human, cultural, economic and social resources and capabilities. Once it is achieved, competitiveness is key to sustainability.

This strategy of the Palestinian tourism sector, though partially in agreement with the perspectives that inform the ways in which to constitute a resistance economy in East Jerusalem, is limited by its neoliberal character. Tourism is one of the main vectors behind projects to commodify both urban spaces and ethnic, religious and national culture and identity, transforming them into assets to be commercialized and eventually consumed by visitors looking to spend their dollars on a unique 'experience' (Harvey, 2005). Once again, we note the contradictions inherent in the economic initiatives of Palestinian resistance in East Jerusalem that are guided by neoliberal rationality. However, instead of hiding Palestinian identity, tourism offers its commodification. Palestinian national culture and identity, which form the base of native historic anti-colonial resistance movements in the territory (Khalidi 2010), are converted to resources organized in particular forms so as to be made available for exploitation. The appropriation of images, actors and radical identities for their domestication and commodification has been a historical constant of capitalism. In neoliberalism, the expansion of the frontiers of commodification of livelihoods and political struggles now has another opportunity for accumulation in Palestinian identity.

However, not even Palestinian businessmen from East Jerusalem or elsewhere in the country have invested significantly to promote tourism in the city, preferring safer options on the outskirts of town or in the West Bank (S. Nuseibeh, personal communication, June 2019; R. Saadeh, personal communication, June 2019; M. Sinocrot, personal communication, June 2019; H. A. Zahria, personal communication, August 2019). Many reported a fear of investing in East Jerusalem and not seeing economic or political results due to colonial restrictions. The few actors that do manage to bypass the settler colonial blockades would rather not risk submitting their economic interests to the political imperatives of defending East Jerusalem. However, as Aref

Husseini (personal communication, July 2019) states: 'This is not the right time to make a profit in Jerusalem.'

The real estate 'boom' that led to the construction of high-end buildings and sophisticated new shopping centres in Beit Hanina and other marginal areas of the city where Israelis tolerate native development does not extend to central East Jerusalem, where many small family businesses, particularly in the Muslim Quarter of the Old City, find it difficult to keep their doors open and are constantly harassed by settler movements. Despite the difficulties faced in maintaining commercial activity, Abu Zahra (personal communication, July 2019), the owner of a small market in the centre of East Jerusalem, says that 'keeping the store open, even at a loss, is important for Jerusalem'. Israelis have arrested Abu Zahra on more than one occasion for supporting political activities in the city.

Adnan Dakkak (personal communication, August 2019), the owner of an Old City souvenir shop that has been in his family since 1936 and a member of the Arab Chamber of Commerce, reports that shopkeepers and the native business community try to organize themselves financially to keep as many stores open as possible. The entrepreneurial community strives to at least avoid the confiscation of property by the State of Israel for non-payment of taxes and to prevent settler NGOs from harassing indebted Palestinians. Another problem that Dakkak reports is the lack of interest of younger generations in taking up traditional family businesses because of the better wages and living conditions they can find in West Jerusalem, Ramallah or abroad, which has already led to the closure of activities of some establishments in the centre of East Jerusalem.

Despite having a degree in electronic engineering from abroad, Dakkak has never pursued a profession in that field due to the importance of keeping the family business running under Israeli occupation. Shopkeepers report a generalized sense of hopelessness resulting from the absence of any assistance that might help maintain their businesses open in an area that remains the main symbol of Palestinian (r)existence and identity in the city. The Old City Shopkeepers Association used to be an important example of mobilization and resistance, but much like other independent Palestinian unions and organizations, it has lost both its internal influence among Palestinians as well as the ability to project external power over the Israelis (A. Dakkak, personal communication, August 2019).

> At the end of the day, people need to make a profit. They don't do it if they can't make a profit. No, they have to make money. They are entrepreneurs, not charities … . On top of that, you have several donors, a lot of money coming from abroad, but at the end of the day, you don't see anything. This is not just because of corruption, but also because people, whether Europeans or the Arab world, say they are going to give money to Jerusalem, but at the end of the day, they don't give any money. They talk a lot, at conferences here and there, but nothing happens. That's why I say that if we're going to do something, we should do it ourselves. (Dakkak, 2019)

Profit and market imperatives keep politics subordinate to the economy. The absence of an anti-colonial imagination that goes beyond neoliberal development have inhibited the resistance practices of various sectors of Palestinian society. Neoliberal hegemony imprisons Palestinians in a labyrinth that hides settler colonial racism and closes off avenues for national liberation. As a result, efforts to strengthen the native economy in East Jerusalem have not been successful in curbing dispossession at the city centre or satisfying the need for self-determination.

Neoliberalism and economics appear to be the only ways to break Palestinian political resistance and allow its pacification. The destructive effects of de-development can become so unbearable they make neoliberal settler colonial traps seem like a more effective strategy. For Salem (2018b), the different Palestinian reactions to this strategy of inclusion without effective integration have been characterized by disunity, discontinuation, fragmentation at the public level and atomization at the individual scale. In the end, these responses would be unable to stop or change the course of the settler colonial project in the city: 'They are responses that aim to maintain survival within the framework of severe suffering, nothing more, nothing less' (Salem, 2018b: 37).

The inability to face and overcome settler colonialism does not mean that Palestinians are unaware of the racist nature of Israeli domination or even of the goals behind neoliberal development policies. This occurs with Palestinian activist-entrepreneurs who equip themselves with market tools to advance a neoliberal anti-colonialism that is alienated from the correlation of forces in the global political economy. Entrepreneurship and neoliberal development nourish the illusion that definitive emancipation would be possible simply by adapting to the hegemonic structures of power. Efforts to form alternative economies can help respond to the native population's material and subjective needs for well-being and dignity, but when imbued with neoliberal rationality, they are swallowed up by Israeli settler colonialism as seen above.

Entrepreneurship allows Palestinians to vent their dissatisfaction, their need to reproduce life and their desire for recognition of their humanity through the market. But does not build a decolonial movement. Entrepreneurship ideological strength derives from not being immediately understood as a form of political normalization as in the old liberal multiculturalism of Oslo-style coexistence. But in post-Oslo, neoliberal multiculturalism picks the market as its preferred space to continue advancing settler colonial interests in an elusive and normalized way. Entrepreneurship cannot be understood as a means of resistance, but merely as a way for Palestinians to affirm their existence in a manner the 'resistance economy' intellectuals understood as static and reactionary *sumud*.

Conclusion: Refusal and emancipation in East Jerusalem

Agendas of entrepreneurship have served as new mechanisms for dispossession and pacification through inclusion in financial markets and are common in the urban peripheries of countries in the Global South, such as Brazil (Davis, 2006). Living in Brazil, which has many similarities and differences with Palestine, gave me the chance to separate Palestine from its uniqueness and compare it to the way things are in Brazil. It led me to look for elements in Brazilian urban peripheries that would help examine the ways in which the racially subaltern populations of these Global South spatialities are continually plundered and pacified.

During the Worker's Party[1] years (2003–16) in Brazil, when progressive neoliberalism and a neo-developmentalist agenda were both in place, the social project of the Pacification Police Unit (UPP Social) and NGO entrepreneurship programmes were key policies that helped advance ostensible policing, military occupation and surveillance in Rio de Janeiro's favelas (Botelho, 2013; L. de Tommasi and Velazco, 2013). If Rio de Janeiro is not that different from Jerusalem, as we have already argued (Huberman and Nasser, 2019), then why should force, weapons, walls, cameras and armoured vehicles always be the preferred objects of analysis when looking at the settler colonial question in Palestine/Israel? My experience with the Palestinians taught me that it was not just soldiers, checkpoints and prisons that prevented the decolonization and liberation of that people. These were and continue to be fundamental reasons, but they are not the only ones. The settler colonial stick always needs a carrot.

---

[1] The Worker's Party is Brazil's largest social-democratic party.

If an Israeli soldier killing a young, wounded Palestinian on the ground without being punished shows that Israel is a settler colony and racist, then a young Palestinian woman starting a business with the help of an Israeli entrepreneur after going to school in Tel Aviv could help hide the same settler colonialism. Seeing the first incident as 'illiberal' and the second as 'liberal', as many do, does not help expose the settler colonial root but reinforces the division between a legitimate and an illegitimate manifestation.

This book criticizes this limited way of thinking about how settler colonialism and neoliberalism are linked. I have shown how the forms of Israeli settler colonial government and Palestinian resistance in East Jerusalem reveal universal dynamics of racial capitalism that work in different parts of the world, mostly in urban peripheries. The entrepreneurship programmes are a key way to look at how counterinsurgency has worked in the South's urban fringes, but they don't get as much attention in the literature as the overtly coercive measures. However, the soft policies of development are key to getting subaltern populations to consent and building a stable and productive order in a more efficient way. Unlike surveillance cameras and military checkpoints, development programmes like those that help people start their own businesses rely on local support, a civil mask and a neutral air that comes from neoliberal ideology. So, they give actions that seem natural the legitimacy they need to build consent among the subaltern.

What distinguishes the neoliberal settler colonial process in East Jerusalem from the rest of Palestine/Israel is the simultaneous coexistence of two apparently antagonistic processes: on the one hand, neoliberal Israelization, and, on the other, the neoliberalization of the Palestinian National Movement. The inclusion and development of Palestinians in East Jerusalem correspond to their integration into the neoliberal market and their forms of control, exploitation and dispossession. The result is the formation of an increasingly neoliberal sociability in East Jerusalem that mainly favours the Israeli population. Progressive neoliberalism provides crucial tools for the Israelis to 'dislodge Jerusalem from their throats' and proceed with the settler colonial project in a way they have not been able to achieve in more than fifty years of history. This integration has led to the formation of a Palestinian middle class of professional collaborators who aid in the administration and pacification of the rest of the native population.

It is important to highlight that this integration does not mean a process of elimination through assimilation, such as has already been seen in other settler colonial contexts. Wolfe (2011) has argued that in post-frontier situations like the United States, politics of integration, development and education, such as boarding schools and the granting of citizenship, were state politics to 'kill the Indian and save the men'. Miscegenation was another biopolitical tool with the same objective. However, this is not the case with the neoliberal integration of Palestinians in East Jerusalem. Although we have shown that some Israelis aim to 'kill the Palestinian to save the men' by making them productive and docile, their objective is not to assimilate them to Jewish-Zionist-Israeli society. As Wolfe (2006) argues, Israeli settler colonialism is particularly exclusivist. Inclusion in settler colonial contexts can mean assimilation, but not always. The Palestinians are submitted to a process of subordinate integration to expand the power of exploitation of native labour and create new subjects that consent to the neoliberal settler colonial order.

Through education, capacity-building and other counterinsurgency processes of attraction, neoliberal Israelization created neoliberal Palestinian subjects in accordance with the needs of the Israeli elites. These Palestinian subjects opt for the most 'rational' and 'objective' ways of resisting and struggling for national liberation, which in some cases means entrepreneurship. They want a stable order to act in the market for their development to achieve political transformations. As a result, mass mobilizations and other practices of resistance, such as the violent ones, became 'irrational' and 'illegitimate'. In doing so, they agree with the security–development nexus that underlies the counterinsurgency rationale of every Israeli policy towards the Palestinians – also deepening the social divisions between the Palestinians.

Recognizing that Israeli technologies of elimination and exploitation have been reorganized does not mean that the elimination of Palestinians in East Jerusalem has stopped. In neighbourhoods such as Silwan and Sheikh Jarrah, the forced dispossessions by the state and settler organizations are in full force. In the end, Israelis are even willing to make Palestinians poorer and stop their economy from growing in order to expand settler colonial control of the land. Inclusion, development and entrepreneurship are options available to some Palestinian Jerusalemites, but not all of them.

According to Decision 3790, the gaps between the Jewish and Palestinian residents of Jerusalem are to be reduced. Nevertheless, Israeli state bureaucracy is structured to act counterinsurgently against Palestinians. It does not matter that some well-meaning individuals have good intentions. Or that some Palestinians may gain economically as a result. The settler colonial structure makes their agency serve the pacification, expulsion, and exploitation interests of the Israeli elites.

The Covid-19 crisis that started in 2020 revealed the fragility of the market-based inclusion measures. Approximately one-third of Palestinians either lost their jobs or had to reduce their weekly hours, with the most affected being young people with low levels of education and in low-skilled occupations. In 2019, 63 per cent of Palestinians who took part in training programmes at the Riyan Center had long-term jobs. In 2020, that number dropped to 44 per cent (Dagoni and Wegner, 2022).

The neoliberal inclusion of the Palestinians in East Jerusalem is still a process inside the realm of accumulation by dispossession, but in a gentler manner to elude the disposed to consent and take part in their own expropriation. I claim that what we are witnessing is like a process of settler colonial recognition. In exchange for recognition, the natives can cease making sovereignty claims that challenge the legitimacy of settler state authority over the territory (Simpson, 2017). In the case of East Jerusalem, I claim a more central role is played by neoliberal actors, such as NGOs and private companies. In exchange for the recognition of their wasted capabilities, the Palestinians can now be exploited in more sophisticated ways instead of being kept as redundant bodies waiting for elimination.

In this process, neoliberal multiculturalism plays a fundamental role. NGOs with a Palestinian mask is fundamental to making the trap legitimate. The illusory separation between economics and politics is reproduced in a division between settler colonialism as a phenomenon exclusive to the realm of politics, while the market would be a space where peace can be built through mutually beneficial, rational and efficient exchanges. This trick has caught several Palestinian activists who believe they can change things from inside or outside the Israeli economic system, but always with the market as their ally, as we have seen in Chapter 4. The racist hierarchies between Israelis and Palestinians are reproduced through depoliticized market relations.

As Fanon notes, recognition in a colonial situation is impossible because it is always trapped in the desire of the Other, the white – in this case, the Israeli Jew – who is represented as a universal, Western subject. The Israeli recognition of humanity and the universality of the Palestinians does not occur no matter how many masks they wear, as in the case of Ameen (Chapter 4). Despite learning Hebrew, studying in Israeli institutions and working with high-tech, he understands that he will never be accepted and recognized as an equal by the settlers. What remains as options are co-optation into the settler colonial structure or exile abroad.

Audre Lorde (2019) has correctly claimed that it is not possible to play on the chessboard of the dominant classes and expect to promote genuine change. You may win some games, but the circumstances will always favour your opponent. Neoliberalism provides the Palestinians with new playing tools that they cannot use to defeat their opponent. Fanon says that the only way to make the dialectic between the subjects and find the universal in oneself and in the Other is for a truly anti-colonial struggle to reject where the colonizer puts the colonized. In this way, we can reach a universal humanity that makes it possible for everyone to be free. In the case of the Palestinians, this means, among other things, rejecting the idea that they are a people who can't adapt to the neoliberal modernity of the West, and accepting what is seen as the only rational way to achieve national freedom. This means rejecting the paradigm of 'neoliberalism as liberation', as Khalidi and Samour (2011) put it.

Palestinian authors critical of neoliberal development argue that economic activity must be submitted to Palestinians' political objectives for self-determination (Arafeh, 2018; Dana, 2014a; Hanieh, 2016; Khalidi and Samour, 2011). This represents a considerable challenge, but it would be the only way to overcome the illusions of the separation between economics and politics and the fetishization of neoliberal development that have limited the formation of a truly counterhegemonic resistance economy capable of containing and destroying settler colonization. As Hall (1988) puts it: 'Politics depends on the power relations of a particular moment. History does not wait in the wings to catch up to its mistakes in yet another inevitable success. You lose because you lose because you lose.' Neoliberal capitalism cannot be used to build these types of power relationships.

Meanwhile, Palestinian acts of refusal in East Jerusalem have kept hope alive. In May 2021, the El-Kurd family refused to let a settler movement take over their land. The refusal inspired Palestinians in East Jerusalem to fight Israeli onslaughts on al-Aqsa and the Mosque Esplanade, turning the dispute into a social uprising. Palestinians in Gaza showed solidarity with what was happening in East Jerusalem by launching rockets against Israeli-occupied territory. Although the response was a disproportionate and inhumane bombing that cost the lives of thousands of Palestinians, the summer of 2021 marked the construction of unity among all Palestinians. The Unity Intifada managed to simultaneously mobilize Palestinians from Jerusalem, the West Bank, Gaza, 1948/Israel and those in exile to take to the streets. It revealed how Jerusalem can serve as the material and symbolic centre of Palestinians' struggle for national liberation. Refusal is one of the main reasons East Jerusalem has remained predominantly Palestinian after more than fifty years of occupation, despite intensive Judaization efforts.

However, the rejection of neoliberal politics brings new challenges for the Palestinian National Movement. The anti-colonial stance involves more than just a dispute for Palestinian minds; it also depends on the organizational capacity of the local society to meet the material needs of the Jerusalemite working and middle classes. There are certain conditions that are unavoidable to economically sustain an anti-colonial struggle that challenges Israeli settler colonial power in the OPTs, including the establishment of a suitable minimum wage, formal protections for the unemployed and the reactivation of social security (Hanieh, 2016). That is, it requires a state power that Palestinians don't have, and the PA cannot fulfil this role because of settler colonial restrictions. The absence of Palestinian institutions that are capable of universalizing socio-economic support to include the native population in East Jerusalem is undoubtedly a limiting factor, but not an impediment. East Jerusalem will need to count on the solidarity of the entire Palestinian people, of the bourgeoisie and political elites and of Israeli and international actors determined to support an anti-colonial mobilization outside the paradigms of neoliberal hegemony.

Winning the city back requires a grassroots movement that rejects the neoliberal settler colonial programmes and provides a material alternative. The Black Panther Breakfast Programme is an example of a community service programme from the 1970s. Its goal was to feed hungry people and feed the revolution. Another significant case is the Solidarity Kitchens of the Brazilian Homeless Workers' Movement.[2] During the COVID pandemic, they started an Emergency Aid programme in the urban peripheries, whereas the Jair Bolsonaro administration was pushing people to work on the streets, mainly the urban informal workers or 'entrepreneurs'. As a result, hunger and death dramatically rose. The Solidarity Kitchens fed those who had no other alternative and allowed them to stay at home, safe from the pandemic. It also allowed the Homeless Workers' Movement – which was portrayed by the media and bolsonaristas as an 'extremist' and 'terrorist' communist organization – to reach people in the urban periphery who are hard to reach otherwise. Moreover, this programme certainly helped Luis Inácio Lula da Silva, the leader of the Worker's Party, defeat Jair Bolsonaro in 2022 elections, winning in major urban centres such as São Paulo, a bolsonarista stronghold. It also gave more than 1 million votes to the coordinator of the Homeless Workers' Movement, Guilherme Boulos, for his candidacy to the House of Representatives – he is the most voted left-wing representative in Brazilian history.

Because of its location and the way people live there, Jerusalem could be a model for building a new kind of solidarity and peace between Palestinians and Israelis. The chance to structure a city in which all Jerusalemites can enjoy a communal way of life must be seized to set forth on the path to decolonization and the emancipation of all. In the same way that its urban space is a vessel for the global movements of capitalism, the regional geopolitics of the Middle East and the national characteristics of the Palestine/Israel settler colonial conflict, Jerusalem can be a centre for disrupting hegemonic orders. As with movements like the Arab Spring, the city is a place where contradictions come together in dramatic ways, despite attempts to make things normal, and misdirection that is driven by ideology. Cities can bring together feelings from all over the world, embracing new ways of life and spreading resistance and insurgency methods. The sumud of Palestinian Jerusalemites and the efforts of some groups to change the ways settler colonialism works show, without a doubt, how powerful resistance practices can be. East Jerusalem has a great symbolic representation for different people. It makes a great place to start a new way of thinking that will finally lead to people's freedom and emancipation.

---

[2] Movimento dos Trabalhadores Sem Teto (MTST).

References

Abdo, N., and Yuval-Davis, N. (1995). Palestine, Israel and the Zionist settler project. In N. Yuval-Davis and D. K. Stasiulis (eds), *Unsettling settler societies: Articulations of gender, race, ethnicity and class* (pp. 291–322). Sage Publications.

Abilio, L. C. (2019). Uberização: Do empreendedorismo para o autogerenciamento subordinado. *Psicoperspectivas*, 18(3), 11.

Abowd, T. P. (2014). *Colonial Jerusalem: The spatial construction of identity and difference in a city of myth, 1948-2012* (1st ed.). Syracuse University Press.

Alami, H. (2019, August). Interview with Hani Alami (Jest), Jerusalem (B. Huberman, interviewer).

Alfasi, N., and Ganan, E. (2015). Jerusalem of (foreign) gold: Entrepreneurship and pattern-driven policy in a historic city. *Urban Geography*, 36(2), 157–80. https://doi.org/10.1080/02723638.2014.977051.

Al-Husseini, L. (2019, June). Interview with Louay Al-Husseini (Arab Chamber of Commerce, Jerusalem), Jerusalem (B. Huberman, interviewer).

Alkhalili, N. (2017). 'A forest of urbanization': Camp Metropolis in the edge areas. *Settler Colonial Studies*, 9(2), 1–20. https://doi.org/10.1080/2201473X.2017.1409398.

Al-Nayzak. (2020). www.alnayzak.org.

Alva, N. (2016). Palestinian workers campaign for social justice. *Middle East Report*, 281, 10–14.

Ameen. (2019, July). Interview with Ameen (Estudante palestino de ciência da computação na Universidade Hebraica), Jerusalem (Bruno Huberman, interviewer).

Amuhammad. (2019, August). Interview with Amuhamad, Jerusalem (Bruno Huberman, interviewer).

Anghie, A. (2005). *Imperialism, sovereignty, and the making of international law*. Cambridge University Press.

Anwar College. (2020). www.anwarcollege.org/ar.

Arafeh, N. (2016a). *Economic collapse in East Jerusalem: Strategies for recovery*. Al-Shabaka.

Arafeh, N. (2016b). Israel's colonial projection and future plans for Jerusalem. *Jerusalem Quarterly*, 68, 14.

Arafeh, N. (2016c). The current state of the markets in the Old City of Jerusalem. *Palestine Economic Policy Research Institute Background Paper*, 27 July.

Arafeh, N. (2016d). *Which Jerusalem? Israel's little known master plans*. Al-Shabaka.

Arafeh, N. (2018). 'Resistance economy': A new buzzword? *Journal für entwicklungspolitik*, 34(1), 91–102.

Arafeh, N. (2020). Jerusalem under continuous settler colonialism (1967–present). *Middle East Insights*, 228, 7.

Arafeh, N., and Khalidi, R. (2017). Local economic development (LED) for the state of Palestine: Economic mapping of Eastern Tubas. *Palestine Economic Policy Research Institute Economic Summary*, July.

Arafeh, N., Samman, M., and Khalidi, R. (2016). Israel's colonial projection and future plans for Jerusalem. *Jerusalem Quarterly*, 68, 14.

Ariella. (2019, July). Interview with Ariella (Municipality of Jerusalem), Jerusalem (B. Huberman, interviewer).

Assaf-Shapira, Y., Gefen, A., Haddad, N., and Yaniv, O. (2022). *Statistical yearbook of Jerusalem 2022*. Jerusalem Institute for Policy Research.

Baidoun, S. (2019, June). Interview with Sahr Baidoun (Madaa Creative Center, Silwan), Jerusalem (B. Huberman, interviewer).

Barakat, R. (2016). The Jerusalem fellah: Popular politics in mandate-era Palestine. *Journal of Palestine Studies*, 46(1), 7–19. https://doi.org/10.1525/jps.2016.46.1.7

Barakat, R. (2018). Writing/righting Palestine studies: Settler colonialism, indigenous sovereignty and resisting the ghost(s) of history, *Settler Colonial Studies*, 8(3), 349–63.

Barel-Sabag, O. (2019, June). Interview with Oded Barel-Sabag (JNext – Jerusalem Development Authority), Jerusalem (B. Huberman, interviewer).

Barros, D. R. (2019). *Lugar de negro, lugar de branco? Esboço para uma crítica à metafísica racial*. Hedra.

Barrows-Friedman, N. (2012). Racism pushing Palestinian citizens of Israel to Ramallah. *Electronic Intifada*, 12 September. https://electronicintifada.net/content/racism-pushing-palestinian-citizens-israel-ramallah/11664

Bartal, S. (2017). Lone-wolf or terror organization members acting alone: New look at the last Israeli–Palestine incidents. *Middle Eastern Studies*, 53(2), 211–28. https://doi.org/10.1080/00263206.2016.1217844.

Baumann, H. (2016). Enclaves, borders, and everyday movements: Palestinian marginal mobility in East Jerusalem. *Cities*, 59, 173–82. https://doi.org/10.1016/j.cities.2015.10.012.

Baumann, H. (2018). The violence of infrastructural connectivity: Jerusalem's light rail as a means of normalisation. *Middle East: Topics & Arguments*, 10. https://doi.org/10.17192/meta.2018.10.7593.

Bhandar, B. (2018). *Colonial lives of property: Law, land, and racial regimes of ownership*. Duke University Press.

Bhattacharyya, G. (2018). *Rethinking racial capitalism: Questions of reproduction and survival*. Rowman & Littlefield.

Blatman-Thomas, N., and Porter, L. (2018). Placing property: Theorizing the urban from settler colonial cities. *International Journal of Urban and Regional Research*. https://doi.org/10.1111/1468-2427.12666.

Blum, B. (2020). High-tech hopes: Addressing Israel's engineering shortage. *Jerusalem Post*, August. www.jpost.com/jerusalem-report/high-tech-hopes-addressing-israels-engineering-shortage-637325?utm_source=ActiveCampaign&utm_medium=email&utm_content=High-tech+hopes+-+Addressing+Israel+s+engineering+shortage&utm_campaign=Premium+plus+August+7.

Boer, D. V. (2016). Toward decolonization in tourism: Engaged tourism and the Jerusalem tourism cluster. *Jerusalem Quarterly*, 65, 13.

Botelho, M. L. (2013). Crise urbana no Rio de Janeiro: Favelização e empreendedorismo dos pobres. In F. Brito and P. R. de Oliveria (eds), *Até o último homem: Visões cariocas da administração armada da vida social* (pp. 169–213). Boitempo.

Boxerman, A. (2020). As mammoth high-tech hub is eyed for East Jerusalem, will it benefit locals? *Times of Israel*, 14 June. www.timesofisrael.com/as-mammoth-high-tech-hub-is-eyed-for-east-jerusalem-will-it-benefit-locals.

Braga, R. (2017). *A rebeldia do precariado*. Boitempo Editorial.

Braier, M., and Yacobi, H. (2017). The planned, the unplanned and the hyper-planned: Dwelling in contemporary Jerusalem. *Planning Theory & Practice*, 18(1), 109–24. https://doi.org/10.1080/14649357.2016.1266505.

Busbridge, R. (2018). Israel-Palestine and the settler colonial 'turn': From interpretation to decolonization. *Theory, Culture & Society*, 35(1), 91–115. https://doi.org/10.1177/0263276416688544.

Chatterjee, P. (1993). *The nation and its fragments: Colonial and postcolonial histories*, vol. 4. Princeton University Press.

Chiodelli, F. (2012). Planning illegality: The roots of unauthorised housing in Arab East Jerusalem. *Cities*, 29(2), 99–106. https://doi.org/10.1016/j.cities.2011.07.008.

Chiodelli, F. (2016). *Shaping Jerusalem: Spatial planning, politics and the conflict* (1st ed.). Routledge.

Clarno, A. (2017). *Neoliberal apartheid: Palestine/Israel and South Africa after 1994.* University of Chicago Press.

Cohen, H. (2010). *Good Arabs: The Israeli security agencies and the Israeli Arabs, 1948–1967.* University of California Press.

Cohen, H. (2011). *The rise and fall of Arab Jerusalem.* Routledge.

Cohen-Bar, E., and Kronish, S. (2013). *Survey of Palestinian neighborhoods in East Jerusalem: Planning problems and opportunities.* Bimkom.

Collins, J. (2011). *Global Palestine.* C Hurst.

Coulthard, G. S. (2014). *Red skin, white masks: Rejecting the colonial politics of recognition.* University of Minnesota Press.

Dagoni, N. (2019a). *Monitoring government Decision 3790 for investment in East Jerusalem.* Ir Amin.

Dagoni, N. (2019b, July). Interview with Noa Dagoni (Ir Amin), Jerusalem (B. Huberman, interviewer).

Dagoni, N., and Wegner, E. (2020). *Monitor report on the implementation of Government Decision 3790 for investment in East Jerusalem.* Ir Amin and WAC-Maan.

Dagoni, N., and Wegner, E. (2022). *Three years since the implementation of Government Decision 3790 for socio-economic investment in East Jerusalem.* Ir Amin and WAC-Maan.

Dakkak, A. (2019, August). Interview with Adnan Dakkak (Old City Shopkeeper), Jerusalem (B. Huberman, interviewer).

Dana, T. (2014a). A resistance economy: What is it and can it provide an alternative? *Rosa Luxemburg Stiftung,* 14 November.

Dana, T. (2014b). The Palestinian capitalists that gone too far. *Al-Shabaka,* 14 January.

Dana, T. (2015). The symbiosis between Palestinian 'Fayyadism' and Israeli 'economic peace': The political economy of capitalist peace in the context of colonisation. *Conflict, Security & Development,* 15(5), 455–77. https://doi.org/10.1080/14678 802.2015.1100013.

Dana, T. (2016). Social struggle and the crisis of the Palestinian left parties. *Rosa Luxemburg,* March.

Dana, T. (2019). The prolonged decay of the Palestinian National Movement. *National Identities,* 21(1), 39–55. https://doi.org/10.1080/14608944.2017.1343813.

Dana, T., and Jarbawi, A. (2017). A century of settler colonialism in Palestine: Zionism's entangled project. *Brown Journal of World Affairs,* 24(1), 23.

Dardot, P., Gueguen, H., and Laval, C. (2021). *Escolha da Guerra Civil, A.* Elefante Editora.

Dardot, P., and Laval, C. (2017). *The new way of the world: On neoliberal society* (G. Elliott, trans.). Verso Books.

Davis, M. (2006). *Planeta Favela* (1st ed.). Boitempo.

De Angelis, M. (2001). Marx and primitive accumulation: The continuous character of capital's 'enclosures'. *The Commoner*, 2(1), 1–22.

Dorries, H., Hugill, D., and Tomiak, J. (2019). Racial capitalism and the production of settler colonial cities. *Geoforum*, S001671851930226X. https://doi.org/10.1016/j.geoforum.2019.07.016.

Dumper, M. (2014). *Jerusalem unbound: Geography, history, and the future of the holy city*. Columbia University Press.

DW. (2019). Young Palestinian entrepreneurs: Business without borders. 20 September. www.dw.com/en/young-palestinian-entrepreneurs-business-without-borders/a-50493101.

Elhan. (2019, August). Entrevista com Elhan (entrepeneur), Jerusalem (B. Huberman, interviewer).

Englert, S. (2017). *The defeat of Hebrew labour?* SOAS.

Englert, S. (2020). Settlers, workers, and the logic of accumulation by dispossession. *Antipode*, 52(6), 1647–66.

Erlanger, S. (2005). An ultra-orthodox mayor in an unorthodox city. *New York Times*, 16 July. www.nytimes.com/2005/07/16/world/middleeast/an-ultraorthodox-mayor-in-an-unorthodox-city.html.

Fanon, F. (1963). *The wretched of the earth*. Grove Press.

Fanon, F. (1994). *Toward the African revolution*. Grove Press.

Farah, M. (2019). The Atarot exception? Business and human rights under colonization. *Jerusalem Quarterly*, 80, 16.

Farsakh, L. (2005). *Palestinian labour migration to Israel: Labour, land and occupation* (1st ed.). Routledge. https://doi.org/10.4324/9780203431658.

Faustino, D. M. (2018). Frantz Fanon: Capitalismo, racismo e a sociogênese do colonialismo (Frantz Fanon: Capitalism, racism and the sociogenesis of colonialism). *SER Social*, 20(42), 148–63.

Fieldhouse, D. K. (1966). *The colonial empires: A comparative survey from the eighteenth century*. Springer.

Fortier, C., and Wong, E. H.-S. (2019). The settler colonialism of social work and the social work of settler colonialism. *Settler Colonial Studies*, 9(4), 437–56. https://doi.org/10.1080/2201473X.2018.1519962.

Foucault, M. (2010). *The birth of biopolitics: Lectures at the Collège de France, 1978–1979* (2008th ed.). Palgrave Macmillan.

Fraser, N. (2017). From progressive neoliberalism to Trump – and beyond. *American Affairs*, 1(4), 15.

Ghoul, D. (2019, July). Interview with Daoud Ghoul, Jerusalem (B. Huberman, interviewer).

Gilmore, R. W. (2007). *Golden Gulag: Prisons, surplus, crisis, and opposition in globalizing California*. University of California Press.

Goldberg, D. T. (2011). *The threat of race: Reflections on racial neoliberalism*. John Wiley.

Gorenberg, G. (2007). *The accidental empire: Israel and the birth of the settlements, 1967–1977*. I. B. Tauris.

Grandinetti, T. (2015). The Palestinian middle class in Rawabi: Depoliticizing the occupation. *Alternatives*, 40(1), 63–78.

Grassiani, E., and Volinz, L. (2016). Intimidation, reassurance, and invisibility: Israeli security agents in the Old City of Jerusalem. *Focaal*, 2016(75). https://doi.org/10.3167/fcl.2016.750102.

Greenstein, R. (2015). Israel, the apartheid analogy, and the labor question. In J. Soske and S. Jacobs (eds), *Apartheid Israel: The politics of an analogy* (pp. 29–38). Haymarket Books.

Grove, J. (2016). The stories we tell about killing. *Disorder of Things*, 6 January. https://thedisorderofthings.com/2016/01/06/the-stories-we-tell-about-killing.

Gutwein, D. (2017). The settlements and the relationship between privatization and the occupation. In M. Allegra, A. Handel and E. Maggor (eds), *Normalizing occupation: The politics of everyday life in the West Bank settlements* (p. 34). Indiana University Press.

Haddad, T. (2015). Neoliberalism and Palestinian development: Assessment and alternatives. In *Critical readings of development under colonialism: Towards a political economy for liberation in the Occupied Palestinian Territories*. Rosa Luxemburg Stiftung Regional Office Palestine and Birzeit University Center for Development Studies (pp. 33–67).

Haddad, T. (2016). *Palestine Ltd: Neoliberalism and nationalism in the Occupied Territory*. I. B. Tauris.

Haider, A. (2018). *Mistaken identity: Race and class in the age of Trump*. Verso Books.

Hall, S. (1988). *The hard road to renewal: Thatcherism and the crisis of the left*. Verso Books.

Halon, E. (2019). Leading Arab entrepreneur: Hi-tech is the foundation for coexistence. *Jerusalem Post*, December. www.jpost.com/israel-news/leading-arab-entrepreneur-hi-tech-is-the-foundation-for-coexistence-612205.

Halper, J. (2015). *War against the people: Israel, the Palestinians and global pacification*. Pluto Press.

Hanieh, A. (2013). *Lineages of revolt: Issues of contemporary capitalism in the Middle East*. Haymarket Books.

Hanieh, A. (2016). Development as struggle: Confronting the reality of power in Palestine. *Journal of Palestine Studies*, 45(4), 32–47. https://doi.org/10.1525/jps.2016.45.4.32.

Harris, C. (2004). How did colonialism dispossess? Comments from an edge of empire. *Annals of the Association of American Geographers*, 94(1), 165–82.

Harvey, D. (2003). *The new imperialism*. Oxford University Press.

Harvey, D. (2005). *A Producao Capitalista do Espaço*. Annablume.

Harvey, D. (2007). *A brief history of neoliberalism*. Oxford University Press.

Hasan, H. (2018). Remembering the 2014 Israeli offensive against Gaza. *Middle East Monitor*, 8 July. www.middleeastmonitor.com/20180708-remembering-the-2014-israeli-offensive-against-gaza.

Hassan, B., and Alsaafin, L. (2017). The battle for al-Aqsa 'has just started'. *Aljazeera*, 22 August. www.aljazeera.com/features/2017/8/22/the-battle-for-al-aqsa-has-just-started.

Hasson, N. (2016). Right-wing master plan envisages mega-Jerusalem in 2040: With invisible Palestinians. *Haaretz*, 28 November. www.haaretz.com/israel-news/.premium.MAGAZINE-rightist-plan-mega-jerusalem-in-2040-with-invisible-palestinians-1.5465629.

Hasson, N. (2017). Hebrew University to become first Israeli school to recognize Palestinian Authority test scores. *Haaretz*, 3 March. www.haaretz.com/israel-news/.premium-hebrew-university-to-recognize-palestinian-authority-test-scores-1.5443610.

Hasson, N. (2018a). Cabinet approves billions to ramp up Israeli sovereignty in East Jerusalem. *Haaretz*, May. www.haaretz.com/israel-news/.premium-cabinet-oks-billions-to-ramp-up-israeli-sovereignty-in-e-j-lem-1.6078168.

Hasson, N. (2018b). Palestinian vying for Jerusalem City Council perseveres despite violence against his campaign. *Haaretz*, October. www.haaretz.com/israel-news/.premium-palestinian-vying-for-j-lem-city-council-perseveres-despite-violence-1.6573895.

Hasson, N. (2019a). Israel's government liaisons to East Jerusalem are mostly ex-Shin Bet. *Haaretz*, August. www.haaretz.com/israel-news/.premium-most-government-liaisons-to-east-jerusalem-are-ex-shin-bet-1.7620845.

Hasson, N. (2019b). Palestinians are attending Hebrew U in record numbers, changing the face of Jerusalem. *Haaretz*, 1 November. www.haaretz.com/isr

ael-news/.premium-palestinians-are-attending-hebrew-university-in-record-numbers-and-changing-j-lem-1.8063702.

Hasson, N. (2020a). Two years in, Israeli plan for East Jerusalem slowly brings about change. *Haaretz*, May. www.haaretz.com/israel-news/.premium-two-years-in-israeli-plan-for-jerusalem-s-palestinians-slowly-brings-about-change-1.8862784.

Hasson, N. (2020b). Israel picks up pace, grants citizenship to 1,200 East Jerusalem Palestinians. *Haaretz*, 12 January. www.haaretz.com/israel-news/.premium-israel-picks-up-pace-grants-citizenship-to-1-200-east-jerusalem-palestinians-1.8384270.

Hermetz, Y. (2019, July). Interview with Yael Hermetz (Riyan Center), Jerusalem (B. Huberman, interviewer).

Hever, S. (2018). Securing the occupation in East Jerusalem: Divisions in Israeli policy. *Jerusalem Quarterly*, 75, 104–14.

Hilal, J. (2015). Rethinking Palestine: Settler-colonialism, neo-liberalism and individualism in the West Bank and Gaza Strip. *Contemporary Arab Affairs*, 8(3), 351–62. https://doi.org/10.1080/17550912.2015.1052226.

Huberman, B., and Nasser, R. M. (2019). Pacification, capital accumulation, and resistance in settler colonial cities: The cases of Jerusalem and Rio de Janeiro. *Latin American Perspectives*, 46(3), 131–48. https://doi.org/10.1177/0094582X19835523.

Hussein, C. (2015). *The re-emergence of the single state solution in Palestine/Israel: Countering an illusion*. Routledge.

Husseini, A. (2019, July). Interview with Aref Husseini (Al-Nayzak), Jerusalem (B. Huberman, interviewer).

Ihmoud, S. (2015). Mohammed Abu-Khdeir and the politics of racial terror in Occupied Jerusalem. *Borderlands*, 14(1), 28.

Inter-agency Task Force on Israeli Arab Issues. (2019). *Government Resolution 922: Five-year economic development plan for Arab society mid-term for Arab society government implementation update*. Inter-agency Task Force on Israeli Arab Issues.

International Crisis Group. (2019). *Reversing Israel's deepening annexation of Occupied East Jerusalem*. Middle East Report No. 202. International Crisis Group.

Ir Amin. (2019). New map release: Settlement ring around the Old City. www.ir-amim.org.il/en/node/2278.

Ir Amin. (2020). *From creeping to formal annexation: Israel's actions under American auspices to actualize 'Greater Jerusalem'*. Ir Amin.

Ir Amin. (2022). Map of Greater Jerusalem. www.ir-amim.org.il/en/node/2618.

ISRAEL21c. (2016). High-tech school for boys opens in Arab East Jerusalem. *ISRAEL21c*, 20 January. www.israel21c.org/high-tech-school-for-boys-opens-in-arab-east-jerusalem.

Issar, Y. (2019, June). Interview with Yara Issar (East Jerusalem Development Authority), Jerusalem (B. Huberman, interviewer).

Jabbour, G. (1970). *Settler colonialism in southern Africa and the Middle East*. University of Khartoum.

Jafari, M., Abdullah, S., Safadi, A., and Salah, S. (2019). *East Jerusalem's economic cluster report*. Palestine Economic Policy Research Institute.

JDC-Israel. (2020). www.thejoint.org.il/en.

Jewish Chronicle. (2019). High-tech is model for shared living, say co-CEOs. 28 January. https://jewishchronicle.timesofisrael.com/high-tech-is-model-for-shared-living-say-co-ceos.

JTA. (2004). New nonprofit aims to boost Jerusalem's ailing economy. *Jewish Telegraphic Agency*, 25 October. www.jta.org/2004/10/25/archive/new-nonprofit-aims-to-boost-jerusalems-ailing-economy.

The Kaizen Company. (2016). Smart-X. www.thekaizencompany.com/project/smartx.

Kassabri, M. K. (2019, July). Interview with Mona Khuri Kassabri (Hebrew University), Jerusalem (B. Huberman, interviewer).

Keidar, N. (2018). Making Jerusalem 'cooler': Creative script, youth flight, and diversity. *City & Community*, 17(4), 1209–30. https://doi.org/10.1111/cico.12339.

Kelley, R. (2017). What did Cedric Robinson mean by racial capitalism? *Boston Review*, 12, Published online: https://www.bostonreview.net/articles/robin-d-g-kelley-introduction-race-capitalism-justice/

Khalidi, R. (2006). *The iron cage: The story of the Palestinian struggle for statehood*. Beacon Press.

Khalidi, R. (2010). *Palestinian identity: The construction of modern national consciousness*. Columbia University Press.

Khalidi, R. (2013). *The Palestinian economy in East Jerusalem: Enduring annexation, isolation and disintegration*. UNCTAD.

Khalidi, R., and Samour, S. (2011). Neoliberalism as liberation: The statehood program and the remaking of the Palestinian National Movement. *Journal of Palestine Studies*, 40(2), 20.

Khalili, L. (2012). *Time in the shadows: Confinement in counterinsurgencies*. Stanford University Press.

Khattab, H. (2019, August). Interview with Hazem Khattab (Co-Impact), Jerusalem (Bruno Huberman, interviewer).

Korach, M., and Choshen, M. (2019). *Jerusalem: Facts and trends 2019: The state of the city and changing trends*. Jerusalem Institute for Policy Research.

Koren, D. (2017). Eastern Jerusalem: End of an intermediate era. *JISS*, 31 October. https://jiss.org.il/en/eastern-jerusalem.

Koren, D. (2018). Memo to the incoming mayor of Jerusalem: Policy guidelines for Eastern Jerusalem. *JISS*, 4 December. https://jiss.org.il/en/koren-memo-to-the-incoming-mayor-of-jerusalem-policy-guidelines-for-eastern-jerusalem.

Laval, C. (2019). *A escola não é uma empresa: O neoliberalismo em ataque ao ensino público*. Boitempo Editorial.

Leichtag Foundation. (2018). Jerusalem renewal. 16 June. https://leichtag.org/strategic-focus-and-grantmaking/jerusalem-renewal.

Lemke, T. (2015). *Foucault, governmentality, and critique* (1st ed.). Routledge.

Lis, J. (2005). The best medicine for Jerusalem. *Haaretz*, May. www.haaretz.com/1.4853342.

Lloyd, D., and Wolfe, P. (2016). Settler colonial logics and the neoliberal regime. *Settler Colonial Studies*, 6(2), 109–18. https://doi.org/10.1080/2201473X.2015.1035361.

Lockman, Z. (1996). *Comrades and enemies: Arab and Jewish workers in Palestine, 1906–1948*. University of California Press.

Lorde, A. (2019). *Irmã outsider: Ensaios e conferências*. Autêntica Editora.

Machold, R. (2015). Mobility and the model: Policy mobility and the becoming of Israeli homeland security dominance. *Environment and Planning A: Economy and Space*, 47(4), 816–32. https://doi.org/10.1068/a140010p.

Mahfouz, M. (2019, August). Interview with Mira Mahfouz (Jerusalem Foundation), Jerusalem (B. Huberman, interviewer).

Makdisi, S. (2018). Apartheid. *Critical Inquiry*, 44(2), 304–30. https://doi.org/10.1086/695377.

Mamdani, M. (2001). Beyond settler and native as political identities: Overcoming the political legacy of colonialism. *Comparative Studies in Society and History*, 43(4), 651–64.

Mamdani, M. (2015). Settler colonialism: Then and now. *Critical Inquiry*, 41(3), 596–614. https://doi.org/10.1086/680088.

Mansour, A. (2018). The conflict over Jerusalem: A settler-colonial perspective. *Journal of Holy Land and Palestine Studies*, 17(1), 9–23. https://doi.org/10.3366/hlps.2018.0176.

Margalit, M. (2018). *Jerusalén, la ciudad imposible*. Catarata.

Markose, A. (2019, July). Interview with Ariel Markose (Jerusalem Model – Leichtag Foundation), Jerusalem (B. Huberman, interviewer).

Marx, K. (2010). *Sobre a questão judaica*. Boitempo Editorial.

Mbembe, A. (2015). On Palestine. In J. Soske and S. Jacobs (eds), *Apartheid Israel: The politics of an analogy* (pp. 8–9). Haymarket Books.

Mbembe, J.-A. (2003). Necropolitics. *Public Culture*, 15(1), 11–40.

Melamed, J. (2011). *Represent and destroy: Rationalizing violence in the new racial capitalism*. University of Minnesota Press.

Memmi, A. (1974). *The colonizer and the colonized*. Earthscan.

Memo. (2020). Prominent Palestinian husband and wife released after brief detention by Israel. *Middle East Monitor*, 23 July. www.middleeastmonitor.com/20200 723-prominent-palestinian-husband-and-wife-released-after-brief-detention-by-israel.

Mohamed. (2019, July). Interview with Mohamed (Palestinian Union of Jerusalem), Jerusalem (B. Huberman, interviewer).

Morgensen, S. L. (2011). The biopolitics of settler colonialism: Right here, right now. *Settler Colonial Studies*, 1(1), 52–76. https://doi.org/10.1080/22014 73X.2011.10648801.

Morozov, E. (2018). *Big tech*. Ubu Editora.

Naftali, Y., Shtern, M., Asmar, A., Kimhi, I., Nahel, M., and Natsheh, M. (2018). Vocational training: A tool for employment integration of East Jerusalem residents. *Jerusalem Institute for Policy Research*, 491, 69.

Nasara, M. (2019). Occupied East Jerusalem since the Oslo Accords: Isolation and evisceration. In M. Turner (ed.), *From the river to the sea: Palestine and Israel in the shadow of 'peace'* (pp. 213–44). Rowman & Littlefield.

Neocleous, M. (2011). 'A brighter and nicer new life': Security as pacification. *Social & Legal Studies*, 20(2), 191–208. https://doi.org/10.1177/0964663910395816.

Neocleous, M. (2017). Fundamentals of pacification theory: Twenty-six articles. In T. Wall, P. Saberi and W. Jackson (eds), *Destroy, build, secure: Readings on pacification* (pp. 13–27). Red Quill Books.

Nesher, M. (2018). *Illegal construction, bloody conflicts and two billion shekels a year: The price of lack of land rights in East Jerusalem*. Jerusalem Institute for Policy Research.

The New Arab. (2020). 'Israeli gentrification': Palestinian business owners fear expulsion for high-tech 'Silicon Wadi' hub in Jerusalem. 8 June. https://engl ish.alaraby.co.uk/english/news/2020/6/8/palestinians-fear-expulsion-for-isra eli-high-tech-hub-in-jerusalem.

Newman, D. (2017). Settlement as suburbanization. In M. Allegra, A. Handel and E. Maggor (eds), *Normalizing occupation: The politics of everyday life in the West Bank settlements* (p. 34). Indiana University Press.

Nijam, M. (2019, July). Interview with Mohamad Nijam (East Jerusalem Development Authority), Jerusalem (B. Huberman, interviewer).

Nolte, A. (2016). Political infrastructure and the politics of infrastructure: The Jerusalem light rail. *City*, 20(3), 441–54. https://doi.org/10.1080/13604 813.2016.1169778.

Nolte, A., and Yacobi, H. (2015). Politics, infrastructure and representation: The case of Jerusalem's light rail. *Cities*, 43, 28–36. https://doi.org/10.1016/j.cit ies.2014.10.011.

Noura. (2019, July). Interview with Noura (Step-Up), Jerusalem (B. Huberman, interviewer).

Nuseibeh, S. (2019, June). Interview with Samer Nuseibeh (businessmen), Jerusalem (B. Huberman, interviewer).

OCHA-OPT. (2019). *Increase in destruction of Palestinian property in the West Bank, including East Jerusalem*. United Nations Office for the Coordination of Humanitarian Affairs–Occupied Palestinian Territory. www.ochaopt.org/content/increase-destruction-palestinian-property-west-bank-including-east-jerusalem.

Owens, P. (2016). *Economy of force: Counterinsurgency and the historical rise of the social*. Cambridge University Press.

Pappe, I. (2006). *The ethnic cleansing of Palestine*. South End Press.

Pappe, I. (2015). The framing of the question of Palestine by the early Palestinian press: Zionist settler-colonialism and the newspaper *Filastin*, 1912–1922. *Journal of Holy Land and Palestine Studies*, 14(1), 59–81. https://doi.org/10.3366/hlps.2015.0104.

Peace Now. (2020). Settlements watch. https://peacenow.org.il/en/settlements-watch.

Peled-Elhanan, N. (2013). *Palestine in Israeli school books: Ideology and propaganda in education*. Bloomsbury.

Peres Center for Peace and US Department of State. (2020). *An overview: The business case for Israeli-Palestinian tech sector partnerships*. Peres Center for Peace.

Piterberg, G. (2015). Israeli sociology's young Hegelian: Gershon Shafir and the settler-colonial framework. *Journal of Palestine Studies*, 44(3), 17–38. https://doi.org/10.1525/jps.2015.44.3.17.

PNN. (2019). Palestine to host first International Conference on Entrepreneurship in Bethlehem. *Palestine News Network*. https://group194.net/english/article/63951.

Poets, D. (2020). Settler colonialism and/in (urban) Brazil: Black and indigenous resistances to the logic of elimination. *Settler Colonial Studies*, 11(3), 271–91.

Porter, L., and Yiftachel, O. (2017). Urbanizing settler-colonial studies: Introduction to the special issue. *Settler Colonial Studies*, 9(2), 177–86. https://doi.org/10.1080/2201473X.2017.1409394.

Prime Minister Office. (2018). Resolution Number 3790: Reducing socio-economic disparities and economic development in East Jerusalem. *Estado de Israel*. www.gov.il/he/departments/policies/dec3790_2018.

Pullan, W. (2011). Frontier urbanism: The periphery at the centre of contested cities. *Journal of Architecture*, 16(1), 15–35. https://doi.org/10.1080/13602365.2011.546999.

Quteineh, R. (2019, June). Interview with Rana Quteineh (Jest), Jerusalem (B. Huberman, interviewer).

Radai, I. (2015). *Palestinians in Jerusalem and Jaffa, 1948: A tale of two cities*. Routledge. https://doi.org/10.4324/9781315670751.

Ramon, A. (2021). *Discovering East Jerusalem: Processes that led to Israeli policy change and government Decision 3790*. Jerusalem Institute for Policy Research.

Ravid, B. (2015). Security cabinet authorizes police to impose closure on East Jerusalem neighborhoods. *Haaretz*, 14 October. www.haaretz.com/.premium-cabinet-authorizes-police-to-impose-closure-on-east-j-lem-1.5408630.

Rawabi. (2020). https://www.rawabi.ps.

Robinson, C. J. (2000). *Black Marxism: The making of the Black radical tradition*. University of North Carolina Press.

Robinson, S. N. (2013). *Citizen strangers: Palestinians and the birth of Israel's liberal settler state* (1st ed.). Stanford University Press.

Rodinson, M. (1973). *Israel: A colonial-settler state?* Monad Press for the Anchor Foundation.

Rokem, J., and Vaughan, L. (2018). Segregation, mobility and encounters in Jerusalem: The role of public transport infrastructure in connecting the 'divided city'. *Urban Studies*, 55(15), 3454–73. https://doi.org/10.1177/0042098017691465.

Rokem, J., Weiss, C. M., and Miodownik, D. (2018). Geographies of violence in Jerusalem: The spatial logic of urban intergroup conflict. *Political Geography*, 66, 88–97. https://doi.org/10.1016/j.polgeo.2018.08.008.

Ross, A. (2019). *Stone men: The Palestinians who built Israel*. Verso Books.

Roy, A. (2016). Reimagining resilience: Urbanization and identity in Ramallah and Rawabi. *City*, 20(3), 368–88.

Rubin, E. (2018). Make high-tech, not war: Israel and Palestinians forge cutting-edge coexistence. *Haaretz*, 11 June. www.haaretz.com/israel-news/business/.premium.MAGAZINE-make-high-tech-not-war-israel-palestinians-forge-coexistence-1.6164479.

Saad Filho, A. (2015). Neoliberalismo: Uma análise marxista. *Marx e o Marxismo*, 3(4), 15.

Saadeh, R. (2015). Jerusalem tourism: Challenges and opportunities. *This Week in Palestine, Jerusalem My Beloved City*, February, 80–6.

Saadeh, R. (2019, June). Interview with Raed Saadeh (businessmen), Jerusalem (B. Huberman, interviewer).

Saad-Filho, A. (2005). From Washington to post-Washington consensus: Neoliberal agendas for economic development. In D. Johnston and A. Saad Filho (eds), *Neoliberalism: A critical reader* (vol. 45, pp. 113–19). Pluto Press. https://onlinelibrary.wiley.com/doi/10.1111/j.1745-5871.2007.00432.x.

Sadeh, S. (2018). Evidence is accumulating that ultra-Orthodox Jews, East Jerusalem Arabs, religious Zionists and secular people can team up to cut the city's 46 percent poverty rate. *Haaretz*, December. www.haaretz.com/israel-news/.premium.MAGAZINE-how-to-turn-jerusalem-into-an-economic-powerhouse-1.6724562.

Said, E. W. (1979). Zionism from the standpoint of its victims. *Social Text*, 1, 7–58.

Salamanca, O. J., Qato, M., Rabie, K., and Samour, S. (2012). Past is present: Settler colonialism in Palestine. *Settler Colonial Studies*, 2(1), 1–8. https://doi.org/10.1080/2201473X.2012.10648823.

Salem, S. (2018). Reading Egypt's postcolonial state through Frantz Fanon: Hegemony, dependency and development. *Interventions*, 20(3), 428–45. https://doi.org/10.1080/1369801X.2017.1421041.

Salem, W. (2018). Jerusalemites and the issue of citizenship in the context of Israeli settler-colonialism. *Journal of Holy Land and Palestine Studies*, 17(1), 25–41. https://doi.org/10.3366/hlps.2018.0177.

Samira. (2019, July). Interview with Samira (urban planner), Jerusalem (Bruno Huberman, interviewer).

Samour, S. (2016). *The Palestinian economy between settler colonial invasion and neoliberal management*. School of Oriental and African Studies.

Saps, M. F. (2019). The Palestinians crossing checkpoints and societal divides to work in startup nation. *Haaretz*, 3 March. www.haaretz.com/middle-east-news/palestinians/.premium-the-palestinians-crossing-checkpoints-and-societal-divides-to-work-in-startup-nation-1.6982.

Sawsan. (2019, July). Interview with Sawsan (East Jerusalem school principal), Jerusalem (B. Huberman, interviewer).

Sayegh, F. (2012). Zionist colonialism in Palestine (1965). *Settler Colonial Studies*, 2(1), 206–25. https://doi.org/10.1080/2201473X.2012.10648833.

Seidel, T. (2019). Neoliberal developments, national consciousness, and political economies of resistance in Palestine. *Interventions*, 21(5), 727–46. https://doi.org/10.1080/1369801X.2019.1585921.

Shafir, G. (1996). *Land, labor and the origins of the Israeli-Palestinian conflict, 1882–1914*. University of California Press.

Shalhoub-Kevorkian, N. (2012). Trapped: The violence of exclusion in Jerusalem. *Jerusalem Quarterly*, 49. www.palestine-studies.org/jq/fulltext/78466.

Shalhoub-Kevorkian, N. (2015). *Security theology, surveillance and the politics of fear*. Cambridge University Press.

Shalhoub-Kerkovian, N., and Busbridge, R. (2014). (En)gendering de-development in East Jerusalem: Thinking through the 'everyday'. In M. Turner and O. Shweiki (eds), *Decolonizing Palestinian political economy: De-development and beyond* (pp. 77–94). Palgrave Macmillan.

Shehadeh, M., and Khalidi, R. (2014). Impeded development: The political economy of the Palestinian Arabs inside Israel. In M. Turner and O. Shweiki (eds), *Decolonizing Palestinian political economy: De-development and beyond* (pp. 115–37). Palgrave Macmillan.

Shihade, M. (2012). Settler colonialism and conflict: The Israeli State and its Palestinian subjects. *Settler Colonial Studies*, 2(1), 108–23. https://doi.org/10.1080/2201473X.2012.10648828.

Shlaim, A. (2015). *The iron wall: Israel and the Arab World*. Penguin.

Shlay, A. B., and Rosen, G. (2015). *Jerusalem: The spatial politics of a divided metropolis* (1st ed.). Polity.

Shlomo, O. (2016). Between discrimination and stabilization: The exceptional governmentalities of East Jerusalem. *City*, 20(3), 428–40.

Shohat, E. (1988). Sephardim in Israel: Zionism from the standpoint of its Jewish victims. *Social Text*, 19/20, 1–35. https://doi.org/10.2307/466176.

Shtern, M. (2015). Palestinians in West Jerusalem: Economic dependency amid violent contestation. *Palestine-Israel Journal*, 21(2), 4.

Shtern, M. (2016). Urban neoliberalism vs. ethno-national division: The case of West Jerusalem's shopping malls. *Cities*, 52, 132–9. https://doi.org/10.1016/j.cities.2015.11.019.

Shtern, M. (2017). *Polarized labor integration: East Jerusalem Palestinians in the city's employment market*. Jerusalem Institute for Policy Research.

Shtern, M. (2018a). *Between the wall and the mall: Geographies of encounter between Israelis and Palestinians in Jerusalem*. Ben Gurion University. www.academia.edu/37854825/Between_the_Wall_and_the_Mall_Geographies_of_Encounter_between_Israelis_and_Palestinians_in_Jerusalem.

Shtern, M. (2019). Towards 'ethno-national peripheralisation'? Economic dependency amidst political resistance in Palestinian East Jerusalem. *Urban Studies*, 56(6), 1129–47. https://doi.org/10.1177/0042098018763289.

Shtern, M., and Yacobi, H. (2019). The urban geopolitics of neighboring: Conflict, encounter and class in Jerusalem's settlement/neighborhood. *Urban Geography*, 40(4), 467–87. https://doi.org/10.1080/02723638.2018.1500251.

Siegman, J. A. (2018). *Enemies in the aisles: On the micropolitics of antagonism in the Occupied West Bank*. University of Chicago Press.

Simpson, A. (2017). The ruse of consent and the anatomy of 'refusal': Cases from indigenous North America and Australia. *Postcolonial Studies*, 20(1), 18–33.

Singh, N. P. (2016). On race, violence, and so-called primitive accumulation. *Social Text*, 34(3), 27–50.

Sinocrot, M. (2019, June). Interview Mazen Sinocrot (businessmen), Ramallah (B. Huberman, interviewer).

Soske, J., and Jacobs, S. (eds) (2015). *Apartheid Israel: The politics of an analogy*. Haymarket Books.

Spivak, G. C. (2010). Can the subaltern speak? In R. Morris (ed.), *Can the subaltern speak? Reflections on the history of an idea* (pp. 21–78). Columbia University Press.

Stoll, I. (2019). Meet the two most optimistic people in the entire Middle East. *The Algemeiner*, 16 January. www.algemeiner.com/2019/01/16/meet-the-two-most-optimistic-people-in-the-entire-middle-east.

Strakosch, E. (2015). *Neoliberal indigenous policy: Settler colonialism and the 'post-welfare' state*. Palgrave Macmillan. http://public.eblib.com/choice/publicfullrecord.aspx?p=4008660.

Tabash, R. (2019, July). Interview with Ramadan Tabash (head of Sur Baher Community Center), Jerusalem (B. Huberman, interviewer).

Tamari, S. (2011). Confessionalism and public space in Ottoman and colonial Jerusalem. In D. Davis and N. Duren (eds), *Cities and sovereignty: Identity politics in urban spaces* (pp. 59–82). Indiana University Press.

Tatour, L. (2016). *Domination and resistance in liberal settler colonialism: Palestinians in Israel between the homeland and the transnational*. University of Warwick.

Taylor, K.-Y. (2021). *Race for profit: How banks and the real estate industry undermined Black homeownership*. University of North Carolina Press.

Tilley, L., and Shilliam, R. (2018). Raced markets: An introduction. *New Political Economy*, 23(5), 534–43.

Tobi, G. (2019, July). Interview with Golan Tobi (MATI), Jerusalem (B. Huberman, interviewer).

de Tommasi, L., and Velazco, D. (2013). A produção de um novo regime discursivo sobre as favelas cariocas e as muitas faces do empreendedorismo de base comunitária. *Revista do Instituto de Estudos Brasileiros*, 56, 15. https://doi.org/10.11606/issn.2316-901X.v0i56p15-42.

de Tommasi, L., and Velazco, D. (2016). O governo dos jovens e as favelas cariocas. *DILEMAS: Revista de Estudos de Conflito e Controle Social*, 3, 26.

Toren, Y. (2019, July). Interview with Yaron Toren (Municipality of Jerusalem), Jerusalem (B. Huberman, interviewer).

Tress, L., and Munin, R. (2015). At annual summit, entrepreneurs seek to rebrand 'social good'. *Times of Israel*, 14 June. www.timesofisrael.com/at-the-annual-roi-summit-rebranding-social-good.

Veracini, L. (2010). *Settler colonialism: A theoretical overview*. Palgrave Macmillan.

Veracini, L. (2015). *The settler colonial present*. Palgrave Macmillan.

Veracini, L. (2016). Facing the settler colonial present. In S. Maddison, T. Clark and R. de Costa (eds), *The limits of settler colonial reconciliation: Non-indigenous people and the responsibility to engage* (pp. 41–54). Springer Singapore. www.springer.com/la/book/9789811026539.

Volinz, L. (2018). Crafting and reinforcing the state through security privatisation: Territorialisation as a public–private state project in East Jerusalem. *Policing and Society*, 29(9), 1077–90. https://doi.org/10.1080/10439463.2018.1489396.

Wac-Maan. (2018). Palestinian workers in Mishor Adumim unionize with WAC, strike for collective agreement. http://eng.wac-maan.org.il/?p=2223.

Wafa. (2020). Rights group says Israel's assault on East Jerusalem cultural centers a flagrant violation of international law. *WAFA Agency*, 23 July. http://wafa.ps/Pages/Details/118622.

Wallach, Y. (2016). Jerusalem between segregation and integration: Reading urban space through the eyes of Justice Gad Frumkin. In S. R. Goldstein-Sabbah and H. L. Murre-van den Berg (eds), *Modernity, minority, and the public sphere: Jews and Christians in the Middle East* (pp. 205–33). Brill. https://doi.org/10.1163/9789004323285_009.

WEF. (2020). Amani Abu Tair. www.wef.org.in/amani-abu-tair.

Weisman, R. (2009). Harvard helps Jerusalem's mayor with strategy. *Boston Globe*, 27 March. http://archive.boston.com/business/articles/2009/03/27/building_up_jerusalems_economy.

Weizman, E. (2017). *Hollow land: Israel's architecture of occupation*. Verso Books.

Whyte, J. (2019). *The morals of the market: Human rights and the rise of neoliberalism*. Verso Books.

Wilson, K. (2012). *Race, racism and development: Interrogating history, discourse and practice*. Bloomsbury.

Wolfe, P. (1999). *Settler colonialism and the transformation of anthropology: The politics and poetics of an ethnographic event*. Cassell.

Wolfe, P. (2006). Settler colonialism and the elimination of the native. *Journal of Genocide Research*, 8(4), 387–409. https://doi.org/10.1080/14623520601056240.

Wolfe, P. (2011). After the frontier: Separation and absorption in US Indian policy. *Settler Colonial Studies*, 1(1), 13–51. https://doi.org/10.1080/2201473X.2011.10648800.

Wolfe, P. (2016). *Traces of history: Elementary structures of race*. Verso.

Wood, E. M. (2005). *Empire of capital* (new ed.). Verso.

Wootliff, R. (2018). Likud mayoral hopeful Ze'ev Elkin says he will work to keep Jerusalem Jewish. *Times of Israel*. 18 October. www.timesofisrael.com/likud-mayoral-hopeful-zeev-elkin-says-he-will-work-to-keep-jerusalem-jewish.

Yacobi, H. (2012). God, globalization, and geopolitics: On West Jerusalem's gated communities. *Environment and Planning A*, 44(11), 2705–20. https://doi.org/10.1068/a44612.

Yacobi, H. (2016). From 'ethnocracity' to urban apartheid: A view from Jerusalem\al-Quds. *Cosmopolitan Civil Societies: An Interdisciplinary Journal*, 8(3), 100–14. https://doi.org/10.5130/ccs.v8i3.5107.

Yacobi, H., and Pullan, W. (2014). The geopolitics of neighbourhood: Jerusalem's colonial space revisited. *Geopolitics*, 19(3), 514–39. https://doi.org/10.1080/14650045.2013.857657.

Zaban, H. (2016). 'Once there were Moroccans here – today Americans': Gentrification and the housing market in the Baka neighbourhood of Jerusalem. *City*, 20(3), 412–27. https://doi.org/10.1080/13604813.2016.1166703.

Zahria, H. A. (2019, August). Interview with Hamzi Abu Zahria (businessmen), Jerusalem (B. Huberman, interviewer).

Zahra, M. A. (2019, July). Interview with Mustafa Abu Zahra (businessmen), Jerusalem (B. Huberman, interviewer).

Ziv, A. (2019). 'Coming in droves': Number of Arabs in Israeli high-tech soars. *Haaretz*, September. www.haaretz.com/israel-news/business/.premium-coming-in-droves-number-of-arabs-in-israeli-high-tech-soars-1.7834716.

Zureik, E. (2001). Constructing Palestine through surveillance practices. *British Journal of Middle Eastern Studies*, 28(2), 205–27. https://doi.org/10.1080/13530190120083086.

Index

Abu Hamed, F. 123
Abu-Khdeir, M. 51, 81
abusive surveillance 4
accumulation by dispossession 30, 33, 37, 46, 168
agriculture 4–5, 57, 101, 110, 132, 157
Alami, H. 141
al-Aqsa Mosque 1, 23
Al-Fanar 92
Algeria 25, 27–9, 38, 85
Al-Nayzak 150, 151, 153, 156, 159
American Road 110
anti-colonialism *see* neoliberal anti-colonialism
anti-colonial uprisings 34
anti-racism 41
Anwar College 105–6, 108
apartheid 5, 9, 54
Apartheid Road 110
Arab Chamber of Commerce and Industry 105, 146, 157, 161
Arab Hotels Association 158
Arab Revolt of 1936 12, 36
Arab Spring 69, 171
Arafat, Y. 18–20
archaeology 16
Ashkenazi Jews 71, 72
Ateret Cohanim 97, 139

Baidoun, S. 147
Barakat, R. 12
Barel-Sabag, O. 63
Barkat, N. 6, 52, 59, 60, 62–5, 67–9, 72–4, 100, 116
Barros, D. R. 32
Ben-Gurion, D. 36
Bermeister, K. 61
Biden, J. 1
Black entrepreneurship 42
Black Panther Breakfast Programme 170

blue-collar labour 7, 100, 101, 111–12
Boycott, Divestment and Sanctions (BDS) 48, 56, 65, 89
boycotts 51, 107, 112, 115, 127, 151
Brabbing, A. 98–9
Braga, R. 53
Brazil 29, 42, 44, 45, 165
Brazilian Homeless Workers' Movement 170–1
British colonization 12
Buraq Revolt 12
Bureau of Indian Affairs (BIA) 35
Busbridge, R. 142, 147

Canada 26, 29
    indigenous populations in 31
capitalism 8, 9, 28, 30–6, 41, 43, 48, 57, 89, 120–1, 136, 148, 155, 171
Chatterjee, P. 32
Christians 10, 11
Church of the Nativity 157
citizenship 15, 31, 33, 90, 103, 167
City Hall 115–16
City of David settlement 5, 61–2, 137, 147, 158
'City without Violence' programme 97–8
civil rights 40, 130, 152
Clarno, A. 28, 39, 40, 55
class 12, 76–80
colonial policies 34
colonial power 48, 68, 83, 85, 86, 132, 156, 170
The Colonial-Settler State (Rodinson) 25
community centres 116–18, 138
confiscation of properties 4
construction of settlements 4
cost of living 2, 17, 54
Coulthard, G. S. 30, 31
counterinsurgency strategy 68, 90, 114–15, 117
COVID pandemic 168, 171

'creative class' strategy 63
culture 64–5, 98, 114–24, 159

Dakkak, A. 161
Dana, T. 89
Dardot, P. 38, 40
Dayan, M. 36
Decision 3790 1, 3, 4, 6, 9, 94–104, 110, 115, 121, 122, 136, 137
de-development policies 20, 23, 104–12, 126
Dell 154
Democratic Front for the Liberation of Palestine (DFLP) 20
demolition of houses 4
depoliticization processes 87
development 5, 8, 16, 33, 34, 43, 45, 65, 84, 87–8, 99, 167
digital marketing techniques 106
direct investment 70, 89
dispossession processes 87
Dome of the Rock 157

East Jerusalem
  development policies in 125
  industrial zones in 110, 113–14
  Israeli settler colonization of 14–18
  neoliberal counterinsurgency in 118
  neoliberal Israelization in 94–104
  Palestinian survival and resistance in 18–23
  personal security in 81
  socio-economic development 81, 99
  spaces of power in 116
East Jerusalem Development Company 98–9, 106, 110
economic needs 33, 68, 103
economic normalization 89
economic peace 58, 87, 102, 131, 133
education 114–24
educational neoliberalism 120
Elad 97
Elhan 148
Elias, R. 116
elimination 5–7, 29
  of natives 30
elites 11, 14, 156–63
Elkin, Z. 97
emancipation 32, 155
Emergency Aid programme 171

employment
  lack of opportunities for 22
  source of 18
empowerment 44, 115
Englert, S. 29, 30
entrepreneurial activity 94
entrepreneurial ecosystems 156
entrepreneurial training programmes 87, 93, 99, 106, 108, 134
entrepreneurship 4, 128, 130, 139, 163
  of Palestinian women 140–8
environmental protection 16
'ethno-religious' groups 61
European wages 56–7
exploitation 5–7, 29
  of natives 30

Fanon, F. 32, 33, 46, 48, 53, 79, 85, 140, 169
Farsakh, L. 29
feminism 41
Fieldhouse, D. K. 29
First Intifada 57, 73, 75, 76, 131
First World War 12
Florida, R. 63
food sovereignty 48, 132
foreign capital 43, 59, 62, 88–9, 95
Foucault, M. 40
Fraser, N. 8, 41

Gallieni, J. 35
gated communities 16, 17, 55, 69, 71, 133
Gaza Strip 1, 19, 39, 51, 133–4, 151, 170
genocide 27, 44
Ghandour, Y. 148
'ghost neighbourhoods' 69, 70
Ghoul, D. 158
globalization, principles of 121
global market 4, 38–9, 90–1
Global Shapers Community 153, 154
'good Arabs' 120, 149
Grassroots Jerusalem 158
Greater Jerusalem 12, 17, 65, 134
Green Line 18, 57, 87–8, 150
Gueguen, H. 38
Gurion, D. B. 13

Hall, S. 169
Hanieh, A. 49

Harvey, D. 33, 37
Hebrew 102, 107, 118, 122, 143, 149, 169
Hebrew University of Jerusalem 17, 120, 122, 123, 149
high-tech industry 88, 92, 94, 134, 148, 150, 151
Hollywood 41
Holy Land Incoming Tour Operators Association 158
homelessness 66
human capital 41–2, 63, 115, 120–1
human rights 47, 69, 82, 130
Husseini, A. 160–1

imperialism 8, 37, 100–1
income source 67
indebtedness, of Palestinian women 140–8
Indian Removal Act 34
inequality 1, 39–40, 54, 82
Internet 141, 154–5
Israel
  civil society 61
  community centres 106
  export and import legislation 107
  GDP 94
  high-tech industry 94
  labour market 3, 36, 90, 118, 121, 142, 144
  neoliberal counterinsurgency in 87–94
  neoliberal mask 148–56
  sovereignty 13, 21
Israel Defence Forces (IDF) 36
Israeli IT Works 92
Israelisation process 123
Israel Land Fund 97
Issar, Y. 110, 111

J-14 movement 72, 79
Jabbour, G. 25
Jackson, A. 34
Jaffa–Jerusalem railway 10
JDC-Israel 93
Jerusalem
  civil society 109
  'creative class' strategy 63
  'good Arabs' 120
  neoliberal settler colonization of 5–9
  political economy of 52

population 2
resistance in 9–14
sale of urban space in 69
settler colonialism in 9–14
social movements in 139
in twentieth century 9–14
Jerusalem 2020 60
Jerusalem 2050 61
Jerusalem 5800 61
Jerusalem Day 1, 4
Jerusalem Development Authority (JDA) 61–3
Jerusalem Innovation Park project 151
Jerusalem Municipality and the Ministry of Education 121
Jerusalem Tourism Cluster (JTC) 157–8
Jest 8, 109, 114, 140, 141, 146, 153, 156
Jewish Agency 14
Jewish LGBTQA+ 59
Jewish National Fund 14, 69, 134
Jews 2, 10, 11, 52, 70, 168
  settlement of 3
  in West Jerusalem 54
Judaization 2, 5-6, 16, 58, 59, 86, 96, 97, 101, 112, 134, 135, 139, 170

The Kaizen Company 87–8
Kassabri, M. K. 123
Kav LaOved 77
Kelley, R. 32
Kfar Aqba 73, 74
Khalidi, R. 169
Khalili, L. 34, 36
Kollek, T. 100
Koren, D. 102–3, 116, 120

labour exploitation 27
labour market 11, 30, 32, 36, 69, 118, 122, 142, 144–7
Labour Zionism 55
land expropriation 7
land ownership 31, 136
Latin America 7, 28, 35
Laval, C. 38, 40, 120
Leichtag Foundation 63, 108
LGBTQIA+ 41
Lloyd, D. 39
Lockman, Z. 77

Lorde, A. 169
Lupolianski, R. U. 59

Madrid Conference (1991) 20
Mamdani, M. 28
Maof 106
market competition 40–1, 105, 114
Mati 106–10, 114, 116
Mbembe, A. 39, 56
Memmi, A. 27, 49
Middle East 17, 69, 171
miscegenation 31, 167
Mizrahi Jews 71, 72, 74
modern capitalism 26
modernization 16
Morozov, E. 155
multiculturalism 41
municipal urban planning 5
Munin, R. 64
Muslims 10, 11
Muslim women 100–1, 141

Nablus Road Open Days festival 159
Nakba 6, 12, 13, 29, 71
Narrowing Socio-economic Gaps and Economic Development in East Jerusalem 1, 82, 95
national security 104
National Security Council 120
native labour
  alienation of 55
  economic vulnerability 57
  exploitation of 28
  power of exploitation of 167
  presence and centrality of 29
Neocleous, M. 37
neoliberal anti-colonialism 128–31
neoliberal apartheid
  class 76–80
  concept of 39, 55–8
  contradictions of 66–76
  race 76–80
neoliberal capitalism 45
neoliberal counterinsurgency 87–97
neoliberal hegemony 8, 128, 130, 156, 162
neoliberalism 8, 36–8, 45, 52, 55, 64, 78, 127, 129, 134, 162, 169
  ideology of liberty 40
neoliberal Israelization 6, 85–7

culture, education and police 114–24
  in East Jerusalem 94–103
neoliberal modernity 100–1
neoliberal multiculturalism 168
neoliberal settler colonialism 36–45
  resisting 45–9
neoliberal settler colonization 5–9
neoliberal urbanism 58–66, 135–9
NGO New Spirit 59, 63, 68, 108–9
NGOs 5, 6, 8, 42, 43, 44, 82, 92–3, 107, 112, 113–14, 143, 153, 161
  entrepreneurship programmes 165
Nijam, M. 98
Nuseibeh, S. 111

occupation 16, 35, 36, 78, 98, 131, 135, 138, 142, 156, 168, 170
1967 occupation 15, 18
Occupied Palestinian Territories (OPTs) 15, 17–19, 48, 70, 77, 87–94, 114, 170
OECD 69, 82, 89, 91, 92, 95, 120
Old City 6, 113, 157
  central region of 61
  'inner ring' encircles 16–17
  Muslim Quarter 112, 161
  population of 10
  Shopkeepers Association 112, 161
Olmert, E. 59, 60, 96
Orange 154
Orient House 19, 20, 22
Oslo Accords 3, 5–9, 20, 40, 42, 47, 129, 131–2
Ottoman Empire 10, 90, 136

pacification processes 35, 87, 98
Palestine
  capacity-building 104–14
  commodification of 156–63
  de-development of 104–14
  economy 104–14
  educational system 82
  elites of 156–63
  industrial zones 104–14
  nationalism 1
  population 3
  property rights 136
  refugees 14, 15
  road system 17
  social clubs 116

survival and resistance 18–23
tech entrepreneurship 148–56
tourism 84, 112, 113, 156–63, 159, 160
urban planners 135–9
youth 148–56
Palestine Communist Party 77
'Palestine Is Open for Business'
    campaign 133
Palestine Liberation Organization (PLO)
    14, 18, 19, 42
Palestinian Authority's (PA) 20–1, 47, 60,
    78, 103, 125, 128, 131, 171
  Ministry of Entrepreneurship and
    Empowerment 154
Palestinian Internship Programme (PIP) 88
Palestinian National Movement 11–12, 56,
    131, 166, 170
Palestinian women
  entrepreneurship of 140–8
  indebtedness of 140–8
  proletarianization of 140–8
  working age 142
Palestinian workers
  COVID crisis 168
  employment of 18
  gentrification of 111
  lack of unity 77
  rights for 77
  unionization of 77
Peres Center for Peace and Innovation 88
police 114–24
political economy 7, 25–30
political freedom 10, 18
Popular Front for the Liberation of
    Palestine (FPLP) 20
Porter, M. 62
post-Oslo settler colonial neoliberal
    urbanism 58–66
poverty 1–2, 42, 43, 68, 88–9, 91, 95,
    142, 144
  rate of 145
primitive accumulation 30, 31, 37
privatization
  education services 86
  public transportation 86
  residential property 70
  risk of 41
  security 86
  urban property 71

weakening of 131
professional training programmes 106
progressive neoliberalism 8, 41, 42
proletarianization, of Palestinian
    women 140–8
Pullan, W. 86

quality of life 61, 63, 93, 97, 108–9, 110,
    118–20, 125, 126, 133

race 32, 58, 76–80, 142
racial capitalism 31–6
racial exclusivity 25
racial self-segregation 25
racial supremacy 25
racial violence 16
racism 8, 31, 32, 44, 55, 140, 124, 140,
    149, 150
racist urban planning policy 2
rationality 99, 101
Rawabi Tech Hub 133–4
real estate privatization process 70
recognition 7, 31, 33, 40, 94–7, 103, 104,
    107, 126, 140, 147, 156, 163, 168, 169
refusal 9, 48, 170
rejection 4–8, 73, 75, 121, 126, 170
resistance
  in East Jerusalem 18–23
  economy 131–5, 163
  in Jerusalem 9–14
right of residence 4, 15, 22
right to housing 135–9
Rodinson, M. 25
Ross, A. 29
Roy, A. 134

Saadeh, R. 159
Saadi, S. 94
Said, E. W. 25, 30
Salem, S. 85
Salem, W. 162
Salman, C. Y. 15
Samour, S. 169
Sayegh, F. 25
Second Intifada 3, 6, 22, 52, 58, 75, 99, 105
security, lack of 104
Segev, Y. 68
Seidel, T. 132
self-employment 147

self-government 41
'self-segregation' 61
settlement 3–5, 11, 17, 18, 21, 35, 61, 72, 110, 116, 123–4, 138
settler colonial government 31–6
settler colonialism
  classic typology of 29
  in Israel 14–18
  in Jerusalem 9–14
  neoliberal urbanism in post-Oslo 58–66
  political economy of 25–30
  racist discrimination 123
  violence in 27
settler colonial theory 9, 26, 29, 30
settler economy 30
settlers 4, 6, 7, 11, 16, 27, 34, 64, 76, 97, 123–4, 147, 168
Shafir, G. 26, 30
Shalhoub-Kerkovian, N. 142, 147
Shin-Bet 98, 99
Shlomo, O. 86
shopping centres 65, 83, 111, 157, 161
Shtern, M. 87
Shuafat Refugee Camp 73, 74
Silicon Valley 41, 155
Sillicon Wadi project 83, 84, 109–10, 113, 155
Singh, N. P. 31
social clubs 10, 116, 119
social mobility 10, 142
socio-economic development 3, 59, 81, 91, 93, 97–9, 115, 117, 129, 131, 144
socio-economic inequality 95
socio-spatial Judaization 5
soft imperialism 42, 130
South Africa 25, 28, 30, 39, 40, 53, 54–6
sovereignty 19, 21, 34, 117, 132, 168
  struggle for 103
SpaceX project 88
spatial reproduction 65
Spivak, G. C. 101
Strakosch, E. 33, 34, 40
subformalization 86
supermarkets 78, 111
symbolic elimination 27

Tatour, L. 47
tech entrepreneurship 148–56
technocratic paternalism 85

Tel Aviv
  airport in 65
  central square in 69
  school in 166
terrorism 16, 116
Time (magazine) 64
Tobi, G. 107, 108
Toren, Y. 96, 98, 102
tourism 52, 60, 62, 84, 98, 112, 113, 119, 132, 156–63
Trump, D. 1, 4
Tsofen 92
2018 development plan 3
2018 Jerusalem development plan 89, 98

unemployment 66, 67, 95
United States 27, 29, 35, 41, 69, 88, 106, 148, 167
urban development 3, 16, 111, 134
urban planning 16, 17, 55, 135–9
urban precariats 53
US foreign policy 35

Veracini, L. 26, 29
violence 32
  of capital needs 33
  of genocide 34
  of politics 41
  in settler colonialism 27
vocational training programmes 108
Volinz, L. 86

WAC-Maan 77
Wadi Hilweh Community Centre 144, 147
Wall Street 41
Waqf 119
war on terror 37
West Bank 1, 2, 7, 13–14, 19, 22, 23, 66, 72, 74, 89, 97, 153, 157, 170
  Palestinian bourgeoisie in 105
Western-style residential condominiums 111
West Jerusalem
  colleges in 122
  skilled labour positions in 67
'white collar' professionals 102, 111–12
Wingate, O. 36
Wolfe, P. 7, 26–9, 39
Worker's Party 165

workers' revolts 66–76
World Bank (WB) 42, 43
World Economic Forum 153, 154
World ORT 121

Yabous Cultural Centre 116
Yacobi, H. 55, 70, 71, 86
Yom Yerushalaim 1

Zaban, H. 71
Zahra, M. A. 112–13, 161
Zionism 9–11, 30, 72, 134
Zionist hegemony 17, 47, 71, 79
Zionist philanthropy 92–3
Zionist settler colonization 9, 11, 30
Zureik, E. 25

www.ingramcontent.com/pod-product-compliance
Lightning Source LLC
Chambersburg PA
CBHW052116300426
44116CB00010B/1689